**Social History, Popular Culture, and Politics in Germany**
Geoff Eley, Series Editor

**Series Editorial Board**
Kathleen Canning, University of Michigan
David F. Crew, University of Texas, Austin
Atina Grossmann, The Cooper Union
Alf Lüdtke, Max-Planck-Institut für Geschichte, Göttingen, Germany
Andrei S. Markovits, University of Michigan

*German Pop Culture: How "American" Is It?* edited by Agnes C. Mueller
*Character Is Destiny: The Autobiography of Alice Salomon,* edited by Andrew Lees
*Other Germans: Black Germans and the Politics of Race, Gender, and Memory in the Third Reich,* Tina M. Campt
*State of Virginity: Gender, Religion, and Politics in an Early Modern Catholic State,* Ulrike Strasser
*Worldly Provincialism: German Anthropology in the Age of Empire,* H. Glenn Penny and Matti Bunzl, editors
*Ethnic Drag: Performing Race, Nation, Sexuality in West Germany,* Katrin Sieg
*Projecting History: German Nonfiction Cinema, 1967–2000,* Nora M. Alter
*Cities, Sin, and Social Reform in Imperial Germany,* Andrew Lees
*The Challenge of Modernity: German Social and Cultural Studies, 1890–1960,* Adelheid von Saldern
*Exclusionary Violence: Antisemitic Riots in Modern German History,* Christhard Hoffman, Werner Bergmann, and Helmut Walser Smith, editors
*Languages of Labor and Gender: Female Factory Work in Germany, 1850–1914,* Kathleen Canning
*That Was the Wild East: Film Culture, Unification and the "New" Germany,* Leonie Naughton
*Anna Seghers: The Mythic Dimension,* Helen Fehervary
*Staging Philanthropy: Patriotic Women and the National Imagination in Dynastic Germany, 1813–1916,* Jean H. Quataert
*Truth to Tell: German Women's Autobiographies and Turn-of-the-Century Culture,* Katharina Gerstenberger
*The "Goldhagen Effect": History, Memory, Nazism—Facing the German Past,* Geoff Eley, editor
*Shifting Memories: The Nazi Past in the New Germany,* Klaus Neumann
*Saxony in German History: Culture, Society, and Politics, 1830–1933,* James Retallack, editor
*Little Tools of Knowledge: Historical Essays on Academic and Bureaucratic Practices,* Peter Becker and William Clark, editors
*Public Spheres, Public Mores, and Democracy: Hamburg and Stockholm, 1870–1914,* Madeleine Hurd
*Making Security Social: Disability, Insurance, and the Birth of the Social Entitlement State in Germany,* Greg Eghigian
*The German Problem Transformed: Institutions, Politics, and Foreign Policy, 1945–1995,* Thomas Banchoff

**Social History, Popular Culture, and Politics in Germany**
Geoff Eley, Series Editor

*(Continued)*

*Building the East German Myth: Historical Mythology and Youth Propaganda in the German Democratic Republic, 1945–1989,* Alan L. Nothnagle

*Mobility and Modernity: Migration in Germany 1820–1989,* Steve Hochstadt

*Triumph of the Fatherland: German Unification and the Marginalization of Women,* Brigitte Young

*Framed Visions: Popular Culture, Americanization, and the Contemporary German and Austrian Imagination,* Gerd Gemünden

*The Imperialist Imagination: German Colonialism and Its Legacy,* Sara Friedrichsmeyer, Sara Lennox, and Susanne Zantop, editors

*Contested City: Municipal Politics and the Rise of Nazism in Altona, 1917–1937,* Anthony McElligott

*Catholicism, Political Culture, and the Countryside: A Social History of the Nazi Party in South Germany,* Oded Heilbronner

*A User's Guide to German Cultural Studies,* Scott Denham, Irene Kacandes, and Jonathan Petropoulos, editors

*A Greener Vision of Home: Cultural Politics and Environmental Reform in the German* Heimatschutz *Movement, 1904–1918,* William H. Rollins

*West Germany under Construction: Politics, Society, and Culture in Germany in the Adenauer Era,* Robert G. Moeller, editor

*How German Is She? Postwar West German Reconstruction and the Consuming Woman,* Erica Carter

*Feminine Frequencies: Gender, German Radio, and the Public Sphere, 1923–1945,* Kate Lacey

*Exclusive Revolutionaries: Liberal Politics, Social Experience, and National Identity in the Austrian Empire, 1848–1914,* Pieter M. Judson

*Jews, Germans, Memory: Reconstruction of Jewish Life in Germany,* Y. Michal Bodemann, editor

*Paradoxes of Peace: German Peace Movements since 1945,* Alice Holmes Cooper

*Society, Culture, and the State in Germany, 1870–1930,* Geoff Eley, editor

*Technological Democracy: Bureaucracy and Citizenry in the German Energy Debate,* Carol J. Hager

*The Origins of the Authoritarian Welfare State in Prussia: Conservatives, Bureaucracy, and the Social Question, 1815–70,* Hermann Beck

*The People Speak! Anti-Semitism and Emancipation in Nineteenth-Century Bavaria,* James F. Harris

*From* Bundesrepublik *to* Deutschland: *German Politics after Unification,* Michael G. Huelshoff, Andrei S. Markovits, and Simon Reich, editors

*The Stigma of Names: Antisemitism in German Daily Life, 1812–1933,* Dietz Bering

*Reshaping the German Right: Radical Nationalism and Political Change after Bismarck,* Geoff Eley

**CHARACTER IS DESTINY**

# Character Is Destiny

*The Autobiography of Alice Salomon*

*Edited by Andrew Lees*

**The University of Michigan Press**   *Ann Arbor*

Copyright © by the University of Michigan 2004
All rights reserved
Published in the United States of America by
The University of Michigan Press
Manufactured in the United States of America
♾ Printed on acid-free paper

2007   2006   2005   2004     4  3  2  1

No part of this publication may be reproduced, stored in a retrieval system, or transmitted in any form or by any means, electronic, mechanical, or otherwise, without the written permission of the publisher.

*A CIP catalog record for this book is available from the British Library.*

Library of Congress Cataloging-in-Publication Data

Salomon, Alice, 1872–1948.
    Character is destiny : the autobiography of Alice Salomon / edited by Andrew Lees.
    p. cm. — (Social history, popular culture, and politics in Germany)
   ISBN 0-472-11367-4 (acid-free)
    1. Salomon, Alice, 1872–1948.  2. Women social workers—Germany—Biography.  3. Women social workers—United States—Biography.  I. Lees, Andrew, 1940–  II. Title.  III. Series.

HV40.32.S35 A3 2004
361.3'092—dc22                                                  2003015479

*With Love and Admiration for
Lynn and Laura,*

*Who Also Teach*

# Contents

*Preface and Acknowledgments*   ix
*Introduction*   1

**Character Is Destiny**

1. A Child with a Garden, 1872–1889   11
2. Apprenticeship, 1893–1899   24
3. Widening Horizon   37
4. London–Berlin   48
5. The Aberdeens, Scotland, Ireland, 1904–1908   61
6. Two Jobs for Life, I: The School for Social Work, 1907–1913   68
7. Two Jobs for Life, II: Officer of the International Council; Canada and First Glimpse of U.S.A.   81
8. Brief Harvest before the Storm   89
9. "The Evidence of Things Not Seen," 1914   101
10. Patriotism Is Not Enough, 1914–1916   105
11. In the War Office, 1917–1919   112
12. Fourteen Years of Democracy, I: Years of Chaos, 1919–1924   121
13. Fourteen Years of Democracy, II: My Foreign Affairs, 1920–1933   133
14. Fourteen Years of Democracy, III: Social Reconstruction, 1924–1929   150
15. Fourteen Years of Democracy, IV: Then Came the Collapse   159
16. The Golden Ring of Friendship   165
17. The Stream of Lava   173

18. The Mystery of Individual Adjustments 181
19. A Spy Stands behind You 188
20. Exit Modern Woman 191
21. The Strong and the Weak 201
22. God and Caesar 209
23. The Pastors . . . Martin Niemöller 214
24. New Lease on Life 220

*Appendix A. The Significance of the Women's Movement for Social Life* 231
*Appendix B. The Revolution of the Mother* 239
*Appendix C. Preface to an Early Version of Salomon's Autobiography* 247
*Notes* 249

# Preface and Acknowledgments

Having published more than two dozen books and well over four hundred articles between 1895 and 1937, Alice Salomon wrote just one more work of any length. After the Nazis forced her to leave her native Germany for the United States, she devoted much of her remaining energy to composing a book-length account of her life, which she titled "Character Is Destiny." Despite the fact that she was quite well known in this country's social-work community and the fact that she had written her autobiography in excellent English, she could not find a publisher for it. It did not become available to scholars until many years after her death. Joachim Wieler, a historian who taught at a training school for social workers in Darmstadt, discovered it in 1981 in the possession of one of Salomon's grand-nieces, Ilse Eden, who was living in California. Soon donated by Eden to New York City's Leo Baeck Institute (a major repository of materials pertaining to the history of German Jews), Salomon's typescript was translated into German and carefully annotated by two other historians, Rüdeger Baron and Rolf Landwehr, who taught at the training school for social workers that Salomon had established in Berlin in 1908. Their edition subsequently appeared with a lengthy postscript by Wieler in 1983 as *Charakter ist Schicksal: Lebenserinnerungen,* under the imprint of the Beltz publishing house.

While writing a chapter on Salomon for a book of my own, I decided to try to enable her to have her long overdue say, in her own words, with regard to her fascinating and fruitful life. Thanks to the University of Michigan Press, to the cooperation of the Leo Baeck Institute, to Ilse Eden, and to several scholars on both sides of the Atlantic who supported my project in a variety of ways, it has finally come to fruition. I much appreciate the encouragement and support that I have received from Ann Taylor Allen, Laurie Bernstein, Belinda Davis, Janet Golden, Lynn Hollen Lees, and Kathryn Kish Sklar. I am particularly grateful for the detailed comments and other assistance I have received from Rolf Landwehr; Joachim Wieler; Adriane Feustel, who heads the Alice-Salomon-Archiv at the Alice Salomon Training Institute in Berlin; and Anja Schüler, author of the fullest treatment of Salomon's life and thought (see introduction, n.1). Thanks go also to Holly Phares for retyping Salomon's typescript and deciphering her handwritten emendations. Finally, I again express my appreciation to Ellen Goldlust-Gingrich for her careful copyediting and to Kevin M. Rennells, of the University of Michigan Press, for his guidance during the final stages of production.

A few more words are in order about my handling of Salomon's text. In general, I have made no effort to edit her prose. Insertions made in pencil on the original document, apparently added either by an unnamed friend of Salomon's or by an editor at a press to which Salomon had submitted it for consideration, had already produced a manuscript that was almost entirely free of noticeable mistakes. In a few cases in which these emendations were difficult to read, I have used my best judgment about how to render the text in a way that conforms to Salomon's intentions. I have occasionally corrected spelling and punctuation, changed capital letters to lowercase letters, and added bracketed words to clarify Salomon's meaning. Unlike the editors of the German edition, however, I have not sought to consolidate her often rather brief paragraphs. My major emendation of the text has been to annotate it. In this regard, I have drawn freely on Baron and Landwehr's notes to the German edition, which considerably eased my labors, although I have not incorporated all of their material and have added notes in cases in which I believed that American readers would require further explanation. I have also attempted to draw readers' attention to scholarship that pertains to some of the issues that Salomon discusses, particularly in the area of social policy.

# Introduction

Alice Salomon was born into a middle-class Jewish family in Berlin in 1872, a little over a year after the foundation of the German Empire at the end of the Franco-Prussian War, and she died in New York City in 1948, more than three years after the end of another conflict that led to the destruction of much of her native country as well as much of what she had sought to build internationally. Although she had been driven into exile by men whose values were diametrically opposed to hers, she led a full and fruitful life that is finally receiving the recognition it deserves. To be sure, her final fifteen years were sad ones. But during most of her life she exuded both energy and confidence, and even toward the end of it she felt that as a whole it had been happy and successful. Whether it was happy is not for historians to say. It is clear, however, that she accomplished a great deal.[1]

Salomon's efforts to expand the sphere in which educated women could act effectively earned her a leading position among late-nineteenth- and early-twentieth-century feminists. Her contributions were particularly significant in the area of education for social work, where she played a pioneering and highly influential role both in Germany and abroad. But she also became deeply engaged in the broader pursuit of greater rights for all women. Working within a transatlantic community of female reformers that included not only Germans such as Helene Lange and Gertrud Bäumer but also Americans Jane Addams and Florence Kelley, Salomon sought tirelessly to advance the well-being of women in general.[2] Toward that end, she performed important functions for many years as one of the leaders of the Federation of German Women's Associations and of the International Council of Women (for which much of the original impetus had been provided by Susan B. Anthony).

Like Addams, who provided American women opportunities to serve as urban volunteers in settlement houses and thereby offered women the chance to pursue careers in the area of social work, Salomon believed that women and men were essentially (and fortunately) different. Addams and Salomon saw these differences as not only physical and psychological but also intellectual and moral as well as inherent and natural. In contrast to much of the feminism in the Anglo-Saxon world (as expressed, for example, by Charlotte Perkins Gilman—but not by Addams), Salomon saw women's rights as based less on male-female resemblances than on male-female complementarity.[3] In line with this belief, she practiced what Germans referred to as a kind of "spiritual motherhood." She devoted herself not to children of her own—like most career women at the time, she remained single throughout her life—but instead to other people's children. Focusing first and foremost on the education of young women whose families had some means in the hope that these women would follow her good example, she encouraged them and others to help improve the conditions under which women from the working classes raised their children. In her view, middle-class women's maternal instincts could and should lead not only to nurturing their own offspring in their own families but also to activities that would contribute—through assistance to women at lower levels—to the betterment of society at large. Salomon's feminist ethic of social service pointed clearly toward the goal of greater harmony among social classes as an outgrowth of a mediating role to be played by women. They were to gain legitimacy for their pursuit of increased opportunities by working toward the triumph of a broadly defined domesticity outside of as well as inside individual households. Women should seek thereby to impart to society as a whole the qualities that ought to inhere in its basic building blocks—namely, families.

Salomon began to move in the direction dictated by such views in 1893. Having led a conventionally restricted life up to that point (her formal education had essentially ended when she was fifteen), she enthusiastically joined a Berlin organization that came to be known as the Girls' and Women's Groups for Social Assistance. The Groups originated for the purpose of giving young, relatively privileged females opportunities both to enhance their social usefulness and to broaden their horizons by means of voluntary activity among working-class families in the German capital. The organization reflected a desire to enlist women from the urban middle classes in efforts to provide answers to the "social question"—the problem of how to improve the living and working conditions of manual laborers and their families—while integrating these people into existing societal structures. Participation in Groups-oriented activities entailed practical charitable work in individual homes and in institutions such as orphanages and daycare centers as well as helping to set up clubs for young female factory workers. In line with a growing tendency among many would-be benefactors of the poor to make social work more "scientific," involvement in the Groups also entailed wide reading about social problems and exposure to stimulating lectures by social reformers. For Salomon, involvement in the Groups served as a partial substitute for formal higher education, which she did not begin to obtain until she was in her thirties, when she was admitted (despite considerable opposition by professors) as a doctoral candidate at Berlin's Friedrich Wilhelm University.

In 1908, with her Ph.D. in hand (she had written a dissertation on the causes of wage differentials between men and women), Salomon refocused her energies on the Groups, taking the lead in transforming their educational component into a formal institution, which she called the Social School for Women. She designed the curriculum with a view to fostering practical knowledge of and feasible solutions to social problems, insisting on the need for a foundation of objective knowledge that would not depend on partisanship for its acceptability. Students took courses not only in hygiene, cooking, and child care but also in public health, economics, history and theory of poor relief, family law, and civics. The students were then required to apply what they had learned in the sorts of places where members of the Groups had previously performed acts of social assistance. The education was intended both to combine theory and practice and to help cultivate a service-oriented mentality. As Salomon stated in remarks she made in 1908 to mark the school's opening, "We wish to give [young women] a *modern education* that will enable them to take part . . . in concrete, practical situations that pervade contemporary life and encourage them to act and accomplish something. Not superfluous knowledge but instead an education that enables them in some way—in the family or in a larger sphere—to serve humanity."[4]

Salomon became deeply involved not only in the training of young social workers but also in legislative efforts to improve women's lives and in attempts to strengthen a sense of identity and unity among female activists both nationally and internationally. She supported a wide range of measures, including the right to vote and enhanced rights to form trade unions, with a view to emancipating women from legally enforced discrimination. In line, however, with her emphasis on gender differences rather than on gender similarities, she emphasized laws to protect women (and their children) from risks—particularly with regard to their capacity for bearing and nurturing children—that men did not face. In this connection, motherhood insurance and limits on the length of the workday were central to her legislative desiderata. She pursued these and other goals in conjunction with large numbers of other feminists in the Federation of German Women's Associations and in the International Council of Women. She became involved in both of these organizations in the late 1890s, rising not long thereafter to positions of leadership that she was to hold for many years. In 1909, her involvement in the International Council's activities resulted in the first of several trips to the United States, to which she felt increasingly drawn.[5]

Internationalism was superseded—in Germany as elsewhere—by sentiments of a markedly different sort during and after the First World War. In many cases, the spirit of openness toward and cooperation with like-minded foreigners receded in favor of dedication to one's own country, the men who were fighting for it, and the families these men left behind when they marched off to battle. Feminists were by no means immune to such feelings, as many of them made quite clear by elevating support for German statesmen, military leaders, and soldiers above solidarity with women who were not German. One of the many instances of growing nationalism among German women was a decision by the Federation of German Women's Associations to boycott a 1915 meeting of women that took place in the Hague for the purpose of pressuring governments to settle their differences peacefully instead of continuing to fight.

These trends pulled Salomon in opposing directions. Although she was quite close to some of the women who did go to the Hague conference—most notably Addams, who played a leading part in antiwar efforts—Salomon declined to attend. She thus bowed to the preferences of most of the German women with whom she was associated, among whom patriotic support for the war effort ran strong. She demonstrated her desire to be of assistance to her country more positively, too. First as a leader of the National Women's Service and then as an employee of the German War Office, she played an important part in efforts to organize social services for women who had been left alone as a result of their husbands' service in the armed forces or who faced new challenges as a result of war-related employment. After the war ended, however, the rifts between Salomon and the dominant elements in the German women's movement became more noticeable. Her decision to attend the first postwar convention of the International Council of Women, held in Norway in 1920, led to her forced resignation from the governing board of the Federation of German Women's Movements and thus to the end of her hopes of becoming the federation's next head. She would probably have been barred from holding this position anyway because of her Jewish origins, but her internationalism provided the explicit rationale for her opponents' moves against her.

Although she had failed to rise to the top position in the women's movement for which she had seemingly been destined, during the 1920s and early 1930s Salomon enjoyed a great deal of professional success, influence, and recognition in the areas of social work education and research into social problems. She served from the outset of the period as the chairperson of a nationwide association of "social schools for women," and she later took the lead in establishing the German Academy for Social and Pedagogical Work for Women, which quickly acquired a division for research. Under her guidance, it published numerous studies of family life and the disruptive influences to which it was being subjected, for which much of the inspiration emanated from the works of Edith Abbott and Sophonisba Breckinridge of the School for Social Service Administration at the University of Chicago. Furthermore, lectures abroad (most notably in the United States) enabled Salomon to build on her earlier contacts with foreign women in ways that led to the 1929 foundation of the International Committee of Schools of Social Work, of which she served as the first chairperson.[6] For these as well as other activities, Salomon received, in 1932, an honorary degree from her alma mater as well as a medal from the Prussian state. At the same time, the training institute she had established for young women, direction of which had passed on to a successor in 1925, was renamed the Alice Salomon School.

In early 1933, a greatly exaggerated incarnation of the nationalism that had already created substantial difficulties for Salomon during and just after the First World War caused her life, like the lives of many others, to take a decided turn for the worse.[7] Salomon had converted to Christianity in 1914, but her conversion did little to assuage the anti-Semitism directed against her. Having already contributed to the tensions that marred her relationships with other German women just after the First World War, hostility toward her on the basis of her Jewish origins contributed still more strongly to her expulsion. The triumph of National Socialism under the leadership of Adolf Hitler meant that the humane values for which Salomon stood were immediately and seriously at risk. As a liberal opponent of chauvinism and militarism—and, by birth, a Jew—she aroused both suspicion and antipathy among supporters and functionaries of the Third Reich. They worked effectively to drive her to the margins of public life while she remained in Germany and were only too happy to seize the pretext of yet more lectures by her abroad to force her permanently to leave Germany.

Emigration to the United States in 1937 was a bittersweet experience. It ushered in a period in Salomon's life that was marked both by greater security and by reduced effectiveness and deepening pessimism. In many ways, living in America represented the fulfillment of her previously expressed sentiment that if she could be reborn, she would like it to be as an American. Although she was living in relative comfort and was obviously far better off than numerous other Germans who had tried or were trying in vain to gain sanctuary on this side of the Atlantic, she can hardly be blamed for the melancholy and bitterness that pervade much of her late writing about recent history and current affairs. Despite her comparatively good fortune, she felt increasingly isolated professionally (Addams had died in 1935), and Salomon was understandably distressed by the direction in which events had taken the world, not only during her final years in Germany but also and even more so thereafter. Both a late lecture (see appendix B) and an early preface to her memoirs (see appendix C) are full of gloom as a result of the violent aggression carried out by people of the sort who had engineered her ouster. Such feelings help to explain why, for many years after her death, Salomon remained largely absent from the realm of historical memory in her native land.[8] Like many others who had emigrated during the 1930s, she stood as a reproach to numerous Germans who had no desire to be reminded of their sins of omission and commission before 1945.

Salomon's relative invisibility in the United States, despite the fact that she spent her final eleven years in this country, has resulted from other aspects of her career. Most obvious is the fact that all of her books—with the exception of her autobiography and one other book[9]—were written in German and that almost nothing of what she wrote has been translated into English. Less obvious but perhaps still more significant is the fact that Salomon's version of feminism was more accepted among German women than among Americans at the time she articulated it and that since her death it has become still less popular in the United States. Since the early twentieth century, feminism on the basis of male-female differences has increasingly been displaced by feminist egalitarianism, as feminist leaders have sought to assert men's and women's similarities. However, some feminists as well as antifeminists continue to frame their arguments along the lines indicated by Salomon and like-minded women nearly a century ago. Her story, told in her own words, thus sheds light not only on her heroic life but also on options that remain alive in the ongoing debate about the importance of gender in modern society.[10]

# CHARACTER IS DESTINY

CHAPTER 1

# A Child with a Garden: 1872–1889

My childhood ended at the close of a chapter in German history. I was sixteen when a whole nation grieved over the death of a beloved sovereign and the fatal illness of his successor. Nobody who lived in Berlin in March 1888 could forget the tragic solemnity of the crowds arrayed to see the procession that carried Wilhelm I, aged ninety-one, to his grave. It was a bitter-cold morning; huge masses of snow had fallen during a month which generally brings spring to Germany. Since before dawn, the population had waited, a living wall against the walls of piled-up snow, to bid farewell to the emperor. For Wilhelm I had been very popular—a good Christian and a God-fearing man, according to his lights, and peace loving, even though his interests were limited to his army. It was known that he had been loath to allow his Iron Chancellor, Bismarck, to push Prussia into three wars of aggression: against Denmark, Austria, and France.[1]

In the case of France, Bismarck had even resorted to the gross deception of publishing a doctored version of one of the emperor's telegrams in order to force a war. During my years at the University of Berlin, the professors of history frankly admitted this and considered it a particularly clever move. The masses of people heard only what they were meant to know: that these had been victorious wars fulfilling the German dream, the resurrection of a united German nation. "Through blood and iron" was the slogan, and I doubt whether many people had qualms about it. We swallowed it as people in other countries had swallowed what their governments had thought fit to let them know about imperialistic moves. "The end justifies the means" was a principle not new in politics, and the new German Empire pleased the people.

Under the influence of Bismarck, Wilhelm had given the nation a liberal constitution including general, equal, and secret suffrage for men; he had contributed an original program of social security to the world's theories on social progress. He remained simple and unostentatious even after the new German unity and grandeur had been achieved, becoming in his old age almost a legend. Liberal groups had looked forward to the reign of Friedrich, his son. In him lay their hope for a reign of peace, of democratic reforms and a stable economic and cultural policy. Now these hopes were blighted. When the old emperor was buried, everyone knew that the days of the new one were numbered. He succumbed after a reign of one hundred days, leaving the throne to rash, vainglorious young Wilhelm II.[2]

At this time I was just beginning to reach out with vague aspirations toward a profession in which I could follow my long-growing desire to help people. It became for me more than a profession. It was a challenge, a vocation, and a calling.

Even as a small child, I had hoped for a career. At five, before I went to school, I wanted to become a teacher, and I began to want to help others when I was twelve. Besides, all my life, as long as I can remember, I wanted to travel and see the world. . . . All those these dreams have come true in strange and unexpected ways.

One of my earliest recollections is the birth of a baby sister when I was three. My older sister and constant playmate had been sent to visit our grandmother in Breslau—not to avoid embarrassing explanations but merely to relieve the household. Nobody dreamed of sex education at that period, nor did any of us doubt the story of the stork. On our vacations in the country we used to gaze for hours at a stork's nest up on the church spire, hoping to witness a delivery. My parents had been married in 1858, and for the next twenty years there was seldom a time when my mother did not have either a child on the way or in the cradle. A son was born in 1860 and another in 1861, who died of diphtheria when he was eight. My mother never stopped mourning the loss of this son, although an infant had died before him and there had been two miscarriages. Then four daughters arrived in the course of only six years. My father was scarcely pleased at the birth of one girl after another, but discomfited mainly, I suspect, at the enforced seclusion of his wife, a damper to his impetuous spirit and love of adventure.

I was the second of the girls. My mother had chosen for me the name of one of Queen Victoria's children, Alice, the Grand Duchess of Hessia, because—my mother told me frequently—the duchess was an exceptionally devoted and loving daughter, a shining example to follow. The two youngest girls had the flowery names of Edith Elfriede and Olga Agnes Lucie.

My parents differed in temperament as well as background. My father and his brothers were products of a family in the early stage of broader education and material comforts. They were rather undisciplined, interested in some form of art or public service, reaching beyond the sphere into which they were born. In my father's case it was a yearning to see the world, a trait I inherited, when from the very beginning I wanted the whole world to be my country. Like all his brothers, my father was in the leather business, handed down for three generations. He seems to have thought that this succession would go on forever. In his will, which I found long after he had gone and when my connection with the leather trade had become exceedingly remote, he expressed the wish that his daughters should marry "businessmen; if possible, men in the leather trade."

His family had lived in a small town in the north of Germany since the beginning of the eighteenth century. His great-grandfather had received concessions for his business and for the acquisition of a house in 1744 and 1764 and a safe conduct from Frederick the Great in 1765. Only in my grandfather's time did the family become established in Berlin.

My mother's people had been bankers since a time before the powerful stock companies had deprived the private and family banking houses of their prominence. She was born in Breslau, the capital of Silesia, and lived there until her marriage. And though it later developed into not too happy a marriage, complicated by clashing temperaments, it was a love match, formed without family interference.

There was neither Jewish tradition nor religion in my parents' home. My father probably did not think at all about religion; he was simply not concerned. This was an "enlightened," liberal period, and many people believed they had grown beyond the riddles of life. My mother was so restrained in her emotions that religious impulses seldom found expression and withered from lack of nurture.

Although Berliners looked down on people from the provinces, the banking family from Silesia considered itself superior to the leather family. In my opinion, the leather family was infinitely more interesting. However, my mother must have had more energy, intelligence, and ambition than the rest of her family. She had worked for a teacher's or governess' examination as a very young girl, a most unusual undertaking for a well-to-do banker's daughter in the fifties. She was to me the most beautiful of women, my yardstick of goodness and virtue, but she must have been exhausted by frequent pregnancies and childbirth, and though she lived to be very old, never very strong or healthy. Nevertheless, she had an active mind until her old age and read a great deal. Her hands were never idle. She knitted stockings for all of us and crocheted miles and miles of lace for curtains, bedspreads, and ultimately for every shelf in the kitchen.

Edith, the sister after me, contracted pneumonia in infancy. She suffered terribly from emphysema of the lungs until she approached adolescence. Sometimes, for months at a time, my mother had to keep her alive during attacks of asthma. If my mother ever had had a capacity for enjoying life, she must have lost it then.

My brother and my older sister were both very good-looking. I was such a thin and weak infant that my mother used to cry when she saw a fat, rosy baby. I seem to have recuperated, judging by my early photographs of a blond curly-haired little girl with bright eyes and as pretty as most healthy and well cared for children. At some unrecorded age, however, my nose became prominent and I became the ugly duckling of the family—tall and lanky. My father considered me the most intelligent of his children, though I cannot imagine what made him think so. I was no child prodigy and I showed no particular gifts; to the contrary, I was slow in learning to speak, until at a belated stage I burst out into whole sentences. Later, when my work often required my speaking in public, the family teased me about hoarding my gifts for a sudden, dramatic display.

During the seventies and eighties, the city in which we were born and grew up was very provincial. Paris, London, Vienna were world capitals. They had picturesque and beautiful quarters, famous palaces and parks, architectural style, great monuments of the past, fine hotels and shops, and artistic entertainment attracting people of every country. Berlin was a capital in name only, no more imposing than the capitals of the many small German principalities. When it was suddenly raised to the dignity of an imperial residence, it developed modern quarters, comforts, and conveniences with American strides, but it could not acquire the dignity and beauty of ancient culture. Its chief distinctions were cleanliness, the integrity of its administration, and the orderly conduct of its citizens.

The Anhalt Railroad Station in Berlin, 1901, at the corner of Königgrätzerstrasse and Schönebergerstrasse. The house in which Salomon spent her youth was located at 28 Königgrätzerstrasse. (Photograph courtesy of the Landesarchiv Berlin.)

Everybody lived economically and frugally—four or five families in the flats of a two- or three-story house. I do not remember ever having visited people during my childhood who had a house to themselves. No technical progress had invaded the home. The old emperor had a bathtub brought from the "Hotel de Rome" whenever he wanted a bath. It was generally conceded that the crown princess, "Frederick," Queen Victoria's eldest daughter,[3] had married into a country still in a primitive stage of civilization.

There were, of course, no public means of transportation within the city. When I was four or five years old, the track for the first tram cars was laid along the original fortifications, the city walls, leading from one city gate to another. The cars were drawn by horses, and there was only one track with a switch for the cars when they met. No child of today can enjoy the movies more than we enjoyed watching the waiting cars and the switching of the rails. Limited and dull as life must have been, to us Berlin was the center of the world and the house we lived in a marvel of beauty. It stood in a street whose name was changed regularly according to military events and foreign policy. While we lived there, it was Königgrätzerstrasse, in memory of the Prussian victory over Austria. Later, when the Austrians became German allies, it was changed to Budapesterstrasse, and under the Weimar Republic it was divided into Friedrich-Ebert and Stresemannstrasse. What the Nazis did, I have forgotten.

My father owned the house we lived in, and we were spread out over a very spacious first floor, which in those days was called the "bel étage." From time to time, as the family grew, a room was added without much architectural planning. Thus it became a maze of dark rooms which could be reached only through my parents' bedroom, through the bathroom or kitchen, or through an open gallery. All rooms had to be lighted with oil lamps or candles. My father had a passion for auctions, where he bought what he considered "art treasures": pictures and bronze statuettes, ivory figures and knickknacks—objects of pride for us—filled the whole house. We children realized in later years that there were quite a few horrors among them. But my mother cherished things for the sake of tradition or because she had grown attached to them. She was distressed and indignant when the younger generation suggested banning doubtful ornaments.

But even for her, days of auction sales were critical. My father had more imagination than restraint. Once an enormous ship made of bamboo arrived without warning, bought from a bankrupt playhouse. It was set in the garden, spurring us to dangerous acrobatic feats.

The garden was our childhood paradise. It bordered on a courtyard where other children were supposed to play, and it was shaded by a beautiful old walnut tree. The garden was reserved for us. No one seemed to be aware of the injustice of this arrangement, but we wanted playmates and as soon as any children moved into the house, we invited them. The garden was unusually large, even for a period when real estate speculation had not yet changed the rural character of the city. It had a tiny hill, a pond, and a fountain; there were all sorts of birds and animals, including a chicken yard, and for a while we even owned two does. There were old-fashioned lilac bushes, fruit trees, and a pergola with grapevines—grapes that never get very sweet because of the pale northern sun. I have never liked any other grapes but these. And no apple—neither an American nor a Meran Caville—compares with the translucent wax apples, as juicy as peaches, from one of our trees. There were enough flowers for the children to cut as many as we wanted. For that matter, there was no one to prevent it, since we had little supervision. The garden implanted in all of us a deep love for growing things, for life as it comes out of the soil, and particularly for flowers, a love we were to keep throughout our years. For me the garden probably did more. This unrestrained existence, this sphere in which no authority prevailed, in which we were our own masters, released my natural bent and my longing for an active, free, and independent way of living.

But there was nothing in this secluded family circle to account for my precocious ambition to become a teacher. Who ever conceived of a girl in our group following a profession? Perhaps my desire was prompted by the teacher of one of my sisters, a lovely young woman who sometimes turned up for a visit. I may have thought that all teachers were as lovable as she was, an idea which I later recognized as an illusion.

A psychologist might suggest another explanation: that my place as second daughter, with the disadvantages involved, may have produced the desire for a position of authority, for a situation in which I would be able to lead. My ambition was inextricably interwoven with the wish to help people, and my adolescent schoolmates and friends knew this when they confided their personal problems to me. I must have inherited this quality from my father, who—though by no means a humanitarian—rushed to the aid of anyone in distress and went so far as to bring home from a business trip to Turkey two little boys whom he had found in a Jewish orphanage in Constantinople and adopted on the spot. According to the professional standards of social workers, which I helped bring into existence, my father's charity without forethought or skill was all wrong. But there was at least a warm impulse behind it, which, alas, is not always evident in those whom we have trained to apply scientific methods.

Looking back, it is difficult to say whether I was a happy child, but I was certainly not unhappy. I was easily frightened. Today we would call it "nervous and excitable." For a while I had crying fits at night and could not be quieted unless my mother took me into her bed. The cause of this I have always attributed to the famous *Arabian Nights.* Possibly I was too young to distinguish between fact and fiction. In one of the stories a huge picture on the wall opened mysteriously like a door and admitted an evil ghost-woman, its living model. I do not remember anything else about it, only that fear gripped me as soon as I saw the picture on the cover. I begged to have it taken away, but my sister and the servants thought it was fun to frighten me. When my mother finally found out about it, the book disappeared. I have never read it since.

I could barely wait for the day when I would be allowed to go to school. I was not quite six years old when that happy first day dawned. People did not fuss over the education of their children. There were no progressive schools, no child-study groups, no psychoanalysts, no rational deliberations about a child's character traits and the best method to develop them in the right direction. I do not believe that this handicapped or damaged us as much as it should have according to the theories of modern educators. Our mothers had a natural relationship with their children and not the cramped attitude of so many modern mothers who have been overfed with psychology. They trusted the influence of love and their instincts for guidance and good example.

When my older sister was ready for school, my father asked a neighbor where he sent his daughters. It was a school in our immediate neighborhood and so, without further investigation, my sister was enrolled there. It turned out to be a Christian school—bent, moreover, on exerting a purely Christian influence on its pupils. In our case, this was successful. My mother did not realize it until quite late. She had suggested to the headmistress that my sister should not participate in the religious instruction of the Protestant children, but there were no other dissenters, and daily chapel was routine. The headmistress warned that such discrimination would harm a young child and reassured her that Old Testament lessons would be given the next term. My sister continued with the class and I did after her, and the two little ones in succession, and when the Old Testament lessons came to an end, nothing was changed. Nobody at home asked us to report, and we were never questioned, while the principal was probably only too glad to leave well enough alone.

I was about ten when suddenly an attempt was made to restore us to the faith of our forefathers. A young teacher came to instruct us, but when he declared that it was a sin for us to say the Lord's Prayer, which we had learned and repeated every day at school, we rebelled. My mother may have thought it was useless, or perhaps she was obliged to economize. She gave in, and lessons stopped.

Every year we brought home the Christmas carols and the beautiful

Advent hymns with their spirit of joyful expectation and recited them for our parents beside the Christmas tree. In the school plays we were shepherds or angels—nobody guessed that one day such children would be "non-Aryan" angels. Children whose education centers around the figure of Christ—his divine drama, his message of love, the miracles wrought by the power of faith—can never forget it. Unless an equivalent is provided (and can there be an equivalent?), it will keep its hold.

I loved going to school, not because I thirsted for knowledge but chiefly because we were kept busy, and this was what I wanted and needed. Learning and being with children of my own age was fun. I cried the day my first vacation started and more passionately when I finished school and had to leave. I was a very lively child. My first report card said, "Alice must learn to be still more quiet," which some friends suggest might be an appropriate inscription for my tombstone.

Although the school standards were pretty low, we did have some stimulating teachers who were not on the staff full time. The staff teachers were mostly young and inexperienced. I was quick at learning. I solved arithmetic problems so easily that I could do my homework in class while the other children were still struggling.

Up to the beginning of the new century, there were two kinds of schools in Germany, as there still are in England: one for the children of the poor, called "people's school"; the other for those whose parents could afford to pay, called "higher school." Mine was of the second variety, yet the girls were not really "selected" as in some fashionable schools, which we nicknamed "velvet-coat schools." Like ourselves, the students came largely from middle-class families.

In certain respects we had a very puritanical childhood, in keeping with my mother's tastes and habits. She spent nothing on herself and no more than was necessary on her children. My sister Kate and I were sent to dancing class in white stockings, black shoes, and rather drab two-toned Sunday frocks. The others, daughters of writers and artists, were far more elegant—two of them, I remember, in light blue from hair ribbons to slippers. My parents were probably much better off than the editor of a Berlin newspaper or some rather obscure playwright, but this was my mother's idea of education. We were kept strictly with regard to material things but otherwise left to ourselves.

Our parents took our good scholarship for granted. My mother was a paragon of reliability and conscientiousness; I do not think that we ever had breakfast without her or that she once failed to see us off to school. And we had to live up to her. We were not praised or rewarded for good reports, nor did anyone coach us. However, like other children growing up in a garden with trees that could be climbed, we were wild and boisterous, sometimes quarrelsome, and willful. Of all of us, the only really selfless and virtuous one was my younger sister, Edith. This was undoubtedly the result of much physical suffering. We nicknamed her "Nieritz" after the publisher of a series of popular-priced stories about goody-goody children who were constantly rewarded for their goodness. Edith loved them, while we, of course, rejected their unnatural demand for sustained virtue.

I tried hard to imitate my older sister, but my methodical bent made it difficult; I had to register, plan, regulate, and arrange things in their order of time and space. I packed my school bag the night before and awoke promptly in the morning without being called. I had bitter arguments with my sister about our common chest of three drawers. I advocated a just and equal division: one drawer for each and a line dividing the third to separate her sphere from mine, a suggestion which she scorned and repudiated. I wanted my own private realm, even though it was only a chest of drawers. I would set myself a time limit on a piece of embroidery and sometimes exceed it by a day so as to have the surprise of a free margin on the next. It irritated my mother when she was in the midst of a spring cleaning or packing for a holiday to see me concentrating, pursuing some work of my own. "Immovable, like a rock in the sea," she would say.

"Something has to be done about it," became a habitual attitude with me, not only when I met with a human problem but when a flower in the school garden looked sickly. My colleagues used to tease me for it. But to this day I say that something has to be done about the troubles of the world, and I have tried throughout my life to do at least a little of what needed doing.

Still, compared to modern girls, I was childish, undeveloped, and inquisitive. I played with dolls until early adolescence, and since I could never get as many as I wanted, I favored paper dolls for playing school. I had a tremendous crush on one of my women teachers, an orphan born and brought up in the Baltic states, who spoke with an accent. The other children made fun of her for this, rousing my protective instinct and thus forming the basis of a friendship. It was rather romantic to have a friend so much older than I who would tell me about her beau and the lawyers' dance she attended every year. Actually, she must have been quite homely and unattractive. But this I discovered only twenty years later, during a terribly disappointing hour when she came to me for advice about her daughter.

I do not remember that we ever had a male teacher with whom we could have flirted. Love and sex were completely outside our orbit. There was no coeducation, no sports or any pastimes for boys and girls together, no movies. Even though the newspapers were much more restrained than they are now, children were not encouraged to read them and never thought of doing so. For all I knew about sex and marriage, I might as well have been brought up on an island inhabited by the female of the species only. The cat got kittens, yes, and we begged that they should not be drowned, but this was the animal world, and we did not ponder it. Procreation was neither as natural to us as it is to country children nor as mysteriously interesting as it sometimes is to city children from sophisticated homes. When we met with the physical effects of adolescence, we considered them a nuisance. Sex was not discussed.

This may have been due to my mother's influence, or it may have been in keeping with the era and with the mores of the bourgeois class. Most of the girls were like ourselves in this respect. If we were repressed, then all of our generation and those before us must have been repressed, too. I believe, however, that we merely matured later—physically, mentally, and spiritually—than children in the bewildering and rapid-paced civilization of today.

The last years of my childhood were overshadowed by sorrow. When my younger sister, Edith, had grown healthy enough to go to school with the rest of us, my father fell ill with pneumonia. Like many men, he was a restless patient and could hardly be kept in bed. He would probably have recovered if he had had the patience to stay home for a while after this attack, but he went traveling again and this time returned with pleurisy. He was an invalid for a year, in bed or confined to his room. From the window he could see the horse chestnut tree in our garden, and through the long winter and the months of early spring he often looked at it, wondering whether he would once more see the leaves unfold and the buds flower. He did not. Almost his last act was to sell the house in which I had spent my childhood. He died in April, at fifty-three, leaving my mother with all the young children.

A memorial service was held in the big drawing room, with curtains, mirrors, and pictures shrouded in black crepe. The burial service was to follow. My uncles did not want us to go to the cemetery, thinking us too young and that the memory might haunt us. My mother said, "A child loses its father only once. I want them to remember it." The two youngest returned to the nursery, while my older sister and I, aged fifteen and fourteen respectively, accompanied my mother and my brother. We were in the street, where a hearse and a number of carriages were waiting, when I heard my uncle say, "The first carriage is for the rabbi and the next for the widow and the orphans." Only then did I understand that I was an orphan, and the whole sadness of it dawned on me.

I did not fully understand what the death of a father implies for his children, nor that a child's potentialities can best be developed by both parents jointly. And though I had inherited many of my father's mental and physical traits, I never loved him as I loved my mother. I was far too young to know much about him, and he had been away most of the time. My mother had never been of a cheerful temperament; life had disappointed her. When my father died, her forces were already spent. The years following his death were unhappy ones for all of us. We had to move to another district, and the nursemaid who had been with us since the younger children were born had to go.

It was like being driven from paradise. All freedom gone. No more outdoor games—the sun and brilliance of life had vanished. No wonder I was thirsting for new outlets.

My brother came home from England to help direct the business. There were financial losses, and my mother economized more than was necessary. My relationship with my brother was difficult then. I had barely known him, and now he came into our lives, an immature young stranger, and assumed authority. The feminist had already been born in me, rebelling when I was expected to wait on him and render all sorts of services at his bidding. Fortunately, my brother married a few years later and disappeared from my daily horizon as suddenly as he had turned up.

My own problems became acute when I finished the "higher school" a few weeks before my fifteenth birthday. Had my father lived, with his love of innovation, he would probably have furthered me in my ambition for greater education. I was at the introspective stage, pondering on things unseen and invisible, on the identity of my physical existence and that of my mind and soul and always on the question of questions, the "cui bono" of life itself. I did not know what to do with my days. I was too young to be admitted to a teacher's seminary. At this period there was no university open to girls, not even a gymnasium in which to prepare for matriculation. If there had been one, I should scarcely have known about it. I had never even heard that there were German women who studied in Switzerland and in the United States of America. Finally, I went to an art school of needlework. This was considered proper and met with no opposition. For five years I spent many hours a day over my embroidery frame convinced that *any* activity is better than none. All my dreams were stitched into the canvas.

Suddenly, at seventeen, I had to face cruel reality with a deeper understanding than ever before. Edith, the child my mother had nursed through so much suffering and for whom she felt a peculiar love, fell ill. Edith had grown into a beautiful child, tall for her fourteen years. Like my mother, she was honest and conscientious—as if she would repay all the loving care she had received. I was very fond of the two little ones, and with the instinct of love I guessed at once that Edith was dangerously ill.

Our doctor diagnosed it as tonsillitis. In the hall he said to me, "You worry about the child. Your mother's condition is far more serious—you ought to be worrying about her!" My mother's health had not been good, and it was said that she had heart trouble. I now firmly believe that it was a functional heart condition, easily explained after the sorrows of the last years. She lived for exactly twenty-five more years. The child died within three days.

When my mother was not with Edith, I was at the bedside. On the third morning I noticed a change. She breathed laboriously and apparently suffered very much. The doctor came, and now he could see more: that it was diphtheria and that Edith's heart was failing. In the eighties this disease was still what it had been in the sixties, when it had robbed my mother of a son—the fiend of childhood. And certainly my sister's heart had been weakened in her earlier, long battle with asthma. The doctor called in a specialist, who told us that the child was lost. My mother broke down completely; she could not even remain with the dying child. Kate and a nurse and I were with Edith during her last cruel agony. From that time on, we had to look after my mother—I am inclined to say we had to "mother" her.

Childhood was definitely over.

CHAPTER 2

# Apprenticeship: 1893–1899

After the death of Wilhelm I, the general outlook was gloomy. My mother impressed upon us our poverty and our misfortunes, which I have since come to realize were relatively negligible and products of her own defeated spirit. My sister married a landowner in Silesia and began having a succession of children. I could easily have embarked on the time-honored job of professional aunt, nursing and "sitting," but fortunately I found work of my own. Shelters had been organized by a wealthy publisher's wife, and I joined a sort of Junior League, a group that enlisted girls for volunteer service in philanthropic and welfare institutions.[1] I had received an invitation to the inaugural meeting in the city hall, and from that day on I worked in a shelter for little girls and in the charity organization society. Since I was given some responsibility, I could not get away, nor did I want to.

The work was characteristic of the low standards of welfare activity during the nineties. Only such children were accepted whose mothers were either widows or who had been deserted by their husbands. Desertion served as a substitute for divorce for people who had no money, and because the mothers had to work, the children were not well kept. They came after school hours, at twelve or one P.M., and remained until seven—a pretty long day. Nothing was done, as it is these days, to develop the intellectual or artistic capacities of the children. They had to do their homework, and when this was finished, they were rewarded (or punished) by having to knit. We Junior League girls helped them with their homework so that none of them would get bad marks at school. This was the ambition of the supervisor, an elderly good-natured woman who had been a seamstress. She had no understanding, of course, of the educational problem involved. Until six P.M., silence reigned, but from six until they went home at seven, the children played games, mostly moving in a circle and singing childish verses.

I visited families for the charity organization—people too old to work or those who had more children than they could support. If there was a husband, it was carefully arranged to keep him in ignorance of the welfare worker's visit, for the men resented charity, while the women were only too glad of the extra money or food.

During the many years I "visited the poor," as it was then expressed, I never ran into actual vice, as my students did ten or twenty years later. By far the worst plight I saw was that of the women in the so-called home industries—later known more appropriately as sweatshops. The women worked to the point of exhaustion, all day and half the night, and yet they did not earn enough in piecework wages to exist without help from the poor-law guardians. Hundreds of pieces of sewing did not bring in enough to support one person, let alone children. Their homes, consisting usually of a kitchen and one room large enough to accommodate a bed, were crowded and unsanitary. Everything was done in the kitchen: cooking, washing and feeding the children, and the sewing they did for the industries. It was the only work they could do while caring for their children at the same time. And of course this type of labor worked to the advantage of the employers; without it, the industries would not have been able to exist.

As I made these first halting steps into a world I had not known before, I also attended lecture courses on sociology and civics arranged by our organization.[2] It was one of the first attempts to devise some theoretical preparation for social work. All this began in the year 1893, when Jane Addams moved into Hull House in Chicago and Lillian Wald in New York went to live on Henry Street to nurse her neighbors. English men and women had preceded us with similar efforts, but we knew nothing of each other.[3] Social work had no history, no rules, no model. It needed creative personalities. It was pioneering and opened a new field.

The story of the early lives of these women who were the first to enter it invariably deals with their sense of unrest. The work claimed them, and they became leaders because it fitted the complex potentialities of their natures. Social work during this period offered an outlet for a certain type of woman. Women in whom the maternal instinct was strong, of creative mind and independent spirit, needed work which could be formed and shaped through their responsibility and initiative. As nurses, they would have been subjected to authority; as governesses, they would have had to bend to an employer's will. Even as teachers, they would have been bound to a strict syllabus and a narrow schedule not of their own making.

I was the product of a society which had not yet shed the shell of paternalism. Poverty, as we know it now, hardly existed. Those were prosperous times. There was no unemployment, and labor as a distinct class was just emerging: no feeling of class struggle moved among the people I knew. But my world was changing. It was approaching a peak of capitalistic and industrial development. There was an ever-growing population in the cities. For some groups of society, technical progress made life easy and more comfortable, for others more hopeless and insecure. I did not realize this before I started out in the League for Social Work. If anyone had asked me whether the working classes had their share of the new amenities of life, I would not have known what the question meant. After all, who did not accept the given order of society as the natural order?

Those who wanted to alter it, the socialists, still a small group in the nineties,[4] were considered as dangerous by the capitalist classes in Germany as the communists are in America today. In 1879 a "Law against the Subversive Activities of the Social Democrats" had deprived labor unions and their leaders of constitutional rights and liberties. Insofar as attempts were made to improve the position of the workers, they were conservative moves, sometimes genuinely mixed with Christian ethics. Bismarck's Insurance Acts,[5] drawn up in connection with the antilabor law mentioned above, were a product of his determination to obstruct radical movements. He reasoned that since labor had been forbidden to strive for better conditions, the state must guarantee assistance. He believed that people with a claim to a regular income, even the smallest annuity, would support the established order. As a result, the insurance law was passed with the votes of the Conservatives only; the Liberals and the Socialists had opposed it!

I remember vividly the discussions of my relatives when the "insurance" came into force. They were annoyed at the new tax, the inconvenience of sending small contributions to various bodies, of pasting stamps into a booklet for each employee week by week. It was the same reactionary attitude which many Americans expressed in their opposition to President [Franklin Delano] Roosevelt's Social Security Acts. Only no one at that time called it a Bolshevist policy—partly because the Bolshevist bogey did not yet exist, and partly because even his most bitter antagonist could not see in Bismarck anything but a conservative. Nobody among the people I knew ever hinted that these laws were a tremendous step toward justice and security, and I myself had to serve my social apprenticeship and to acquire my own social philosophy before I could understand it.

Our League for Social Work came into existence through the efforts of a group of progressive people. Most of the young women who joined came from these same families or from the families of friends.[6] It was an equivalent of the Anglo-Saxon settlement movement. We were asked to render modest services to the underprivileged, then called simply "the poor," and to prepare ourselves for responsible citizenship. For us, yet knowing nothing about public affairs, citizenship did not mean "rights" or "suffrage" but obligation and service. Help for the poor meant only charity.

How sheltered we had been! A woman some years older than I undertook to investigate the condition of women in factories. She carefully drafted a questionnaire and, while talking to each woman, filled in the blanks. When the answer to the question, "Are you married?" was "No," she filled in the next column automatically with the comment, "Therefore no children." The working women, however, soon pointed out to her that one did not imply the other.

In the welfare work in which we started, we discovered other needs and organized new institutions to cope with them. We fought for labor laws for children, and when they were passed, it proved necessary to provide school meals to make up for the loss of the children's wages. We sponsored the first children's courts, which followed in the wake of the child-labor laws and were set up under a special judge assisted first by volunteers, later by professional social workers, of whom many were my students. They investigated home and family circumstances and personal character traits as a basis for court procedure and might well be called forerunners of psychoanalysis. Later, these same social workers became probation officers.

We also introduced Hospital Social Service in Germany and started a Consumers' League to improve working conditions in shops and factories. We traveled and lectured throughout the country and sent petitions trying to interest parliament in better poor laws, in the administration of which we wanted women included.[7] We agitated for extension of the Insurance Acts, especially with regard to maternity benefits, and for labor laws in the sweatshops. At that time, the Poor Law Board acted in favor of industry rather than of the people. The needy were understandably reluctant to sign away their possessions, meager but often precious to them, in order to collect relief that was moreover totally inadequate for decent living requirements.[8] They lived in crowded, airless tenements, prevalent in North and East Berlin, with steep, dangerously rickety flights of stairs, several large families sharing one hall toilet. We wanted the poor to be treated humanely so that they need not fear applying for relief. The restaurant and tavern owners became opponents to be reckoned with; with the advance of women social workers into the slum districts, they anticipated a falling-off of trade. I remember being puzzled during one meeting at the restlessness of the men in the audience, who would keep leaving briefly and returning. It did not occur to me, in my innocence, that this might have had an indirect bearing on the quantities of beer they drank.

Our families were anything but enthusiastic about our work. It had taken some strategy to make it acceptable to my mother. Much more difficult were the uncles who occasionally took an interest in their orphan nieces. They warned my mother not to let me run about in poor districts lest something "happen" to me. For to them poverty was identical with the "underworld."

What "happened" was very different from their lurid expectations. On my part it was a violent moral reaction. The contrast between my own circumstances, which my mother considered bleak, and those of the people among whom I worked overwhelmed me. I rebelled against the injustice and the unequal opportunities. I wanted to take the pictures off the walls at home, the rugs from the floor, to have the simplest clothes and to spend nothing on them. This was a passing mood, and gradually I formed the opinion that pictures and rugs and decent clothes should be accessible to all. But during the first decade of my work, I could not see a man doing heavy and dirty labor in the streets without wondering why he did not attack people like me who were free from drudgery.

We were serious about it as only young people can be, and we expected others to take us seriously. We wanted to change the world and believed we should be able to do it. The first thing we accomplished was to change our own lives. Now my days were filled to overflowing. No more elaborate plans to give my life some substance—the time of uselessness, of empty expectation and blind hopes, had gone.

Among the early projects which I started with some friends in Berlin were the Working Girls' Clubs. Having been luckier in the accidental matter of birth, we wanted to use some of our ease and freedom to give these girls a share of the good things we enjoyed: education, books, flowers, recreation, and decent lodgings. In Germany this was pioneer work, and we started it with the pocket money of a handful of girls. We gave what we had. I argued with my mother about every piece of furniture in the house that I considered superfluous. She complained that she expected me to arrive with a moving van some day and leave her in an empty home. My mother did not like change, not even of furniture. We rented premises for the club, which was open at first only in the evenings. We salvaged an old piano, sent out printed invitations, served refreshments, and fostered reading, acting, and needlework. Later, when the club expanded and gained more support, there were living quarters for the members.[9]

I do not know whether the factory girls gained more than material advantages. We certainly learned many things from them which we could not get out of books or lectures. We had invited our younger sisters to one carefully prepared party in order to interest them in the work. The program was proceeding nicely when a textile worker, apparently a well-mannered girl, stunned us with the most vulgar catch-song I have ever heard. It was not quite so easy as we had thought to teach "culture." Mainly we were afraid our younger sisters might gossip, which would have led to new controversies at home.

A few years later, when the standards of the club had risen, we had the members perform one of the loveliest plays of Goethe, *Die Geschwister,* and they really did exceedingly well. It must have cost them much effort to learn those long parts, late at night after working hours. Our audience was enthusiastic. About that time, the same play was produced in one of the best Berlin theaters. Thinking the girls would be thrilled to see professional actors in the roles they had played, I asked the producer whether he would let them have complimentary tickets. He sent the best in the house, in the dress circle, and they went. But they were not impressed. "Very nice, indeed, Miss Salomon, very nice," they said. "But we acted with much greater passion."

The clubs brought me face to face with a crucial question which confronts all conscientious social workers. We were violently attacked in a socialist paper in an article written by Lily Braun, a prominent feminist who had recently been converted to socialism.[10] She implied that the object of these clubs was purely selfish; namely, to alienate the girls from the labor movement by satisfying their needs and thus stave off the collapse of the capitalistic system. I do not know whether she really believed this or whether she hoped that her bitter and unjust attack would improve her position among the socialists, who were rather suspicious of the bourgeois renegade. However, I could not accept such a serious charge lying down. I went to see her and pleaded for fairness, but she remained aggressive and adamant.

From then on I asked myself what she had asked me: "Can social work help bring about a better world? Is it not merely a palliative, a compromise? Should not the social system be radically changed? Reform or revolution? Where should we go?" I had not arrived at an answer.

Meanwhile, the head of our group had become very dear to me. Of the many outstanding and remarkable women whom I met through my work, two have had a deep, abiding influence on my life. Jeanette Schwerin was the first and Ishbel Aberdeen the second.[11] One made me aware of the wide perspectives, the *Lebensinhalt,* or content, of my work. The other possessed a spiritual strength that helped me to acquire unshakable faith and convictions, without which I could not in turn have influenced the younger generation as I did.

Frau Schwerin was then about forty years old, twenty years my senior, but she looked much older and quite insignificant except for her vivid brown eyes. Nobody would have noticed her in any gathering until she began to speak. Then she aroused general attention. She was short, with a pale complexion that made her look anemic. She had soft, smooth dark hair and wore simple and unornamented clothes. Her father, a doctor, had been one of the organizers of an institute for adult education of small craftsmen and tradespeople. With this background she was, for her time, exceptionally well read and cultivated; her interests had been mainly in the liberal arts. She was married to a doctor and lived among her husband's clients in a lower-middle-class district. Her only son was more or less a problem child, and her marriage was not happy on the whole, but her home became a center of culture for many prominent men and women, and I learned there that liberalism is more than a political and economic doctrine—more than an opposition movement to the conservative state. Frau Schwerin grew very fond of me and became a loving friend.

It is strange to think that she did not take part in social work until she was nearly forty. But before her premature death six years later, she had drawn on all classes for fellow workers and was known all over the country. Without Frau Schwerin, the work of our Junior League would probably have remained ephemeral and amateurish. She had a deep sense of moral obligation, a practical gift for discerning real issues, and it was she who first recognized and stressed the bond between welfare work and feminism. They belonged together. Her power of expression enabled her to hold any crowd, and though she was a most womanly woman, she felt with the intensity of a creed that women must have a place in public life and the opportunity to protect and defend humanity everywhere. She filled our minds and hearts with this belief; she carefully trained groups of girls and women to meet any requirements in social work so that later, no government official might hinder us with the excuse that, being women, we were incompetent. In recruiting she had a formula: to get women of the leisure class to *leave* the home for work that would help the working women *return* to theirs.

She was naturally drawn into the feminist movement, and she took part in building up the National Council of Women,[12] which had been organized by suggestion of the International Council of Women in 1894. Frau Schwerin was far too modern to believe that social progress can be made without the cooperation of all interested groups. Therefore she worked persistently for an understanding with the women of organized labor.

But although Frau Schwerin commanded general respect, she could not break down the prejudice implanted in the socialists by their doctrine. Class feeling had begun to run high, and the antagonism and distrust among political factions was mutual and passionate then in "united" Germany, as it was later in the days when it helped Hitler into the saddle.

During the summer of 1896, an International Conference of Women had been arranged in Berlin. It was an insignificant affair, as the ties between women of different countries were still casual. But it acquired dignity through a meeting in which Frau Schwerin played the decisive part.

The subject to be discussed one morning was "In which spheres can women of all classes cooperate successfully?" The time for each speaker was limited. Lily Braun, with whom I had had the encounter about factory girls, was still in the most passionate phase of socialism. She went to the platform and burst out violently, as if she had been insulted, that she had consented to speak merely because she wanted to denounce the bourgeois lack of understanding in allowing her only twenty minutes for a labor problem. She invited the foreign visitors who wanted to hear her to a meeting the socialist women were holding the same evening. Writing it down after all these years, it seems rather silly. Evidently she still wanted to challenge her recent friends and coworkers in order to gain standing in her new affiliation, where she was not fully accepted.

At the time it seemed dramatic. Those in authority fluttered about at a loss how to deal with the incident. Frau Schwerin went to the platform and asked to be allowed to answer. In all simplicity, without a trace of rancor, she stated that Lily Braun's behavior was unfair. She went on to explain how many handicaps and injustices were shared by all women irrespective of class, describing the fields in which we could cooperate to mutual advantage. "Even though the socialist women oppose us, we would never fight them. Women against women, mothers against mothers; this would be unheard of in the history of humanity." Nothing could have been more impressive than this serene response to a violent display of hostility. It was the answer of a peacemaker, of a woman in a woman's natural role. She made the meeting memorable.

For years I worked together with Frau Schwerin, acted as her secretary, and represented her at meetings when she was too ill to go herself. I spent more time in her home than in my mother's. I doubt if my mother ever realized what this guidance and friendship meant to me—at least not until it came to an end. I was hectically busy, being inclined to give myself wholeheartedly to the task at hand. There were times when I almost forgot that I had learned to read. But Frau Schwerin insisted on giving me books—today they are old-fashioned but then they were up to date, without sentimentality, and instrumental in forming my social philosophy.

Tolstoy's *What Then Shall We Do?* became my textbook.[13] It taught me to see the wrongs we inflict on others through sheer carelessness, and even now I cannot hear a factory whistle calling the employees to work before dawn without thinking of his powerful contrast between the lives of the rich and the poor. It has done more for me than many a course in social psychology can do for a social worker.

Disraeli justified all we did to bridge the gulf when he compared the two classes to two nations, with different languages, different customs, with thoughts and sentiments like those of different continents, subject even to different laws and jurisdictions. Ruskin's *Sesame and Lilies* seemed to have been written for us, as indeed it was for a similar group: "Whatever else you may be, you must not be useless and you must not be cruel." And Goethe's *Wilhelm Meister* still moves me, more than ever here in my adopted country, with his sentence, "Not where I am at ease, but where I can be useful, there is my fatherland!"[14]

In the nineties everybody read novels dealing with social problems: Mrs. Humphrey Ward's *Marcella* and *Robert Elsmere;* and even more popular was Walter Besant's *All Sorts and Conditions of Men,* with a preface of a few words: "I have been told that this is an impossible story, but I cannot understand why it must remain impossible!" The stir it made raised enormous sums with which he realized his dream of a "People's Palace" in the East End of London, the first center for adult education and recreation.[15]

I sometimes wonder if the current, realistic social problem writers will inspire another generation to reform as did Walter Besant, and most of all Charles Kingsley and Charles Dickens.[16]

Such were the years of my apprenticeship. Some people thought it a strange sort of life for a girl. But I had found my place. Perhaps Frau Schwerin had a presentiment that her life would be short. It seemed as if she consciously prepared me to succeed her. In any case, she molded my methods and ideas.

She had been seriously ill for some time, although she summoned just enough energy to keep out of bed and drag herself around. It had been planned that I should accompany her to a meeting of the National Council of Women in Hamburg in the fall of 1898, until at the last moment she realized she could not travel. I had to take her place, without benefit of her chaperonage for my "national debut." In those days women did not travel alone—it was not done. My mother insisted on taking me to the station, unable to do more. At the Hamburg gathering we got acquainted and discussed the current questions and problems: higher education for women, the opening of professions to women, getting women as factory inspectors and city welfare officials. The Council was then the only national group controlled by women in Germany and embodied the first attempt to unite women of all religious and political creeds to work together for social welfare and women's rights. The importance of the meeting was established mainly in the fact that it took place.

The following year Frau Schwerin had planned to take me with her to the International Council of Women in London. Again the idea was not abandoned until the last moment, even though she knew she was dying. That I could no longer doubt after my return from London. My mother had been waiting for me to accompany her to the Swiss mountains and could not be persuaded to put off our departure. A few days after arriving in Switzerland, I was called back. Frau Schwerin had died. It was a terrible blow. My affections had been deep. I knew that my work must be rearranged and the question of new leadership was dubious. People warned me not to try to continue what she had started. Once more, life seemed empty.

Through the centuries, philosophers and poets have testified to the belief that the road to new life is entered through the gates of loss. I should then have sailed right into some new and exciting experience, preferably marriage. I was twenty-seven years old, and if ever there was a moment propitious for marriage, it was then.

My mother had no desire whatever to see her daughters married. Perhaps she had been too deeply disappointed herself, or possibly she was one of those women who suffer under the marriage relationship. For her generation, the curse "In sorrow thou shalt bring forth children" was doubly true. The "honorable estate" meant, after all, that they obey their husbands like chattels in all things.

On the other hand, I would have bitterly resented any attempt at an "arranged marriage" on the part of my mother if she had been so inclined. But why did I not marry? Journalists and interviewers have frequently asked me. I always replied, "Because I could not get the men I wanted and did not want the men I could get." This is quite true. Women do not decide this matter according to a principle or a theory.

While I was in my twenties, it never occurred to me that I would not marry. Tradition was too strong in us. We thought unmarried elderly women a bit queer. In some provincial cities, girls were allowed to "go out" for three winters only. If they did not achieve the desired result by then, they had to withdraw and leave the field to the next age group, probably a reflection of the surplus female population in Europe.

But I was too absorbed in other interests to have time to go about and meet young men. Above all, I never attracted the right sort of man.

I was not good-looking, I was not wealthy, and worse, I was serious and thoughtful. I expected men to live up to my ideas of equal moral standards for the sexes, and such men rarely existed in a bourgeois society where they were compelled to delay marriage until they could provide for a family.

Many girls in my group would have disdained a suitor whose manners and clothes did not come up to their snobbish tastes. Patent leather shoes were more important than character. Although I was less shallow, I doubt that I would have been unconventional enough to choose without regard to social standing and the prevalent class consciousness. In one case, where a man of unimpeachable background courted me from the moment we were introduced, I was simply not attracted. Other suitors in whom I was deeply interested could not offer me the sort of union I wanted, in connection with my work and ideas. Disappointment in love is one of the saddest experiences, sadder than the death of a beloved being. For years I could not see a child without feeling pangs over my lost hopes. But in looking back, I have been thankful that none of these attachments led to marriage. Passion rarely lasts a lifetime. With my faculty for great joy and affection went a faculty for deep unhappiness. Sooner or later, I should have realized that it had been a mistake for me.

After such interludes, I had to find my way back to my former pursuits and to restore to them an undivided mind. This was not easy, but I think that I came out of these conflicts a better worker, more capable of understanding the human problems of others.

Falling in love does not end at any prescribed age—certainly it did not end for me in the period with which this chapter deals. What was it then that ultimately kept me from marriage? Recently, when I read Edna Ferber's autobiography,[17] I was struck by her analysis of the problem. She confesses that it must have been her love for her mother that barred her, because she allowed her mother's needs to dominate her personal life. I have considered this as an explanation for my own celibacy. But I knew that I should have left my mother any day if there had been a probability of happiness. Nor would she have tried to keep me from it. In the end, it was my work, which had already estranged me from my background, that made me reluctant to form a union which could not combine love with common interests and convictions.

I remember a talk on this subject, many years ago, with Lillian Wald and a mutual friend—neither of them very happily married. Both insisted, "The single life is much easier for a woman." I claimed that few German women would share this view and asked whether their attitude was determined by the Puritan strain in their upbringing. They denied this. "German women are oversexed," they said. I said, "They depend on marriage, because they have few opportunities for work and because German civilization stresses marriage as the exclusive career of women."

I thought at that time—and still believe—that married life is easier because the duties of a married woman are obvious, especially if she has children. She need not make decisions about what to do with her life. In that sense, most of the struggle eludes her. She knows where she belongs. But I am equally convinced that some women are made to be single. In the days of my youth, particularly, it was difficult for a married woman of an active nature and a sense of moral values to keep her integrity. Today, when general values have changed, when her sphere has broadened and she can gain financial independence, it is easier. Whether a woman develops into a personality depends not on marriage alone but, equally important, on her capacity to accept—positively—what comes her way. To be able to do this is not merit but divine grace.

CHAPTER 3

# Widening Horizon

After appearing as a substitute for Frau Schwerin at the biannual meeting of the National Council of Women in Hamburg in 1898, I was asked to lecture for women's clubs and leagues all over Germany. Then, in 1900, the Council elected me a member of the board of officers.

This was quite sensational. So far the youngest on the platform had not been under sixty years of age. A novelist of the period had described the women at such meetings as "black shadows," and there I was—twenty-six years old, in a very short light dress, radiating eagerness and unbounded enthusiasm. I spoke on a subject that was currently dominant, on the need for women as factory inspectors, a need stubbornly ignored by male officialdom. I pointed out that women were in a better position to understand and attend to the problems of child labor, sanitary facilities for women workers, women with children, and women in pregnancy, questions that might prove embarrassing or immaterial to male inspectors. In spite of my youth, or perhaps because of it, the audience liked me.

The National Council was organized as a loose federation of women's societies and clubs, preferably of national bodies, and did not accept individuals as members. From the beginning it appointed committees to work on special problems. At once, I was elected to the committee propagating the appointment of women as factory inspectors, and I organized the first women's employment and vocational guidance bureaus. I found friends among the Council's women in all parts of Germany, and this was very encouraging.

The German Council developed rapidly. Progressive German women were probably more inclined to band together than the women of Latin countries. In France, for instance, a woman could usually gain by herself what she wanted from a cabinet member or from the head of some department—whether it was the right to study, or a degree, or a job which no woman had held before. The Frenchman is more inclined than the German to accede to the wishes or complaints of the individual woman. Consequently, French women were less compelled to stand up for each other, to organize. It took them longer to articulate the claims of women in general.

In Germany, however, where men in official circles were intent on keeping women confined to kitchen and nursery, women had to back a request in large numbers before they could make themselves heard. At the time of the Hamburg meeting, the National Council was still in a rather humble stage, but it soon grew into a body representative of what might have been called the "modern women." The younger women who came in after me developed with the Council in status and influence. The feminist movement became popular among the liberals, and we began to reap a harvest.

There were many gifted women of my own generation in the Council, some foremost in intellect, others in practical matters, and a few rare beings endowed with an innate harmony of mind and soul. Women artists, painters, musicians, and scholars kept in close touch with our welfare movement. We felt like one family. It was a period of flowering after centuries when women had been repressed, without scope or opportunity, without property rights or even the right of guardianship over their own children.

We counted our years by the Council meetings: the years of Heidelberg, Danzig, Gotha, Nuremberg. We had not only long days of scheduled activities but long nights of private talk. We thrashed out work, family, love, friendship—between women, between a woman and a married man; love without marriage; education, labor, politics and parties, people and countries, women in professions. . . .

I belonged to the group that wanted to penetrate into the social service of local and state administrations. Self-governing bodies could appoint none except enfranchised citizens, and so women were kept out. There were "fathers of the city" but no "mothers." Men directed the poor-law administration and the school board; they supervised municipal nurseries and hospitals and approved foster homes for children who were boarded out. They cannot have been very happy with many of these duties, yet they were loath to turn them over to us.

This state of affairs existed all over the country, and our struggle lasted for years. We petitioned the Prussian Diet to have the law changed. We would even have been satisfied to become advisory members without a vote. But after legal difficulties were overcome in 1902, there was always some new excuse for refusing our claim when we applied to the Berlin municipality. Most of the poor-law guardians were men of the lower middle class who held their meetings in beer restaurants. They drank and smoked liberally while they passed their decisions on records, each one of which represented the life and sorrow of a family in desperate need. This practice would have been considered improper in the presence of women, and they did not want their evenings spoiled. However, we carried our point by doggedly proposing a candidate whenever a vacancy occurred. Gradually, women began to get in.

The interests of the women in the Council varied, and our temperaments sometimes clashed, although new loyalties, apart from those traditionally concerned with marriage and motherhood, held us together. There were doubts and problems. Should I attempt to take over Frau Schwerin's work in the Council, or return to the rank and file, to the Charity Organization Society and the direction of the girls' clubs? And who was now to head the Junior League, which had initiated my friends and me into social work?

It is astonishing how many pretenders turn up for every vacant throne, even one so insignificant as the presidency of a local society of volunteer welfare workers. The question was settled by Emil Münsterberg, the head of the Berlin Poor-Law Department and an adviser on our board. He said, "We have a choice. We can ask a woman with name and position. But such a woman would be likely to think that her name is sufficient contribution. Or we can choose someone who has neither name nor position but who will put heart and soul into the work. She will make a name and position for the association and for herself." Quite to everyone's surprise, he suggested me. I was elected.[1]

Our work grew with the change in political, social, and cultural forces. The era of economic liberalism was nearing its end. The universities began to stress the social sciences and social research. National and international associations were formed to influence public opinion. In the Junior League we had long realized that social work needed systematic preparation, an understanding of the legal and economic structure of society and of the human side of poverty. Accordingly, in the fall of 1899 we announced a one-year, full-time course to prepare professional social workers—the first on the European continent. It was a most modest undertaking, and today it seems unbelievable that we always looked back upon it as the cradle of schools for social work. The scheme was haphazard and more or less amateurish—an experiment. The main thing was that the students had to devote a whole year to social work. We had no permanent rooms at our disposal, no money, and no teaching staff except people of the administration or professors who came each for ten lectures on public health, child welfare, poor law, and charity. We could afford little publicity. Yet a handful of students turned up. Social work did not yet offer possibilities for earning a living. A new profession, and the education for it, is not "ready made" nor suddenly born but developed gradually.[2]

So far the steps taken by Catholic orders and Protestant groups to help the poor, the destitute children, the cripples and prisoners, were based on religious education and regarded as a religious service. We were convinced, however, that something other than charity was needed—the devotion and undivided time of people who would develop this into a true profession.

It took nine more years and an impulse from outside forces to put education for professional social workers on a systematic basis and organize the first school of social work. But we were hardly aware that our beginning was actually the starting point of the new profession, which was to raise community standards through better care for the underprivileged, attracting thousands of people all over the world. It was the inauguration of a highly satisfying career for humanitarian men and women. Nor did I foresee that for the next thirty-eight years, until I had to leave Germany, education for social work was to be my constant preoccupation. Our experiment created forever-widening orbits, like a stone thrown into a pond. It gave impetus to a growing need. Other groups started similar courses, and a few years later, the National Association for Poor Law and Charities[3] endorsed the plan and recommended further institutes for the education of social workers. The movement grew from a local to a national one, and ultimately I was to be asked to unite, as far as possible, the schools of all countries into an international body.

At this crucial time in my career I owed much to a young man, Friedrich Wilhelm Foerster,[4] who had been equally close to Frau Schwerin. He had (what was always suspect in Germany) radical pacifist ideas, which he had expressed in an article that had caused him to be sentenced for lèse-majesté. I once told him that I had inhibitions against disclosing deeply felt and treasured convictions when speaking in public. He was quite emphatic: "Unless you're willing to give all you have, all you are, the innermost core of you soul—stay home. If you merely want to tell people something they don't know, you can write. In addressing a meeting you must make an effort to inspire people. Let a hundred people laugh at what means most to you. But if you win *one*, it's worth the sacrifice." I never again talked at a meeting without trying to live up to his advice.

Labor loomed high on my social-work horizon. The socialist movement grew strong after it had been freed of restrictive laws. I knew that I must decide where I stood. For women twenty years older than I, this had been no problem. They were, rather, liberal; socialism had not yet affected the bourgeoisie and the intellectuals. Some women of the leisure class wanted to help organize women's trade unions, as Lady Dilke and Margaret MacDonald did in England, and Mrs. Raymond Robbins and Mary Dreier in the United States. But in Germany the class-war theory had too firm a hold on the minds of organized labor. Unless I became a party socialist, such an attempt would be impossible.

I had met many socialist leaders at the house of a relative who had joined "the party." He was a man of both wealth and idealism, generous with his time and contributions. There I came to know August Bebel, the head of the Socialist Party.[5] Bebel had been a carpenter and was self-educated, having gained his leadership through a combination of great intelligence, charm, and enthusiasm. He was good-looking, of medium height, with a mop of light hair and radiant, compelling blue eyes. He spoke with vigor and persuasion, even in private conversation, and was much more the type of old-fashioned craftsman than I had expected in a man who wanted to revolutionize the economic system. Although he talked of theories and economic creeds, he had basically a practical nature interested in results.

Bebel was one of the first men in Germany to take women's problems seriously. He wanted [to win] women for socialism under a program of equal rights. His sensational book, *Women and Socialism,* written from a materialist standpoint, could be sold only secretly in the ten years during which the Socialist Party was outlawed; nevertheless, ten editions were brought out.[6] Its readers were probably mostly men, for it was too revolutionary in matters of marriage and sex to appeal to women. Bebel proposed equal rights long before German women claimed them and overcame theoretically all opposition to this among Socialist men, incorporating his ideas on woman suffrage in the party program of 1891. Although practically it may not have influenced the individual attitude (often a dominating one) of a man toward a woman or of a husband toward his wife, still it was proved that forty years of proclaiming a principle implied a moral obligation when the provisional government, calling a national assembly in 1918, stuck to its guns and gave the vote to women.

Bebel made many attempts to win me for the Socialist Party. A socially minded woman from the privileged class was considered a valuable acquisition, both for purposes of propaganda among working women and for the psychological effect of such an allegiance on her own class. He tried to convince me that the class-war theory was no more than the expression of an economic fact. But I would not join a movement that rejected the principle of conciliation.

During a labor dispute that aroused violent excitement and antagonism, I decided to see for myself what could be done. In August 1903 a strike involving five textile factories in the small Saxon town of Crimmitschau had resulted in a general lockout of 7,500 workers, 4,000 of whom were women. The whole population of 23,000 was affected. By the end of the year it had become a desperate struggle, hinging on the modest demand for a ten-hour day. At Christmas I went, without introduction, to talk to the employers, the mayor, the government officials, the clergy. In a small industrial town, the professional people depended to some degree on the factory owners, and there were family ties between these two groups. All of them were hostile toward labor. When the employers talked about good living wages for families, they meant those in which a man and wife and several grown-up children worked. Families like these did not exist, for women with grown-up children were rarely strong enough to continue work in the mills.

I discussed the problems with the labor leaders and visited the workers' homes. Those women who worked had no time for children and housekeeping. They solved the problem simply by not keeping house. The children were boarded out in foster homes, permanently or by the day. Here the problem was reduced to plain arithmetic: one woman sent her two children for the day to her sister, who had three younger ones. With three small children it did not "pay" to board them out.

These women had been working half-time from the age of twelve, before child labor between twelve and fourteen had been forbidden by law. At fourteen they took full-time jobs. When they were married, they continued working, and the first child was handed over to the grandparents. If more than two children were born, the mothers stayed at home and increased their income by looking after other people's children. There was no family life. It was the women who kept up the strike—who rebelled most bitterly.

The town swarmed with police troops; under army protection, the employers imported foreigners as strikebreakers. The air was thick with hatred. All this time the government could easily have offered a solution. The ten-hour day had been due for some time—had the government drawn up a bill and whipped it through, Crimmitschau would at once have reverted to peace. (The bill was passed three years later.) My trip had failed. The only thing I could do was to try to arouse public opinion by writing articles. A government official effected a conciliation soon after my visit.

On my return to Berlin I met a "liberal" professor whom I told about my futile effort. His comment was, "Soon we shall be obliged to organize for the protection of employers."

This was almost more than I could bear. We had to contend with Liberals who wanted liberty for the strong to exploit the weak, Socialists who wanted a new order or nothing, Conservatives who were ready for concessions so long as they served their own aims. If I had not been in the feminist movement from the start, my experience in social work alone would have urged me to join those women who knew that there is no wealth but life and that life must be valued and protected.

Meanwhile, in the year 1900, the Prussian universities had finally been opened to women, a year or two later than those in southern Germany.[7] The struggle of women for admission to the universities had been long and hard and had met with the most stubborn resistance designed to keep them on a low educational level in order to eliminate possible competition in the professions. It was too late for me, I thought. I did not have sufficient education to meet the entrance requirements, and my teaching (social science and economics in vocational schools) and writing absorbed me altogether. I had published *Social Duties of Women,* contributed to the *Handbook of the Women's Movement,* the parts dealing with social work and with labor laws for women, and brought out a collection of articles and speeches, *What We Owe Ourselves and Others,* dealing with the obligations of women of the leisure class to do valuable work, thus making their own lives more dignified and at the same time pay their debt to the underprivileged.[8]

A change came into my life, unexpectedly like so many, through my friendship with a pioneer university student who had won her Ph.D. in economics. Else von Richthofen was a baroness, of a distinguished family, beautiful, gifted, and charming. She came from southern Germany and met her many Berlin relatives at a family dinner. Having thought that something so disreputable as a university education must mark a girl, they were incredulous at her long hair, her white dress—and because she did not smoke. Nor was her mother, at home, enthusiastic. While Else worked during holidays, she would look over her shoulder and sigh, "I only hope you won't be sorry later that you've studied so much." She meant that it might spoil her daughter's chances of marriage.

The university was proud of her, and there was hardly an unmarried don who would not have proposed to her had he had the courage. But they too believed that a woman university graduate—even one so attractive as Else—would not marry. She was appointed the first woman factory inspector with university education and on a common footing with her male colleagues. After a few years one of her former fellow students, editor of a socialist magazine, did propose and was accepted. It caused an uproar; everyone who had not dared was convinced that the man who had got her was not nearly good enough.

It was indirectly through her that I entered the university.[9] After Else's graduation one of the professors, the very progressive Max Sering,[10] gave a party in her honor and she suggested that I be invited. Taking me in to dinner, Sering asked me why I did not study, now that the way was clear. I mentioned requirements, but he insisted that exceptions could be made for people with merit, and he would be glad to help. It happened before I really knew what I wanted. My application was accepted. For women, the university was still surrounded with romance, and after eight breathless years of social work, I was mentally starved. I doubt if any student of the present day can imagine the bliss that we, the first little group of women, felt at having access to the accumulated wisdom of centuries. We learned to see coherence among the different spheres of learning, to begin to understand the search of mankind for truth and knowledge. It was enormously exhilarating.

This was the flourishing period of economic and social sciences. Gustav Schmoller and Adolf Wagner were at the summit of their careers.[11] Sering was an excellent teacher and a brilliant personality. The three of them took some interest in me. A group of tutors admitted me to a club of the more mature students in which we discussed the fruits of our own research.

As women, we were stirred by the idea that the achievement of each one of us would be credited to women in general. We knew that the standards set for us were more severe than those for men, but we liked this. I had been brought up in a family of businessmen and had never questioned the belief that people must be miraculously endowed to earn a university degree. Now I saw how many mediocre boys achieved one. It was impossible for me, since my attendance permit did not include taking examinations. Then, suddenly, events took another startling turn.

During a course in economic theories, one of the tutors, Alfred Weber,[12] was explaining the "theory of marginal values." In a flash I realized that here was the explanation of unequal wages for men and women. I began research at once and turned in a manuscript that was, from a feminist point of view, sheer heresy, since it proved unequal wages to be an inherent law of a free and uncontrolled economic system.[13] However, my new approach at least indicated the direction in which the problem could be attacked.

Professor Weber read it, called it a fine piece of work, and asked me if I intended to use it as a thesis for a Ph.D. degree. Overwhelmed, I managed to counter that I could not take a degree in Berlin because I had not matriculated. He said, "There will be some way out."

"But," I said, "I don't know anything about philosophy, and it's a prescribed subject!"

Weber was unimpressed: "You should not hesitate to take your place where you belong." That settled it.

I had been afraid of philosophy because I had never grasped what it was about. I took it up now and discovered that the greatest thinkers had searched for the meaning of life and for answers to riddles of the universe, with some of which I had been preoccupied ever since I was fourteen. I learned from the great philosophers that men's knowledge has boundaries, that there is a realm of the impenetrable. It made me more deeply religious than I had ever been before. If I had learned nothing else, I would still be grateful for having been compelled to enter this most beautiful garden of knowledge.

Then the blow fell. The dean of the faculty, an Egyptologist, objected to having women in the university. Possibly his absorption with ancient cultures made him averse to modern movements. German men can be very rude, and in my case he typified those who were "men of wrath" to their families and subordinates. Hardly glancing at my papers, he threw them on the floor and said, "You have no education whatever."

I objected: "I know I'm self-educated, but my teachers are of the opinion that this has not interfered with my academic work. I come by their request." The dean refused to submit the matter to the faculty. But he had not reckoned with the anger of my temperamental professors. Taking it as a personal insult, they sent a report to the Ministry of Education. But the university faculties were then among the few free, self-governing institutions in Germany, and even the minister was powerless to force the issue.[14] He advised me to submit my application once more at the beginning of the new academic year, after another dean had been elected.

I was disgusted. I wanted to get back to productive work and no longer attended lectures; being older than most of the students, I could learn faster out of books.

The following February the "permission" arrived. According to regulations, I had to call on every professor to ask if he were willing to examine me. With some of them this was mere form, but it was shortly before the start of Easter vacation, and none of my professors of philosophy were free. I applied to Professor Riehl, who had recently joined the faculty. He was a highly cultured man with lovely, if somewhat pedantic, manners. "If you know enough," he said, "I shall consider it an honor." So it was done, and I got my Ph.D.

I bought and smuggled into the house a new black dress. "The men appear in frock coats, the ladies in black without ornament," the charming new dean, Professor Bauschinger, had told me. It was he who later, at the graduation ceremonies, took my oath "to search for the truth and to confess it." No one among my friends knew about that day. I left the house by the back door, leaving a vague message for my mother. When I returned, I joined her in the sitting room and let her tell me the story of her afternoon. I waited until she was ready to give me her attention. Suddenly she looked at me and said, "You're wearing a new dress. You know I don't like to see you in black. Why did you buy it?"

"I needed it for my Ph.D. examination. I've just passed with honors." She did not admit how pleased or surprised she was and pretended she had known all along: "Only I have never asked you. I knew you wouldn't tell me the truth and I would not tempt you to lie."

My celebration party was rather uncommon. To emphasize the feminine character of the event, and perhaps also because I preferred it, there were, rather than beer or wine, mountains of cake and whipped cream. Finally, a last difficulty arose, this time for the dean, who had to arrange for the printing of my diploma as PHILOSOPHIAE DOCTORIS ET ARTIUM LIBERALIUM MAGISTRI. They looked in all the dictionaries, but the name *Alice* simply did not exist in Latin. This seemed to me rather symbolic. In the end, the dean compromised by giving me a Latin suffix.

I considered my degree as an ornament—no more than a badge certifying my membership in the educated clan. Yet it proved indispensable to me in the struggle for bread which inflation was to impose upon all of us. It provided me with credentials for professional social work. The time had passed when amateurs could lead the movement.

CHAPTER 4

# London—Berlin

My nebulous childhood ambition to have the whole world for my country was never quite realized, but travel was at least relatively easy before the First World War. No passports were needed on the continent, with the exception of Russia, and there were no customs or currency restrictions. I never got all around the world, but I went as far west as Vancouver and San Diego and as far east as Budapest and Kiev. Most of this I owe to the International Council of Women, the mother organization of all the national groups.

The representatives of a majority of the women of the world met in London the summer of 1899 to attend the quinquennial meeting of the International Council. There I first heard of the principle that anyone holding an international office was to serve, to act, and stand for the interests of the body as a whole, that she must become international-minded and while holding office remain uninfluenced by the policy or bias of her particular nation. This was upheld by Lady Aberdeen, the president of the International Council, at all times. It was a code to which I was bound for most of my life and one which brought me into frequent conflict with the women of my own National Council.

The International Council had been formed in Washington, D.C., in 1888, at the fortieth anniversary of the first American Women's Rights Convention.[1] This had been a result of Susan B. Anthony's[2] first trip to England—a plan truly American in its conception, a rational structure of international, national, and local councils combined with the vision of an ideal: to pool the efforts of women of all classes, creeds, and nations for the advancement of their sex and the welfare of mankind. It was long before the League of Nations had been conceived, but this was a Women's League of Nations, with all the birth pangs such an ambitious body was bound to have. It was built on air. There were no national organizations that could join. They had to be created, and someone was needed to take the project in hand. It took five years to find this person.

The Countess of Aberdeen was in Canada, as the wife of the viceroy, when she received a telegram asking her to accept the presidency of the International Council of Women. She wired back, "What is the International Council of Women?" The information she got in answer won her support. Lady Aberdeen had just returned from Canada, at the end of the viceregal term, when she appeared in London as president of the Council. It would have seemed incredible to me then, in 1899, that she was to become my dearest and most intimate friend for life.

International meetings were not as frequent as they are now, for although travel was less hindered in some ways, women rarely had the independent means necessary for going about on their own. It was to everyone's astonishment that thousands of delegates came from all parts of the world. London was flooded with them. Preparations had been excellent, it was a brilliant affair, and I saw London in the limelight.

I mixed mostly with less conspicuous people, but some of the celebrities left me with indelible impressions. There was Baroness Alexandra Gripenburg from Finland, tall and broad-shouldered, firm of mouth and chin, with cropped hair—long before it became the fashion—and vibrant with energy. Everybody envied and admired Finnish and Scandinavian women for the rights they had won. Finnish women were enfranchised in 1906, Norwegians in 1907, while we in Germany did not even dare ask for the vote. My English was then still very feeble; I understood English such as spoken by the baroness, with an accent much like my own, far better than the correct variety, and this made the Scandinavians great favorites with me.

The American delegation included Mrs. May Wright Sewall,[3] who had conceived the idea of a permanent international women's council together with Susan B. Anthony, and Charlotte Perkins-Stetson (later Gilman), who had just published a revolutionary book advocating a development that seems quite natural today: married women to achieve independence by their own earnings and aided by a community system of housekeeping.[4] Another distinguished American was the Reverend Anna Shaw, the first woman to be ordained.[5] She conducted a service in one of the churches of London for the members of the Congress. There were also women from remote countries like Tasmania,

New Zealand, Canada, South Africa, China, and Argentina. Apart from a few brief acquaintances made during my former visit to England, I had scarcely known any non-Germans before this meeting. I had never before met an American.

England was represented by a number of titled women, duchesses and countesses; by women of wealth and position like Mrs. Creighton, the bishop's wife, and the Rothschilds. But the outstanding British delegate was Josephine Butler, one of the most courageous women of the century.[6]

Mrs. Butler had been the first woman to devote herself to the victims of prostitution. At the same time, she wanted to form a basis for dignified sex relations. When the British government with the support of Parliament introduced state regimentation of vice in the eighties, she had organized a crusade against the law and against the injustice and hypocrisy of the unequal code of morals. She had carried her campaign into politics by holding meetings in industrial districts, pledging the voters to support opponents of regimentation. She was viciously slandered and persecuted, attacked by newspapers, government officials, politicians, and above all by the medical profession. It often became impossible to secure a hall for her meetings, and innkeepers were threatened that their buildings would be set on fire if they dared take Mrs. Butler in. She had been in danger many times. Still, her faith kept her going until she had brought public opinion around to a regeneration of moral values affecting every order of society.

At the time of the London meeting, she was an old woman, almost wholly retired from public activity. I should have expected her to show the scars of battle, of thirty years spent in slums, among prostitutes, fighting gangs of procurers. But no trace of bitterness was left. She seemed wise and restrained, and in spite of her frail transparency, radiating a spirit of goodness. Her name already had the glamour of a legend.

There were business meetings of the Council attended by two or three delegates from each affiliated national council. Though these sessions were also open to the public, few people ventured in, and most of them left quickly. The intricate details of constitutions, standing orders, bylaws, and so forth were not alluring. But lectures were held, besides, on almost everything else: laws, professions, women in industry, on the stage, in literature; on marriage and the family; on labor and social work. We chased about London from one hall to another, attracted either by the topic or the speaker.

One of the most impressive figures was Susan B. Anthony, the crusader for woman suffrage from the United States. In spite of her age—she was then in her eighties—she did not miss a thing. She still looked a little Quakerish, although she enjoyed fine clothes and looked very stately in black silk and a flowered hat. She was tall and haggard, with a fine, thin mouth, vivid eyes, and white hair. She was treated justifiably like a prima donna, but her sense of humor also allowed teasing about her specialty, woman suffrage.

Believing it would help the cause of suffrage if a sovereign were to give the congress official recognition, she told Lady Aberdeen, "If the congress were being held in the United States, I should ask the president to receive you. Could you not ask the same of Queen Victoria?" Lady Aberdeen approached the queen's advisers. Queen Victoria agreed, and a reception of the executive committee was arranged. Susan B. Anthony was the most pleased of all. She was typically American in her love of meeting royalty but also thoroughly democratic, with no notion of class superiority, and her judgment was not blinded when she said afterward, "The queen is a living refutation of the theory that public life is detrimental to women's instincts. As a mother of nine children, and as head of the largest household in the world, the queen has always excelled in devotion to husband and children and in domestic duties. But in matters concerning the rights of women, the queen is conservative. There have been movements for three reforms affecting women during her rule. One for fighting venereal disease, the second for a change of property laws, and a third for woman suffrage. On any one of these subjects a word from the queen would have been of the greatest importance to the welfare and the progress of women. I am inclined to believe that it was a lack of knowledge of this, rather than a desire to conform to public opinion, that influenced the queen in remaining silent." However, the queen's reception was a precedent and improved the position of progressive women wherever we met.

Beatrice Webb was a famous scholar in the social sciences and the model for women with academic aspirations.[7] I had been thrilled not only at the prospect of meeting her but at being scheduled to appear with her on the same platform and deal with the same subject, "Protective Labor Legislation for Women." She had been born into a family of great wealth—as she expressed it, "the class accustomed to give orders, while never receiving them from others." Her social group, promoters and manufacturers, looked upon labor purely as a commodity. "Water is plentiful and labor submissive," her father had written in a report. She had left these surroundings for research among dockyard workers, a rather unusual undertaking for a young woman. She had investigated conditions in other industries and in the cooperative movement, and married, very unconventionally, Sidney Webb, who was a socialist of the milder brand. They worked and published together, spending much of her considerable income on a houseful of secretaries who did research.

Mrs. Webb was just forty years old when I met her, good-looking but not beautiful. It was nobody's fault but my own that I had expected a romantic figure with the inner urge of my colleagues—someone like Mrs. Humphrey Ward's "Marcella."[8] I took it for granted that after becoming famous herself, she would be interested in the work of other women. Instead she was detached, unemotional, typically a scholar. She pronounced that she had been led by thirst for knowledge, not by love for her neighbor. She was opposed to woman suffrage, and what upset me most, rejected protective legislation for working women. This was decades before a "woman's party" or an "open-door movement" had come into existence with the object of sweeping away special regulations for the protection of women. To me the issue was simple and unassailable. We asked not for privileges, for preferential laws, but for an adjustment to women's greater vulnerability arising from specific organic functions imposed upon them by nature. Working women in all great industrial countries have expressed themselves in favor of protective laws. In my address to the congress, I stressed this attitude.

Mrs. Webb's argument was not determined by a theory of women's rights as it was later in America. She thought in different categories and dimensions from feminists and social workers. Her idea was to wait and collect the material on which to base political action for future help to millions of laboring people, men and women, rather than respond at once to the urgent need of a few hundreds of thousands of women. Certainly there is something to be said for both sides. But I was chilled by this lack of spontaneous reaction to human hardship. I wanted to work for both, the immediate and the ultimate end, and on my return to Germany I was careful to prevent such controversies from arising in our own Council.

Lady Aberdeen was the central figure of the London meeting. She looked more royal than anyone I had seen—like a queen out of a fairy tale. Although she belonged to a social circle that was remote for all of us, she worked with the lowliest of us on equal terms. She had great diffidence, and yet, because of her grace and her charm, she was the dominating power. For me she was not much more than an apparition—always on the platform at the head of the receiving line, far away from me, with the rank and file. I saw her as one sees a picture in a gallery or an actress in a play.

She was in her early forties, very tall, with beautiful carriage. She wore wonderful, constantly varied clothes and jewels, tiaras, necklaces, brooches, and bracelets. This may sound queer, but it suited her. Her eyes were dark blue and inward looking; she had a sweet voice and a lovely manner of bending down to someone smaller than herself.

Without Lady Aberdeen and her connections, the meeting could not have been so successful. All the famous London homes were open to us. We were invited by the beautiful Duchess of Sutherland to a reception at Stafford House, by Lady Rothschild and Mrs. Leopold de Rothschild to a magnificent garden party at Gunnersbury Park, by Lady Battersea to view her famous gallery with pictures by Rubens, Tintoretto, and Burne-Jones' celebrated *Golden Stairs.* All this overawed the delegates, many of whom had never entered the houses of the mighty in their own countries.

The names of many of these women in the Council have little meaning for the generation of today, but they were pioneers in human freedom and responsible for many of our present rights. Looking at an album of photographs recently, it struck me how young they all must have been. I had forgotten this as we grew into advancing years together.

One highly important resolution was adopted at the London congress, although it has remained a crucial one in the International Council ever since—the unanimous decision to work for peace and international arbitration. This, in 1899, was supported alike by French and German women! The delegates from Germany were a handful of advanced liberals who understood the indissoluble bond between the progress of women and democratic ideas. The German Council, too, was still a small, uninfluential body, an avant-garde. Otherwise, the delegates would hardly have dared to endorse a peace resolution, for the average German was always suspicious of peace propaganda and even more suspicious of all international contacts and affiliations.

Later on, when the German National Council had grown and assimilated more conservative women among its members, it lost enthusiasm for a vote on international arbitration. Every word had to be probed for possible meanings and consequences. The bulk of German women remained cautious and guarded, and when the First World War broke out, our pledges were treated as invalid. The tumult swept away all promise.

It was never quite clear to me what moved the modest group of the German Council of Women to extend an invitation to the Women's International to hold their next meeting in Berlin. In 1904, Lady Aberdeen and the rest of the membership arrived as our guests.

To entertain hundreds of delegates and to attract large audiences was, considering the attitude of the German public, not without risk. We had no influential backing, and we were expected to arrange a public demonstration for peace, at best a controversial subject in Germany. It might easily have developed into a fiasco. But as it happened, the convention turned out beyond our fondest hopes.

Since Berlin is smaller than London, the affair was on a smaller scale. And in a way it was more integrated. All the meetings were held in one huge building, the Philharmonie, equivalent to New York's Carnegie Hall, so that the delegates were not obliged to run about tracking them down. We proved that women, too, possessed the organizing ability known as a peculiar trait of the German nation.

Our board had been looking for a "woman of the world," one with means and accustomed to social functions, to act as head of the local committee on arrangements. We asked Hedwig Heyl, who was the owner of a factory which she had directed since her husband's death.[9] Early in her marriage she had already shown interest in the welfare of her husband's employees by starting cooking lessons for their wives and daughters and an afternoon club for the children. She advocated domestic efficiency as a source of sound community life. She was indeed a genius in practical things, but she could neither think nor express herself clearly. Her speeches and articles kept us in a constant state of anxiety. It was pleasant to work with her, but she had queer ideas about the younger women with academic educations and was

Members of the preparation committee for the International Women's Congress in Berlin, 1904. Alice Salomon is next to the woman at the far right. (Photograph courtesy of the Pestalozzi-Froebel-Haus Berlin/Archiv.)

convinced that none of us could cut a slice of bread or boil an egg. As hostess to the thousands of people at the congress, however, she was unsurpassed. I was her assistant and became responsible to a large degree for the whole program.[10]

Our meetings overflowed. Many, if not all, of the famous women leaders of the world appeared to lecture. Lady Aberdeen came with her daughter, Lady Marjorie Gordon. Susan B. Anthony was with us again, for the last time, with her following: Anna Shaw, who held a sermon that Sunday in the American Church; Ida Husted Harper, the biographer; Adelaide Johnson, the sculptor; and of course Mrs. May Wright Sewall.

Mrs. Sewall, one of the founders of the International Council, had been elected in London to succeed Lady Aberdeen as president. It is almost impossible to describe her. She was a teacher from Indianapolis, where she ran a private school with her husband. She was a typically middle-class woman, clever, ambitious, impulsive, easily hurt and slighted. She was not as democratic as we had expected from an American—in her exaggerated sense of importance as president of the Council. Perhaps she did not realize that we represented merely an attempt to build up a world parliament, rather than the accomplished structure.

She was plump and flabby-faced, with narrow eyes, curly white hair, her head always a little bent. When I met her she was already elderly, rather overdressed and in very light colors, which seemed strange to Europeans. She was a great talker, both at meetings and in private, and spoke well, with pathos, quickly running the gamut of emotions. No actress could do better and, indeed, there was much of the actress in her. She loved the limelight and wanted more than her share of it, which made relations with her rather difficult. She was constantly surrounded by a devoted group of friends, who formed a sort of claque, and she spent far too much money. When she was not pleading for funds for the Council, she was trying to extricate herself from personal financial difficulties. At such periods she had no time for the affairs of the Council and did not answer letters. This was a source of frequent headaches for the board. Mrs. Sewall traveled in great style, with her satellites and a number of large trunks and boxes filled, probably, with propaganda literature. I have seen her take them back full to overflowing with dried roses, remains of the bouquets she had received at meetings. They would have filled a house.

She gave lavish parties for delegates and speakers and finally for the pages, and the rumor was that after she had left Berlin the hotel bill, including all items resulting from her hospitality, was presented to the German Council.

From 1904 on, Lady Aberdeen was again president; Mrs. Sewall remained on the board as an honorary president, and I saw much of her until the war broke out. After her death we heard that she had long ago joined a spiritualist society and been in constant communication with the beyond. Among other things she had learned to play the piano in a trance and continued to play, although, it was said, she had never before touched a key. This kind of activity may explain much that seemed odd and even incomprehensible about her.

Since the queen of England had received the officers of the International Council, the German empress could not refuse. After a number of people had been approached in the order of their rank and their proximity to the court, the audience was granted, even with some interest, no doubt mainly because our leading woman was a countess and a former vicereine. But from that time on, certainly, official circles in Berlin were well aware of the existence of progressive, academic, professional, and working women and less fearful that recognition of their pursuits would overthrow the German Empire. After the audience, relations were established between our group and the ladies-in-waiting or, as they were called, the "empress' ladies," some of whom were very charming, clever, kindhearted, and diplomatic. They went about in court carriages which bore the court emblems, attracting crowds of people who were, in spite of socialist propaganda, royalist at heart and gathered whenever one of them came to see me, convinced that Her Majesty was in the house.

The most memorable event of the conference was the peace meeting which had caused us so much trepidation. It proved what the Nazis have since impressed upon the world—that the masses can be swayed in any direction by the magnetism of glamorous trappings and the legend of a personality. Bertha von Suttner,[11] who had been announced as the chief speaker, had never before appeared in Berlin, and her name drew crowds. When I arrived more than an hour before the meeting was scheduled, I found the entrance of the Philharmonie besieged, with the police appearing on the scene to keep order. The hall was filled within a few minutes after the doors were opened, and I had to arrange for an overflow meeting.

Of all the women leaders I have known, Bertha von Suttner was the most adventurous. Perhaps it would be more accurate to say that she was by background, nature, and education an adventuress, while becoming more or less by chance the famous leader of a movement. She was the author of the celebrated novel *Lay Down Your Arms,* but she might never have started to write if she had not been forced to go into exile after a clandestine marriage.

When I met her, she was at the peak of her fame. She was about sixty and had lost her husband a short time before. She was beautiful, with strongly marked traits of the Austrian military caste that had produced her—neither particularly intellectual nor spiritual, but with statesmanlike intuition and a keen political sense. Born after the death of her father and brought up by a gambling mother, her youth was spent mostly in spas and in a general atmosphere of frivolity. When she was compelled to earn a living, she accepted a position as governess, characteristically with a titled family, and soon after secretly married her employer's young son, who had not yet finished his studies and had besides no inclination for a career. His parents objected bitterly, and when the young couple found themselves stranded without a home or means to live, they decided to spend their honeymoon with a friend in the Caucasus, the Princess of Mingrelia, whom Bertha had met at one of the spas, where they played roulette. After this, they lived like refugees in various small towns of the principality, giving lessons and doing odd jobs. They lived near the scene of the Russo-Turkish war, and her husband sent reports on the situation to the Vienna newspapers which were accepted and fairly well paid. This spurred her ambition. She made up her mind to try writing and experimented with an article called "With Fan and Apron," continuing to write rather insignificant essays. After nine years of voluntary exile, when they had proved they could stand on their own two feet, the baron's parents asked them to come home.

Meanwhile Bertha von Suttner had come under the influence of the philosophers and scientists of her period—Darwin, Spencer, Carus, Sterne, and Buckle[12]—and was firmly convinced of man's unlimited capacity for progress. She had become an advocate of free trade, peace, and a universal religion. Altogether, it was the shallow, popular rationalism of "enlightenment" which was the essence of her writings. The book that made her famous, *Lay Down Your Arms,* was not her life story, as most readers believed. It was written not as an emotional experience but deliberately as propaganda for pacifism, every word right out of her imagination.

It has always been a mystery to me how a sensitive woman could live through all the wars in which her country was entangled between 1859 and 1878, amid the victims of devastation, without being involved emotionally, but her attitude remained purely intellectual and rational. It was no humanitarian urge that moved her to protest against these horrors, but theoretical conviction, a reasoned belief in the evolution of mankind.

It had been extremely difficult to find a publisher for the book. They all feared confiscation for "attacking the established order." It finally appeared in 1890, placing her among the ranks of the great. Before her marriage, she had spent several weeks as secretary and supervisor in the household of Alfred Nobel in Paris, and it was she who later suggested that he use the profits of his dynamite works for the work of peace, who sponsored the plan for his foundation. She had clear judgment, sharp critical powers, and a sentiment which was more of the mind than of the heart. This together with an immovable will made her easily one of the most unusual women I have ever run across.

Her speech at the Berlin meeting was a masterpiece. She knew that women as they were could not change the world, that they still had to learn to judge for themselves each situation within the framework of mankind: "The woman who can summon enthusiasm for a war and be willing to sacrifice the husband and the sons she loves, stands higher than the one who is not capable of such sacrifices. But another and still higher stage is reached by the woman who rebels against war, not because war threatens her home, but because she realizes that war is a scourge for all mankind. Modern women will revolt against war not because they are daughters, wives, mothers, but because war checks the development of civilization; because it is pernicious and objectionable from every point of view—that of morals, economics, religion, and philosophy." She spoke of the women of the Sabines, who in bygone times prevented a war by throwing themselves between the two belligerent armies. "Now," she said, "our task is not to prevent one war but to eradicate the institution of war for all time."

The acclamation was tremendous. The girl I had chosen to present a huge bunch of roses to Bertha von Suttner was kissed in return and raved, "I shall never wash this cheek again!" Bertha von Suttner died immediately before the [First] World War broke out; she was spared the disillusionment of having to see the values for which she had lived blown to bits.

Apart from such excitement, the delegates also accomplished a good deal of serious work. The International Council of Women once more unanimously passed a resolution to form a standing committee—this time on woman suffrage. This was even more revolutionary than the decision made five years before in regard to peace. Peace, after all, was an abstract principle, since war seemed remote. But woman suffrage was highly controversial. The International Council was bound to be cautious, as it included women from the most outlying villages as well as from those regions better prepared for an energetic policy in favor of the franchise. The resolution was therefore no small victory for the progressive faction.

I had observed from the first the particular position of the young adherents to the movement and decided that we must act to bring the succeeding age groups in. I kept up this policy during the sessions of the International Council in Berlin by arranging for a meeting of girls. Our hall had a capacity of four thousand, but we squeezed in five thousand youngsters. They looked lovely in their light summer frocks, in their eagerness and excitement. I had brought all the most famous women, the "stars," to speak to them. For a woman at the turn of the century there were two great experiences in public speaking. One was to address an audience of men and see their prejudice give way to immensely gratifying appreciation. The other was to talk to a hall full of girls, stirred to enthusiasm as we presented ideas of which they had never yet heard.

We spoke to them of mental horizons which had been closed to us in our own early days—opening before them. We talked about professional careers as one way to a full and blessed life. About social obligations we told them that many of women's time-honored duties had been taken over by the community and that the younger generation would have to fulfill them in a new setting.

The meeting delighted not only the girls but the speakers. Lady Aberdeen and her daughter, who had become attached to me during these weeks, were enthusiastic, and on their way home, Lady Aberdeen wrote to ask me to spend Christmas with them at their ancestral home, Haddo House in Scotland. Her daughter, Marjorie, was to be married and would be there with her husband.

Thus I came to know more and more intimately in succeeding years a most extraordinary family and to form a friendship that has spanned three generations.

CHAPTER 5

# The Aberdeens, Scotland, Ireland: 1904–1908

The Earl and Countess of Aberdeen epitomized the modern ideal of a union of love in conjunction with a union of work and interests. Lord Aberdeen regarded women as partners and comrades of men, equally responsible for the life of the family and of the community.[1] They consulted each other on all things. He adored her and made her, as she expressed it at the time of his death, after more than fifty-five years, "blessed above women." If she was the stronger personality and perhaps somewhat obscured him on occasion, he did not mind.

It took me more than forty-eight hours to travel from Berlin to the far north of Scotland, by train and boat and train and bus, in midwinter during the Christmas rush. I had not the faintest idea what to expect when I got there, although I had heard that the Scots were a democratic and unprejudiced people; that, at the same time, Scotland had a very ancient nobility, a hierarchy of ranks and titles; and that the moors and highlands were owned by a handful of feudal families.

Lord Aberdeen once told me of a Western Union clerk in an American city who had asked him, "How do you spell the first word of your signature?" He meant the word *Lord.* I was not quite so unprepared, but the British are inclined to understate their positions and properties, to give their castles unostentatious names. I had a lot to learn.

Haddo House was part of an enormous estate holding about one thousand tenants. The walled-in park and the seventeen hundred acres surrounding it were breathtaking. The house had been built during the Adams period and was filled with portraits of generations of forebears. Around it were terraces with flower beds of wallflowers and forget-me-nots in summer, and the trees each had a small placard recording the history of the planting, many of them bearing the names of kings and queens and prime ministers, as well as ancestors. There were stables and kennels and greenhouses and a huge building for festivals and theatricals. The private chapel, built by Sir George Street at the time of the Aberdeens' wedding, was a masterpiece.[2] The Aberdeens cherished and faithfully kept the Scottish traditions. The men wore kilts in the tartan of their clans, bare knees, and beautiful silver spades in their belts. A bagpiper waked us in the morning and went around the dining room at night, piping what seemed to me not very melodious folk music.

John Campbell Gordon, seventh Earl of Aberdeen, was the grandson of that prime minister, the fourth Earl of Aberdeen, who was said never to have smiled again after he had failed to save his country from the Crimean War. My host was just as conscientious, and in a social sense. In his youth he had assisted Lord Shaftesbury, the great philanthropist, and he was looked upon as a successor. When he inherited the title and the estate, he must have been a tremendously wealthy man.

Ishbel Marjoribank, the daughter of Lord Tweedmouth and later the Countess of Aberdeen, had met him when she was fourteen years old. He was her ideal of what a man should be, then and until the end. Lord Aberdeen was very good-looking, very much a Scot, slim and tall, dark haired and dark eyed. He had the sweetest disposition of any man I have ever known and a rare capacity for self-effacement. When I was staying with the Aberdeens in Ireland in 1914, after the war broke out, the police informed him that even a guest of the viceroy had to register as an enemy alien. It was characteristic of his protectiveness toward everyone around him that he took me to the police station himself, to shield me. What he once wrote about his own father, "One of the humble and holy men of heart," applied to him as well.

He was also one of the great figures of the empire, although he was not a great statesman. He served twice as lord-lieutenant (viceroy) of Ireland, in 1886 during Gladstone's administration and again from 1905 to 1915, when Campbell-Bannerman had formed the cabinet.[3] Between the two Irish periods, he held office as governor-general of Canada, from 1893 to 1898, and represented the sovereign as lord high commissioner at the General Assembly of the Church of Scotland. Since these were administrative posts, Lord Aberdeen was obliged to hold himself aloof from politics, a circumstance quite in keeping with his gifts and inclinations. He had the Scot's love for the beauty of his country, for poetry, music and folklore. He was more interested in the humanities than in politics. During his last viceregal term, he frequently remarked to me, "I want peace, not power." And so it happened that much of his time and attention was given to promoting his wife's social and philanthropic ventures.

Lady Aberdeen had a Liberal background. The Gladstones were continual visitors in her father's house, as was John Bright, and her older brother was a whip of the Liberal Party. Like her family, she was a staunch Liberal, although she had inherited nothing of the business talent that had made her father successful and her grandfather director of the East India Company and senior partner of Coutts' Bank. She possessed the faculty of making each one of her friends feel especially loved, and when she talked of someone who meant a great deal to her, her voice was tinged with a kind of caress. Rarely, if ever, did she have friends who were not interested in her causes: the welfare of Scotland, of Ireland, of Canada, liberalism, public health, and very prominently, the International Council of Women. Her capacity for work was astounding. Wherever she and her husband lived, she built hospitals, started campaigns against tuberculosis and infant mortality, organized nursing services and playgrounds, revived folk arts and industries. She kept everyone around her busy as well, and the house was always full of experts on town planning, folk dancing, rural institutes, health exhibitions, and medical specialists. She maintained that one could train himself to live on four hours' sleep a day. We never believed this, however, for even though she did not stay in bed much longer than that, she slept in cars, on trains, and on boats, and her friends saw her at many a meeting with her eyes tightly closed.

She was, at times, a great speaker, particularly in a friendly atmosphere. She had none of the characteristics of an orator but could say wise things of the kind that do not come from the mind alone, being essentially of the spirit. With infinite patience, she would stand for hours at the end of a meeting or a lecture to receive everyone's greetings, introductions, and requests for favors. The friends who waited for her were usually less patient, since it probably meant that their president would be late for her next appointment. She was kind to everybody, consistently kind as only a person with complete inner harmony can be. She had the heightened sensibility often found among Scots, almost mounting to a sixth sense, and so was easily frightened when she felt antagonism. But she seldom revealed it. Her peculiarities were sometimes difficult to understand unless one saw her in her home. She had the walls of her drawing room done in pale blue, and her clothes were just as colorful, even when she was old and had grown enormously stout. I remember a morning in a European capital when we were expecting her at a meeting and someone told me, "Lady Aberdeen has arrived. She is in the lobby in a pink suit surrounded by bags and suitcases." It was a strawberry-colored Scottish tweed in which she had traveled, and it did look startling.

While living on the social scale of the nobility, the Aberdeens worked steadily to change the social order, to make huge incomes from landed property impossible. They supported a land tax with which they made themselves poor, at least for their station in life. Inherited treasures gradually passed from their hands. It has scarcely been realized in other countries that the tax laws on landed property, sponsored by Liberals like the Aberdeens—themselves members of the feudal caste—completely broke the power of the old nobility.

They were so exceptional, however, that people of their own class went out of their way to try and weaken their public influence. Among the "slanderous" stories that went the round one told how the Aberdeens, while representing the Crown, insisted on dining twice a week with their servants. Queen Victoria was so shocked by this bit of gossip that she asked Lord Roseberry, the prime minister, to make an official inquiry. And a famous author wrote in an article that Lady Aberdeen, as guest of a Canadian magnate, had told a parlor maid, "Take off your cap. I hate to see this symbol of servitude!" In Ireland they were almost boycotted by the Conservative landlords who disliked the Aberdeens' passion for Irish home rule. They were too much the friends of the working class to be popular among the rich.

Their children had been brought up simply, the two younger sons educated to earn their living as businessmen. The second son worked as an apprentice in a shipyard and later became a partner in a refrigerator plant. The younger son was trained as a banker and spent some time with the Dresdener Bank in Berlin. One day when some Canadian notes had come in, he dumbfounded the clerks by remarking that the picture on them was that of his parents. To foreigners the intricacy of the British social system is bewildering. But the principle is simply to have the younger children of the nobility drop back into the ranks of the commoners, while every year outstanding people from all fields of endeavor are knighted; this forms connecting links between the nobility and the rest of the population and keeps the class system from becoming rigid.

An attempt to portray Lord and Lady Aberdeen would fail without mention of the mainspring and source of their lives, their all-pervading and abiding religious faith. Everything they did was religion, in the literal sense of the word, a radiation of inner light and integrity. Lady Aberdeen told not without humor about having set out for their honeymoon to Egypt with boxes full of religious pamphlets to distribute among the Arabs, as well as medicine chests.

In their early days they had worked in the evangelistic movement that had aimed to win back the educated and upper classes from their religious apathy, a result of the recent great discoveries of science. In this connection they became acquainted with Professor Henry Drummond, the author of *Natural Laws in the Spiritual World.* He had been on a scientific expedition in Africa when the book had appeared; it made him famous and is published in most living languages. With the American evangelists Moody and Sankey, Professor Drummond became one of the founders of the Christian Student Movement. He developed a close friendship with the Aberdeens, and for years, until his early death, they were together whenever possible. If anyone besides her husband ever exerted a profound influence on Lady Aberdeen, it was Drummond with the broad character of his teaching. His picture remained on her desk, and in the foyer leading to the chapel.

Like Drummond, the Aberdeens had friends of different denominations and religions. They were broad in outlook and drawn to those who had the same basic values, whose religion was more than a habit or sentiment, whose faith gave a transcendental meaning to their existence.

A few months after my return to Berlin, the newspapers reported on the general election in Great Britain, which resulted in a large Liberal majority. With the forming of the cabinet, Lord Aberdeen was sent once more to Ireland as representative of the king. The clamor for home rule was growing insistent, and it was known that the Aberdeens were strongly in favor of it. The Irish population would not have welcomed a viceroy with a different attitude. This time the Aberdeens stayed in Dublin for nine years.

For the International Council this meant seeing less of our president, who would be very much taken up with other duties. I doubted, too, whether our personal relationship would survive. But a year later, when I was invited to speak on a labor problem at a conference in London, Lady Aberdeen read my name on the agenda. I received a note written in the round letters she formed with a quill (disdaining the use of more modern pens), asking me if I could arrange to cross the Irish Channel for a visit to their present home.

The Aberdeen estate in Scotland had seemed royal to me. But this was a real court. Lady Aberdeen welcomed me in her boudoir and told me the names of her guests, the time for dinner, and where to appear, adding, "I hope you will not be afraid." This conveyed nothing to me. When the time came, I found a number of young men assembled, in uniform, black coats with pale blue lapels and lots of gold braid—aides-de-camp and attachés—but the host and hostess were still missing. They were the last to arrive, announced by the butler as "their excellencies," and all the ladies curtsied in British court style. It dawned on me that this was court ceremonial. After dinner we drank the king's health in fresh glasses, and no one ate after the viceroy had finished. We curtsied again and left the dining room backwards, facing the viceroy as we withdrew, and in the drawing room we rose every time he left his chair to speak to another guest. There were guards of honor in front of the house and outriders for our carriages, drawn by teams of four. Strangely enough, people become accustomed to that sort of thing and perform the functions automatically, so that it is not even a nuisance except for those about whom all the fuss is made.

I often traveled with Lady Aberdeen to distant parts of Ireland, where she inspected houses that were to be remodeled into hospitals and sanatoria. The poverty of the people, exploited and wronged for a century by the absentee landlords, was appalling. The homes of the tenant farmers were scattered on plains and hills, more like toy huts than houses. They sheltered men and beasts; families rich in children—and families who gave this wealth away, letting the children go overseas, while the good earth went untilled: the result of an unjust system of tenancy. There were long stretches of terrible loneliness, woods and lakes and regions that were inaccessible except in summer, and then only by boat once a week. In spring the woods were filled with flowering rhododendrons, part of the colorful pattern of the greenest of green countries, of a people largely red haired and blue eyed. The Irish had surprising character traits, they were humorous in spite of their poverty, quick-witted, and with a streak of mysticism. Yet they grew wild and ferocious in their fight for independence. Life was never dull there.

The mansions of the privileged were hidden away in gorgeous parks. Was it that their way of life should not be seen—or that they should not be faced with the distress, the houses in decay, burnt down and not rebuilt, the forsaken homesteads? Whenever we were in the neighborhood of some such house belonging to a friend of Lady Aberdeen, we went and stayed there for an indefinite period. She completely lacked any sense of time. Before she departed, a message would usually have to be sent to "keep the train waiting." I cannot say that stationmasters and conductors ever greeted us enthusiastically.

I sent my mother press clippings from Ireland on the "functions" which Lord or Lady Aberdeen attended—a sort of viceregal "My Day" [i.e., a diary]. After the names of the aides-de-camp who "attended" their excellencies was noted, "And accompanied by Dr. Alice Salomon." Sometimes reporters went so far as to describe my modest outfit as "a black merveilleux suit and a picture hat." My mother had begun to enjoy what she called my "success," perhaps mostly because our relatives had originally disapproved, and every recognition that came to me justified her in allowing me to work out my life as I wished. However, she never missed an opportunity to say to me, "It's not really that you are so gifted. You just had the best of luck." And with this I have always agreed—until this day.

CHAPTER 6

# Two Jobs for Life

## I: The School for Social Work, 1907–1913

In 1900, when the new civil code had come into existence in Prussia, the subjection of women was still upheld in spite of progressive women's passionate propaganda. As before, the husband alone was entitled to manage the common business affairs, to administer the capital or earnings of himself and his wife, to dispose of or speculate with his wife's possessions and dowry, unless a legal arrangement had been made prior to the marriage. If the parents differed with regard to the education of their children, only the will of the husband was valid. Who can wonder that women so restricted, treated as minors even within their own families, had remained timid in matters of politics? While women in other countries embarked on a spectacular suffrage campaign, we theorized—discussing heatedly whether suffrage was a point of departure or a goal. Women in Germany, together with students and apprentices, were forbidden to join political societies and to take part in meetings dealing with political issues. This law dated from 1850 but had been reaffirmed in 1887. What then could we do? Everything came under the heading "politics": petitions relating to the constitution, administration, legislation, the rights of citizens and the foreign policy of the state. Under this obsolete law, a women's trade union was dissolved for discussing the import tax on sewing thread, another because it had arranged a lecture on conditions in the state hospital.

Finally, some fortuitous incidents brought about its repeal. Early in the new century the reactionary League of Agriculturists, representing the big landowners, held an annual meeting in a circus in Berlin to discuss bread-and-butter interests, taxes on imports, etc., and for this event all the country squires came for a gay and profitable week in the capital. Many brought their wives. Some of the wives, having nothing else to do, accompanied their husbands to the sessions, where political talk was rampant. The police, probably in awe of the leading men, allowed them to take seats in the hall, and the liberal press did not fail to point out that the squires' wives were permitted that which would send lesser women to jail. The minister of the interior, challenged, then ruled that women might only be admitted to listen in a "segment" apart from the men who shared in the proceedings. At about the same time, the Society for Social Reform,[1] a progressive body, was organized by a group of influential men who wanted the cooperation of certain women considered experts in the field of labor legislation. However, under the law, women were not eligible for membership.

The Society for Social Reform did not accept the situation lying down. They petitioned, together with the women's clubs, but even von Bülow, the progressive chancellor, refused to move.[2] Then the society decided upon a test. They asked one of the first women economists, Helene Simon,[3] to address their annual meeting in Cologne in 1904. The subject was mild enough: "The Reduction of Working Hours for Women and the Protection of Adolescents in Factories." The police sent an order stating that the speaker was not to be admitted to the hall. In the end, her lecture was delivered by a male member, while she was allowed the privilege of listening from a "segment" with instructions "neither to show signs of approval or disapproval" of her own lecture! This finished the law. It was not only a disgrace, it had become ridiculous and was repealed soon after.

At that time I was faced with a personal problem. Since my youngest sister had married recently and I was alone with my mother, I found it increasingly difficult to leave her for long periods. She had had a roaming husband, and I felt that she should not have to undergo the same experience with a daughter who was so like him. It seemed desirable that I should settle down. But how? With a Ph.D. from Berlin University and the recommendation of my professors, I might have chosen a career as university instructor. But German universities did not include vocational schools; they were exclusively centers of academic teaching and for promoting research. It was a medium alien to my nature, too remote from life, a means and not an end. Anyone with the same academic qualifications could do this just as well. I had a gift for leading and influencing young women, as other people are fitted to teach small children or adolescent boys or to nurse the sick. I wanted to continue as a missionary for social work and for a social philosophy among young women. I had wasted so much time without aim and substance that I wanted to release a younger generation from the desert of uselessness. In the words of the Epistle to the Hebrews (2:18), "For in that he himself hath suffered being tempted, he is able to succor them that are tempted."

Again circumstances worked in my favor. We had fought for and obtained a reform of the school system for girls in Prussia which was, with minor changes, copied, subsequently in other parts of the Reich.

For boys the grade school led to various types of "gymnasium," a high school primarily devoted to either the classics or mathematics and modern languages. This led in turn to the university, after a curriculum of twelve years. No equivalent of the American colleges existed. For girls there was nothing but the grade school followed by finishing schools with a total curriculum of ten years. Private attempts to prepare small groups of gifted girls for entrance into the university did not solve the problem.

We wanted a girls' high school that offered the same standards and credits as the boys' and would lead to the university. Instead, a reactionary plan was drawn up in 1907, providing a few such schools for a small minority only but generally a new type of high school for the age group from seventeen to nineteen. This plan combined subjects from all fields of learning in a motley pattern with courses in household economics and child care. It was the finishing school all over again, "finishing" neither the girls nor their education. The women teachers were horrified. If there had to be a special type of junior college for girls, they wanted something with a central idea. One of their leading women suggested that the course in social work which I had directed since 1899 might be a starting point, and the Berlin club of women teachers asked me to address them on the subject. I prepared an alternative to the government plan, stressing education for citizenship and a really systematic foundation for professional social work. The "college" was to combine lectures and classes with supervised fieldwork, the subjects to be arranged in logical sequence; classroom lectures directed toward the field of practice and practical experience to be tested and used in class discussions. The plan included the main features which later became typical of the European schools of social work. When I had submitted it to the teachers' club, one of the mem-

*Two Jobs for Life* 71

**Alice Salomon, 1908. (Photograph courtesy of the Alice-Salomon-Archiv Berlin.)**

bers asked me, before we left the hall, whether I would head such a project in cooperation with the Pestalozzi-Froebel Haus—an institution with a great reputation in training kindergarten teachers and teachers of home economics.[4] She thought it would be a good idea to have the courses for professional social workers affiliated with this sort of junior college.

The plan developed at a rapid pace. A committee was formed. But we had no money! Some friends guaranteed a small sum, which, by the way, was never claimed. I made out a budget and managed the publicity. The Pestalozzi-Froebel Haus offered us the use of some rooms for certain hours at a nominal charge. We decided to begin in the fall of 1908, provided we could secure at least ten students for each class, but soon more than eighty had registered. I opened the School of Social Work in 1908 with an address on the words of Carlyle: "Blessed he who has found his work. He need not ask for any other blessing."[5] A few years later, when a house of our own was dedicated, this motto was inscribed on a lintel over the entrance, and thousands of young people have gone in and out under its encouragement. I too had found my work at last, the job I had wanted since early childhood.

There seemed to have been girls all over Germany, and in some of the neighboring countries, just waiting for our school. The administration of the school was more or less of a "one-woman" job, for I alone worked full time, and I saw every girl who applied before admitting her. Usually they were accompanied by their mothers or by both parents—not that I cared especially to meet them or to be influenced by their social position. But often they wanted to look *me* over before entrusting their daughters to me, to be assured about the possibility of future jobs.

There were, of course, no set regulations or requirements for admission in the early days except graduation from secondary schools and a minimum age of seventeen years. Once in a while I deviated even from this low standard. In one case a girl, a Polish expatriate, applied. A committee member who believed that a little supervision would do me no harm insisted that the girl was really too young. "Her hair is still down," she said, "and tied with two white bows!" The girl herself has often reminded me of my answer: "Even a girl with bows in her hair may have a heart for human suffering, and outstanding intelligence. She will mature in time." She was Marie Ginsberg who—once more exiled—joined the staff of the League of Nations and is known to thousands from all parts of the world, every one of whom would testify to the validity of my judgment in her particular case.

On the other hand, I reserved the right to decide after a term or two whether I considered a girl qualified for work that demands a human approach and the capacity for selfless devotion. With rare exceptions, I got this kind during the early years, girls who were intent more on giving in life than on "getting."

Luckily enough, for some years we could work out our scheme and begin a system of education without being hampered by a government and its officials.

After the profession had been universally approved and the opportunities for employment grew plentiful, the character of the student body changed gradually: many came to prepare for jobs that promised the goal and ideal of Germans, namely "security" and a pension. Pioneer devotion subsided. Much later, after the revolution in 1919, the

Socialist Party proposed that this profession above all others be made accessible to girls from the working class, and we arranged an experimental six months' course for them. Most of them did well. They were a chosen group, and we made provisions to have the most gifted take the full two-year school course.

The first years of the school were in every way wonderful. I had the finest staff a school of social work could demand. Among us were the head of the Poor Law Administration and the president of the Charity Organization Society, as well as all the women who were leaders in social and public work—brilliant and exciting personalities. But soon other schools of this type were established, some of them well endowed or supported by rich municipalities. Sometimes the trustees tried to lure me away, and then they competed for my teachers. Many of the leading women in public life became principals of schools of social work. This meant for me a constant search for new ones and the task of breaking them in. Hardly any of them were professional teachers, they were specialists in other fields: law, medicine, philosophy, economics. I attended their classes for a term or two, whether they liked it or not. Usually they did not like it. But none of them yet had a teaching technique, and it was also desirable to see that a certain objectivity was maintained.

There was no "ready-to-buy" science of social work which we could use in teaching. The staff had to develop it themselves. There were no textbooks—we had to write them.[6] Ours was genuine teamwork, a most intimate cooperation, coloring the school with the peculiar character that education for social work needs: the drawing together of teachers and students, the readiness on our part to do more than teach, the readiness for guidance in all problems which arose for the students in work and life. I was kept feverishly busy teaching economics, the history of social work, its theory and methods. But more than that I tried to impress on the students that social work should bind its adherents to certain precepts of living.

Half the student body came from other cities, and we had to find homes for them until we started our own dormitory and hostel in 1922. I recommended a high-class boardinghouse in our neighborhood to one girl who apparently wanted an excuse for living in Berlin. Her snobbish and fussy mother kept insisting, "But my daughter has style." I assured her that many of our students were no less fashionable. The mother's behavior should have warned me, but obviously the young girl—or perhaps I should say the young lady—was not happy at home, and I felt I should try to rescue her. It turned out that she was not much wiser than the parent.

Very often I had to iron out family problems when girls were opposed by their middle-class families in wanting to follow a profession. This was the period when an analogy to the ancient father-son conflict had newly arisen between mother and daughter. The mothers were strangers in professional and public life, a world the daughters had to conquer. Mothers could not lead them into this land of promise, and often they could not be convinced that there was a promise in it.

It was a frivolous period for wealthy people, and some grew wealthy rather fast. One girl, Edith, urged me to help her get away from home. Her parents were nice people but decidedly the "society brand." They had refused all her demands for a serious education, and they thought their friends would suspect something wrong in the family if their only daughter were absent. What could I do? The girl was so depressed she frightened me, and yet I could not secretly oppose the parents. I promised to look around for a job she could fill but added that she would have to fight it out at home in case I found an opening. A few weeks later the headmaster of one of the supermodern schools wrote that a girl assistant had left suddenly and he needed someone to look after the children's health, attend to first-aid and odd jobs. If my friend wanted to come she would be welcome, but *at once.*

I forwarded the letter to her, saying, "The next step must be yours." The following day her parents appeared in my home. I have never witnessed such an outburst of rage on the part of a refined and educated man in the presence of his wife and a strange woman. However, I got him over it by advising him to let her go for a short time and he would probably see her return with a new appreciation of her home life. This was the most brazen lie I ever told. I knew this bird would not fly back, at least not back into the lap of luxury. She got her share of the kind of work she wanted by marrying a famous educator. For me, extracurricular efforts like this often developed into lasting friendships.

During my marriageable years I had wanted a dozen daughters. Somehow I had never thought of children in terms of boys. Now I got the girls, hundreds and hundreds, and I looked upon them all as my adopted daughters.

After several years of the school, it was evident that the classrooms and offices loaned to us by the Pestalozzi-Froebel Haus had become

Alice Salomon with some of her pupils in the roof garden at the top of her school, ca. 1915. (Photograph courtesy of the Leo Baeck Institute New York City.)

most inadequate. It became imperative to find better quarters. In 1913, I spent the summer holidays in Berlin since my mother could no longer travel and I could not leave her; and during the unaccustomed quiet of July in Berlin, my imagination ran riot. I decided to build a house for the college. We had been self-supporting, as salaries were modest and there were great numbers of students. We had even been able to accumulate some reserves. I knew I could appeal to friends and former students to contribute to a building fund, and I had unbounded confidence that the plan could be carried out.

Very few people, I think, have ever gone about the building of a house so lightheartedly and with so little legal formality as I did. The Pestalozzi-Froebel Haus, which owned almost an entire block, allowed me to use one of their backyard lots, and within a few weeks I had a thirty years' lease in my hands; then construction began. The lease was signed by a trustee for the Pestalozzi-Froebel Haus and by myself for the school. No other signature was attached. I got some financial help from friends and students, but since that was not nearly enough, I made additional and rather hazy plans. As principal of the school, I arranged with myself, as president of the women's social work organization, a loan of ten thousand marks. In return the association was promised, for an indefinite period, the use of an office room. This paper I, only, signed—in both capacities. I also drew up a written agreement between myself as principal of the school and myself as a private individual to lend the enterprise a considerable sum of money out of my own capital, to be gradually repaid.

No one except myself could understand this confusing hodgepodge of contracts. The astonishing thing is that no one ever attempted to. Some years later when we asked a head man of the municipal administration to become chairman of our board of trustees, he accepted office without going into the matter. Only in 1925, when I resigned from the school and the new principal was determined to be engaged legally, was the labyrinth of documents investigated for the first time by a municipal administrator.

He told me that none of these *chiffons de papier* had any value and that it was perfectly absurd to build a house, and a pretty costly one at that, on such perilous foundations. He laughed at my ignorance of business affairs and my casual optimism. But what did it matter! I had always disliked red tape and was convinced that institutions grow better and become stronger with a moving force behind them rather than a large endowment and a legal constitution. Anyway, for twenty years I spent most of my days there, and the house was the center of much activity. If I had bothered about legal securities and waited for formal contracts, a move that would make the heart of every good civil servant rejoice, I should never have got the house.

Fortunately, the building was complete in brick and mortar in 1914 when the war broke out, before the shortage of labor and materials could stop construction. Since it was almost my own house, I wanted to keep my hands in touch with growing things in memory of my childhood. I had the pavement in front of the house replaced with garden mold and planted two hundred square yards with early and late shrubs and flowers—none for midsummer, for we closed during July and August. An apple and a cherry tree were planted there too, and every year when I returned from my vacation I was given a jar of preserved cherries, though I often wondered if they had really all grown on my

The building of the Social School for Women in Berlin-Schöneberg, completed in 1914, with a roof garden. (Photograph courtesy of the Alice-Salomon-Archiv Berlin.)

little tree! Our schoolhouse had one of the first roof gardens in Berlin, with wisteria and crimson ramblers and real grass plots that a Swiss student euphemistically called "meadows."

Like all living organisms, an institution goes through stages, especially an institution dedicated to a new profession. The school had, naturally, periods when things did not run smoothly, comparable to the diseases of childhood and the difficult symptoms of adolescence.

The first Flower Day in Berlin brought on something of a crisis.[7] It was arranged by a kindly old man who was the president of some charities with rather old-fashioned methods of which modern social workers did not approve. However, having seen "Hospital Day" in London, it seemed to me a recommendable way of raising funds, although for Germany it was quite new to take up a collection for social institutions in the streets. There was, unhappily, on my staff a charity organization leader who took a definite stand against Flower Day. He considered it his and the school's duty to interest the people specifically in the institution or case to which they contributed. Indiscriminate giving, with motives other than pure aid, he thought lacking in ethical standards. He contested "dances for the benefit of the lame," "dinners for raising funds for the hungry," and "theatricals for providing shelter for the homeless." He made a public appeal to prevent Flower Day, to impress upon people what he considered its "immorality." He pictured all sorts of undesirable scenes which might arise—girls molesting men in the streets or vice versa—over the business of asking for pennies and urged me to sign his appeal.

I agreed partly with his argument. I too disapproved of questionable and tactless money-raising methods, but I did not consider Flower Day one of them. I did everything to persuade him of its validity, but, though he was a man of high ethics, he could never see another person's point of view. He was inclined to think that attitudes he did not share were not only wrong but due to a lack of moral principle. Finally I gave in for the sake of peace and friendship and signed his appeal, so as not to hurt his feelings. In consequence, another member of the staff, the teacher of social hygiene, resigned, refusing even to finish his course. He was, as I had been quite unaware, an organizing member of Flower Day. He wrote a letter stating that since I had signed a document condemning the plan as unethical, I could not possibly approve of him as a teacher, and he never again set foot in the school. It was an irreparable loss. So few people at that time had specialized in social hygiene.

Another bad episode occurred years later when we had a student whose capacity for vicarious suffering had made her a radical communist. We had then introduced a form of self-government, a community of staff and students to discuss and decide together on new developments for the school. A weekend house and various neighborhood activities resulted. This particular girl proceeded to organize a rebellion. She felt these were half measures and wanted complete control of the school for the students, although she did not elaborate on who was to teach and how money was to be raised. She nearly upset the whole show. In our small-scale democracy, we had the same experience the nation's politicians underwent. Self-government requires a slow process of education. We had overestimated the capacity of our stu-

Alice Salomon at work, ca. 1915. (Photograph courtesy of the Alice-Salomon-Archiv Berlin.)

dents for independent thinking and had not taken into account the upheaval which demagogic agitation can cause. I had to take a firm stand.

The affair confirmed a principle I had always supported—to keep politics out of the school. Social work, for which we trained our students, is one approach to the problems of society. Politics is a different one. Even when the aims may coincide, the means do not. We had students and teachers who belonged to different parties, and this was beyond question, even desirable. But in the classroom a teacher must explain and interpret objectively the approach of all parties and creeds toward social problems and help the students to evaluate opinions and principles removed from their own. Above all others, the principal of such a school, though he must be outspoken about social reform, should not become a propagandist. He must be an impartial authority. If this is not so, the spirit of unity, necessary to this type of school more than to any other, cannot be maintained.

Before continuing with the school in its more mature stages, I should not neglect to say more about my other job for life, the International Council of Women, for my time was divided. However, it could not split my interests, for I soon realized that international work and social work are work alike for the welfare of mankind, that social obligations govern society as a whole, and that the social conscience has no boundaries.

CHAPTER 7

# Two Jobs for Life

## II: Officer of the International Council: Canada and First Glimpse of U.S.A.

For Americans, Europe is much nearer than America is for people on the European continent. Americans have to cover such enormous distances when traveling in their own country that a trip to Europe seems proportionately a small undertaking. There is besides an American tradition that considers a visit to ancient centers of Europe an educational or cultural asset. At the start of the century, very few Europeans thought this would soon become almost equally true of the New World—that there, too, were many things to be learned, of a different kind.

Consequently, many of us were surprised when the International Council of Women resolved in Berlin (in 1904) to hold its next quinquennial in Canada. We put little faith in such a utopian plan; they could not possibly handle such large delegations. None of us seriously contemplated crossing the Atlantic for a meeting. And what was Canada to us anyway? A vast pink region on the map, of which we knew nothing. But five years is a long time when still ahead of us, though often short in retrospect. The officers of the International Council recognized these difficulties and that Canada had to be made attractive, meanwhile, if the meeting was to come off.

They held an interim meeting in Geneva, a central location, in the fall of 1908, not only to keep the various groups interested but also to have the Canadians submit their plans and present the trip in an appealing light. Without misgivings I went to Geneva—not yet the Geneva of the League of Nations, the international center it was to be after 1919. In 1908 it was just a quiet Swiss city with picturesque ancient quarters, a very conservative Evangelical population, and an incomparable view of the lake with the huge white mass of Mont Blanc rearing behind other mountain ranges, sometimes hidden in the clouds for days, sometimes glowing overpoweringly.

It was a fine place for quiet work, and I should have enjoyed it had I not suddenly been confronted with a new job. The Council was preparing to elect new honorary recording and corresponding secretaries. Somebody suggested me for recording secretary, an office I had held in the German Council for years. Lady Aberdeen thought for a moment. "No, not recording secretary," she said, "but corresponding secretary," for whoever filled this office was in constant touch with her. I should have felt honored—but my school was to open in a few weeks. I had planned to give it my exclusive attention and not to be diverted by any one of my many former activities. It was only a remark made about the difficulty of working with Lady Aberdeen, who was much too occupied with other projects, that induced me to accept the nomination. And it was some comfort that a nomination is not an election, and I could still hope to get out of it. However, there was no doubt that I had to go to Canada to be there in case they did elect me.

The Canadians reported on their preparations. They had secured reduced rates on one of the Canadian liners. They assured us that traveling second class (it was not yet dignified by the term "tourist class") would be ever so comfortable. We would find hospitality everywhere we went. It sounded as if one needed scarcely any money at all. The meeting would be held partly in Montreal, partly in Toronto. Afterward they planned to take us all across the continent to the Pacific coast by chartering a Pullman train, and we would return as the guests of the United States Council. They also advised us on the sort of clothes we needed for the heat of the American summer—since clothes remain a universal preoccupation of women, whether they are council-, club-, or businesswomen or homemakers. One of the Canadians urged us to buy black silk underwear and dresses that did not show dust and soot and not to bring fine white things requiring frequent washing and pressing. There would be no time for that, for we would seldom stay in one place for more than a day. With my German upbringing I thought black things, dirty and sooty on my body, an abomination. But how often I later regretted not having brought one thin black dress I could have kept looking neat.

The British were much better prepared. They had learned the geography of Canada in school, and the names of rivers, mountains, and cities had some meaning for them. Many of them, too, had relatives in Canada whom they visited after the trip. The Germans of that day only sent their sons overseas if they did not do well at home, and though I had some problem cousins, they were not sent away, and I had, alas, no relatives in the New World who had grown rich and who would have been so useful not only on this trip, but later when Hitler turned me out.

Somehow I had not included America in the scheme of my life. There were other continents luring me. I had hoped that when I became free to travel, I might go to Australia. This may seem a strange desire, but I was engrossed in welfare problems and laws to improve the living and working conditions of the masses, and some of the Australian states had Labour governments with the most progressive social legislation in the world: an eight-hour day, minimum wages, industrial arbitration courts. I should have liked to see if it worked out.

But now I crossed the Atlantic for the first time, together with most of the delegates on the White Star liner *Laurentic*. It was a lovely ship, glittering, clean, and white. Today it would be considered a baby craft for its mere seven thousand tons, but to me it was a wonderful and mysterious structure. The *Laurentic* took the northern route toward Montreal, passing icebergs although it was June; the temperature fell and we heard the foghorn for several days. The ship had to move slowly or stop altogether for hours, and she dropped behind schedule.

When we approached the Canadian coast, Lady Aberdeen sent a radiogram—then the very newest invention—asking us to leave the boat for a reception at Quebec. She had arrived ahead of us and was anxious that we should not miss seeing one of the most romantic of cities, the oldest post in the north of the continent. We had a supreme view of the city rising on a promontory formed by the St. Lawrence and St. Charles Rivers, built on terraces dating back to the time of Cartier and Champlain. The St. Lawrence was the mightiest stream I had ever seen, so wide that the opposite shore was invisible and navigable even for large transatlantic steamers. We could well understand that the battle between the French and the British for possession of the colony had been fought here. The same evening we went on to Montreal, where we stopped for a few days, seeing the city and holding part of the quinquennial session.

Then on to Ottawa and Toronto. Wherever we arrived we were told to line up at the station (depot it was called then), and the hostesses lined up across from us. The name of each hostess and delegate was called out, and two strangers utterly different in background, experience, and standards had to make friends for better or worse for a day and a night, sometimes longer. Most of the meetings of the International Council were held in Toronto, and on the last day my fate was sealed. I was elected honorary corresponding secretary of the International Council of Women.

A woman had to be strong or else very enthusiastic to weather the trip to the Pacific Coast, twenty-three days in a Pullman car, after most of the Europeans had started back to Europe. One hundred of us, speaking all sorts of languages, were crowded together in a train of four cars. The day we started, the heat was suffocating and the humidity almost unbearable. Lady Aberdeen, who was accustomed to travel in state, was so frightened for us that I had to promise to send her a wire after the first night and report whether we had survived without casualties.

The washrooms were our greatest affliction. Since we got off at the same time, we all headed for them simultaneously, and thirty-five years ago the cars were not so well equipped as they are today. One of the Britishers hung up a placard: "Don't wash, it's no use anyway."

We were never alone—not for a moment—during those weeks, day or night. On our westward route across the continent we generally traveled by night and stopped somewhere for the day. The Canadians were delightful hosts. Every morning we were received by the mayor of whatever town we were passing through, by the local Council of Women, and by the photographers. Then the local members drove us around in their cars to see the schools or hospitals, the sights. From sheer exertion our facial muscles developed a perpetual frozen smile. When we returned to our Pullman berths we were exhausted. Sometimes we grew irritable with councilwomen above and in front and in back of us and with others settling on our berths for talk when we were ready for sleep.

Yet it was a unique and wonderful experience.

We traveled across flowering prairies covered with tiger lilies, pink eglantine, blue flowers, black-eyed Susans; past forests often swept by fires. The Rocky Mountains reminded me in a more rugged way of Switzerland. We passed fruit ranches and lakes and met some Indian tribes at railroad stations—all new and exciting things. We had a public meeting every evening for the local council and local population, for in return for their trouble they were eager to see the strange women who had come from so far away. As the only officer of the International Council on this trip west, it was my lamentable duty to speak each time. These addresses were all more or less of a complimentary nature, not unlike after-dinner speeches. But considering that there were a hundred women in our party who were obliged to listen to them over and over, I strove desperately for variations on the theme of the International Council—the unity of women of all classes, creeds, and nations in working for the welfare of humanity—and our motto, "Do unto others as you would that others do unto you."

In Vancouver we left our train and took a boat to Victoria on Vancouver Island. The governor of British Columbia held a reception in the beautiful Government House on top of a hill with a glorious view of the Pacific. We were all in our smartest clothes—if they could be called that after fourteen days in suitcases—and were given roses big as peonies, grown on the Pacific Coast. I had inquired about speeches and was told there would be none. I thought for once I need not collect my wits. Suddenly, His Excellency mounted a platform and welcomed us. The responsible Canadians whispered at once, "You must reply," and when the governor had finished, I climbed up with the courage of a soldier before battle. I spoke of the marvelous reception given us everywhere: in Quebec, Montreal, Ottawa, Toronto, Port Arthur, and Fort William; in Winnipeg, Regina, Edmonton, Calgary, Banff. I said that in the East, people had told us our enthusiasm was premature, that we should wait until we saw the West. And really it had become more and more beautiful and exciting all along. "And now," I ended, "that we have arrived in this most beautiful city of . . . of . . ." and there I stopped. I had completely forgotten the name. After a few seconds, that seemed to me hours, the audience realized what I had forgotten—they shouted from every corner of the hall, "Victoria, Victoria!" We all began to laugh.

Traveling at such high speed through Canada was an object lesson on economic history. Going from east to west was like living history in reverse. The further we went, the greater became the contrast between the forms of civilization we saw and those which are accepted as the natural order in Central and Western European countries. The eastern cities seemed much like English provincial cities and yet with a touch of the past, the streets bordered with trees, every family in a house of its own, the houses bedded in gardens without separating walls or fences, according to the pleasant American custom. Then the prairie cities looked to me the way European medieval market towns must have been, cities with no life of their own but acquired from the surrounding villages and farms—mere centers where the farmers brought their implements and staples and where their wheat and wool was stored and shipped. When we branched off toward the north, it reflected a much earlier period of history. We saw people in the process of settling on the land, burning down the forests, fertilizing the soil with ashes. We saw them living in log houses, in huts, in tents . . . depending on the time that had elapsed since their arrival. It must have been like this in parts of Europe about a thousand years before, when migration gave way to permanent settlements. In the West, we came lastly upon the imprint of older civilizations, Chinese quarters, Spanish missions, and in the houses of the rich, beautiful examples of the Oriental arts and crafts, purchased in trade with the countries beyond the Pacific.

No library could have taught me so much as this trip. People who live in densely populated areas have an economic and social outlook which is not only limited by lack of space and by the peculiar form of their economic system; their point of view is distorted because they take for granted a thousand things with which others do not reckon under natural conditions. No one in Central Europe has a true conception of the world until he has seen a more recent civilization.

We went back across the United States from Seattle to Chicago. My first contact with the U.S.A. is rather blurred in my memory. One week for a country which is practically a continent in itself was too short, and we were all dog tired. The United States Council of Women had only few local councils. Although the idea of a hierarchy of local and national councils had been conceived here, it was apparently not easily applied under U.S. conditions. The Council must have had considerable difficulty in finding people en route to offer us hospitality. Our hosts took us, of course, to see all the "biggest and best" structures. In Seattle we saw mountains in the process of being removed and houses and hotels transferred to the same spot some hundred feet lower. Then we boarded the train in which we lived until we reached Chicago.

An hour or so before the train was due at Salt Lake City, several women, Mormons and Gentiles, joined us, and a heated struggle began over the Mormon versus the Gentile hospitality. The Mormon invitation had been accepted long ago, and the International Council delegates could not possibly refuse it, since our program was to bring about "a better understanding between women of all races, creeds, and classes." Thereupon the Gentile women of Utah decided to stay away from us. We spent the day on the shore of the lovely lake, on a pier, and in an amusement park somewhat like Coney Island. We went into the water too heavy with salt for anyone to sink. In Denver we stopped again, and in Colorado Springs, and rode up to Pikes Peak, the highest attainable altitude before the time of airplanes. There was a moment of breathtaking beauty on the train one morning when I pulled the curtains and saw the sand dunes of the Colorado desert, like pyramids lighted up by the rising sun. For a moment I thought, "This is a dream. This is Egypt!" I had never heard that nature had produced such a likeness nor that a desert need not be just a sandy plain.

From Denver we went to Chicago, where an official luncheon had been arranged. The mayor gave us a particularly warm welcome, because, as he said, the greatest citizen of Chicago was a woman. I asked someone to point out Jane Addams to me. In appearance she was like all other women. She adapted herself in the matter of nonessentials, which is the wisest course for people who have to defend their principles. Yet her lined face revealed that her decisions had not been easy. I met her then and many times afterward and found her a most compelling woman. Hull House and the stockyards were said to compete as the greatest attraction for visitors in Chicago. I went to see Hull House that time and lived there repeatedly as a guest in later years. The stockyards I left for others. They were not in my line.

I left our party in Chicago and went on alone to New York, where I spent a week before returning to Europe. It was the first week of August, one of the hottest New York ever had, and the air was heavy with moisture—though now that I am a New Yorker I know this can be said of every summer. I was worn out, and I knew there were new obligations in store for me. But even the little of New York life I could absorb filled me with enthusiasm. I went home convinced that the United States is the paradise for women.

I had been tremendously impressed by the position of American women. In Germany we had a female surplus of nearly two million. In the United States males still predominated. Certainly, the numerical ratio of women, and the carryover of the even lower one of colonial times, explains to some extent the value and dignity accorded them in

America (and other young countries) as compared with Europe and its overwhelming numbers of "superfluous" women. America had, at any rate, enough men to go round as husbands. They are wonderfully generous to their women in material things when they can afford it, and where there is not enough money they take for granted that they should share in the more unpleasant chores of the home. I shall never forget the wife of a young scholar who, when I rose to help clear the table, said indignantly, "In our house the men do that work." Off he went with the male guests to wash the dishes while his wife entertained the women in the living room. I had never seen anything like this before. It would have shocked a strong German male!

But what struck me most was how women had developed in this era of freedom. There were more independent and courageous personalities among them than in the older countries—women with intelligence, political knowledge, initiative, and the warmest human impulses. If I named some of them it would be unfair to others. They exist in this living generation as well. They have been and are the untiring conscience of the nation.

Back in Berlin I told my friends that in case I should be reborn once more as a woman, my only wish was to be born an American. When, thirty years later—far too late to develop a new personality—I sought refuge and a new country, it did not take more than one night to realize that my new country could only be the United States.

CHAPTER 8

# Brief Harvest before the Storm

In front of one of Berlin's historical buildings there stands a work of art—two chariots of bronze drawn by two rearing horses which are reined and curbed by the driver with great strength and exertion. Popular wit had labeled this monument "Checked Progress and Advancing Reaction." It would be a fitting description of Germany during the decade before the First World War. These years were not only tense in world politics but difficult internally and unproductive in social reforms. The emperor, although formerly cherishing the dream of a "social monarchy," had become hostile toward labor, and several cabinet ministers were dismissed for favoring a more progressive policy. Since the turn of the century, "big business" was increasingly reactionary and constantly demanded antilabor laws. The socialists, on the other hand, were doctrinaire without being constructive and followed a policy of negation. Still, new ideas gradually took hold of individuals and small groups: Protestants, Catholics, liberals, professors of economics, and social workers. Numerically they were insignificant, but by exercising constant pressure they brought about improvements, some of which have already been mentioned—regulation of child labor, of home industries, the ten-hour maximum working day for women, and extended protection for mothers before and after confinement. It was a harvest rich in new applications of ethics and a sense of social justice, and it had been created by a change of heart.[1]

These "modernists" among politicians and statesmen were bent on using the gifts and abilities of women, and we began to work together in some of the important national leagues and conferences. However, if a woman was given a leading position, we could always expect one of the reactionaries, some man of wrath, to attack. The officials in the administration—always conservative—remained deaf to our petitions for reform. So we set out to try to influence them by other means. The method, so common now, was quite new when we organized an exhibition to draw attention to conditions in the sweatshop industries, the first held in Germany and demonstrating the imperative need for protective laws. I had always taken a special interest in these workers, who were exploited more than any others. Once, while teaching social sciences in a fashionable institute, I tried to make the students not only know but feel their plight. I illustrated this through the case of a woman I knew well. I described the room, small and dark, in which the mother lived and slept with her children, in which she was supposed to work and cook and wash and nurse the little ones. I told them how many blouses or coats she had to make in order to earn less than a minimum for existence and that she worked fourteen hours a day and seven days a week. When the lesson was over, the principal said to me, "Miss Salomon, you are all wrong. When you describe the grievances of this woman, you put yourself in her place. You tell the students what *you* would suffer under these conditions. The woman you speak of has not been brought up like you. She does not miss the things you miss, the fresh air, the cleanliness, and so on."

It was this attitude that brought together politicians of different parties, organized labor, and women leaders for the exhibition in 1908. Two of us were chosen to open it at a public meeting—Friedrich Naumann[2] and myself. Naumann was a man well known in politics. He had been a Lutheran minister and had come to the conclusion that Christian preaching is deficient without Christian action. He had given up his ministry hoping to organize a political party with social *reform* as the objective. This was contrary to the socialist program, which aimed at revolution as a means toward social justice; he also differed from them in being a German rather than an internationalist. His party, which he called National-Social, advocating democratic monarchy and industrial democracy, remained ineffective, a small group of educated and public-spirited people. Later he joined the Democratic Party in order to get into parliament. He was very popular and an excellent speaker, and between us we tried to interest great numbers in the exhibition. But the exhibits spoke louder than our words could have. Many people were deeply moved, and thousands came every day. One result was the formation of a league of workers in the home industries. The government, however, kept aloof. Shortly after, we intervened in a strike of workers in the garment industry, and many of my young friends served as pickets, undoubtedly without mentioning their whereabouts at home. Not until 1911 did we succeed in getting the sweatshop industries protected by law.

That same year I was asked to speak on the "Protection of Motherhood" at the National Conference on Poor Law and Charities, as it was called before it became the National Conference for Social Work.[3] The members of the association were mostly public administrative bodies of municipal and governmental departments. The delegates received a generous allowance for their congresses, so that they were not obliged to function as economically as we were at women's conferences, nor did they work so hard. They had a pretty good time, and where I met these men, I saw much more of the surroundings than I usually did. At women's congresses I used to say jokingly, "It does not matter at all *where* we meet. We shut ourselves up in some hall to discuss more or less the same things everywhere."

However, much of the work of the Poor Law Association was accomplished before meetings. The two or three topics on the agenda were thoroughly investigated by an assigned member long in advance. The results were published and sent to the others previous to the meeting of the congress, and the delegates were expected to have read the reports, presenting only the main issues, and to be prepared for discussion. Often they were not.

I have already mentioned how thrilling it used to be to speak in a hall filled with men for whom a woman on the platform was like a first night in the theater. The woman could make a hit or be an utter failure. And the future attitude of these men toward "modern women" depended on her talk. Such events were usually preceded, like my university episode, by some skirmish.

I was to speak, as the first woman, at a meeting in Hanover.[4] When the Committee on Arrangements met the day before the opening of the session, another man of wrath, the head of the Welfare Department of Hanover, abruptly moved that my lecture be canceled. The subject, he said, was too controversial. The people of Hanover were conservative and would not tolerate these new immoral theories.[5] He had not read a line of my book, *The Protection and Insurance of Mothers*,[6] but at that time a "free-love movement" veiling itself with the name "League for the Protection of Mothers" was widely discussed, and he took it for granted that I would condone it. This was the last thing I would have done. I was indeed very unpopular among women who intended to make a sociological program of "free love." I thought they were extremely foolish. Legal marriage, after all, had been formed as a safeguard for women and their children.

The other board members refused to allow any interference with my lecture. What I said to them on this occasion was and is still characteristic of my approach toward women's problems.

Nature, I maintained, has imposed on women special burdens. No legal or economic emancipation can alter this fact. Rarely can a wage-earning woman combine work with motherhood without conflict or sacrifice. During certain periods of her life, a mother is economically dependent and needs protection. This does not invalidate our demand for equal rights. The protection she gets is a necessary compensation for the physical burdens she must bear in the interest of the race. Among women working in mills and factories, the period of pregnancy, confinement, and nursing produces many needs, often distress, sometimes martyrdom.

I drew attention to the married mother who was in danger of being forgotten because of the free-love movement. I wanted to restore the comprehensive meaning to the words *protection of mothers* and outlined a practical program for the benefit of all, married or not, according to their needs. As for the unmarried mother, I claimed that if an illegitimate relationship is deemed wrong, it is wrong for both the man and the woman, and that the man should share fully in the responsibility.

Point by point, I criticized the existing laws bearing on the problem—the factory and other labor acts, the health insurance act, the civil and criminal code, the poor law and its administration. I showed up the inadequacy of private agencies and submitted a charter for the protection of all mothers.

I concluded with a dramatic appeal, urging the audience to keep in mind the distress of women who bring children into a world where, even in the hour of their birth, no light shines for them; of women who have to wrap their babies in rags, who after a few days must drag their tired bodies to the kitchen range and to the washtub. I asked them to compare this with the picture of the women of their own class, attended by doctors and nurses, relatives and servants, mothers in whose arms the babies are placed, bundled daintily in white linen. I urged them not to let their consciences sleep until the mothers of the nation were protected as they should be.

This was not what my opponent had expected. Liberal in regard to individual rights, progressive in regard to social justice, and conservative in ethics: this is what I was then and am today. The audience was wonderfully enthusiastic. It turned out to be one of the golden days of my life.

To battle against obstacles is an exhilarating experience and bears its own reward. I am also convinced that, in spite of the vicissitudes, it was easier for a woman of my generation to make a career than for a man. There were so few of us that people paid more attention to what we did. If we did well, we got on well. I once told a colleague who despised ambitious people that we had no right to judge them. We were made public figures long before we were ready. We never knew how it felt to be confident of one's ability without the opportunity to prove it.

Very different from my occupation with these sordid and sad problems was my part in two exhibitions where I became acquainted with the German empress. The first was an international fair of folk arts and crafts presented by the Lyceum Club and directed by Hedwig Heyl, who had been hostess at the Berlin Meeting of the International Council of Women. Frau Heyl had assembled a group of women with close contacts in foreign countries, each of whom was to arrange an exhibit and take over a stall. I represented Ireland and the Irish Industries Association. They sent me—besides tweeds and rugs, their great specialty—quantities of beautiful, expensive lace, needlepoint, Carrick nacross,[7] and Irish crochet. I feared I would not sell a single piece, but apparently the heritage of my forbears—their business talent— asserted itself, and before we closed I was sold out.

An amusing sidelight of the empress' public appearance were instructions given us beforehand not to encourage Her Majesty in buying, as she had only a limited sum to spend at the fair. We were presented when she arrived, and then she made the rounds. At my stall she picked out a huge scarf with a lace border in the pattern of the Irish shamrock. I had tried hard to get rid of it, without success. The empress bought it at once. A minute later, another lady, who was friendly with the emperor, came to order a copy.

The second exhibition where I met the empress, not as a saleslady but as a guide, was also planned by Frau Heyl. It was a more important show, "Women in the Home and at Work," and opened in 1912. Frau Heyl had always been good at raising money for her institutions; in this case she persuaded the gas company to undertake the financial responsibility. At a time when electricity began to compete with gas, the gas company saw an excellent opportunity for advertising. Frau Heyl meant to demonstrate the equal value of homemakers and wage earners and to evoke mutual appreciation. She managed the homemakers' division. There were hundreds of different kitchens and homes of various sizes and materials, planned by women architects and furnished by women interior decorators. I was in charge of the other department, covering women in agriculture, industries, trades, and professions. We had exhibits from ten thousand women; half a million people came to see our show within one month, and we held a congress in connection with it. The "modern woman" became popular, almost fashionable, and in Germany that meant a lot.

Everybody knew that the empress had a limited outlook, that she was decidedly more interested in domestic than in university women, more in charity and nursing than in social reforms. I was to conduct her through the hall for trades and professions. Again the marshal came to arrange her visit in advance. This time there was no difficulty about buying—as we sold nothing—but he told me how little time the empress could spend, since she had other functions to attend that day. We discussed the leaders to be presented and the exhibits to be seen, and he agreed to all of them, until we came to women in industry—shop assistants, typists, telephone operators. He said there was no time. I told him there had to be time. It would have to be out of the time allotted to other sections. I explained that these women were representative of a much larger group of the population—of Her Majesty's subjects, was the correct phrase—than any others. They were just as respectable, and under no circumstances should they be slighted. After some dispute, I won.

It was a privilege, but not a particular pleasure, to accompany the empress and to present all these people. She was tall and good-looking and favored the same long skirts and tall hats that were until recently so characteristic of Queen Mary. She was most conscientious and sincere, but she lacked the gift of easy conversation, especially of beginning one, which was really one of the most essential amenities for royalty, since people were not supposed to speak until they were addressed. There was always a painful moment when they were presented, and on this memorable occasion I had to break the rules to get her started.

A few years later, some of the leading women were asked to give a series of private lectures for the crown princess, who was again expecting a child—the primary duty of women in exalted positions. It was considered a suitable time to prepare her for some of her future duties as "mother of the country." When the lady of honor gave me a draft of the program, I missed one of the suggested topics: "Equal Moral Standards for Men and Women." I said so, but the reply was evasive. It seemed the subject was considered unfitted for royal ears and perhaps it was feared that the princess would talk it over later with the crown prince, which, according to current rumors, would not have been desirable.

I was reminded of a story that was widely repeated and seemed to me typical of the prudishness which clung to royalty a little longer than to ordinary women. A model research institute to fight infant mortality had been built with a fund given to the royal couple as a silver-wedding present. The house was named after the empress, "Auguste Victoria Stiftung." Soon after the opening, the empress came to inspect it and asked each woman her name and her husband's trade. One after another answered that she had no husband. When the empress realized that this was an institution for unmarried mothers, she turned around, and the rumor was that she said, "And to this I have to lend my name?"

I could not possibly have taken part in so many activities outside my school had it not been for the eager cooperation of my students. This often brought interesting people to the college; at other times, the students met them when acting as ushers at congresses. Consequently, they learned about life and social problems in a wider sense than they would have merely in the classroom or in some limited field of social work.

Although I moved among progressive women, I was bound to encounter some who were as reactionary as the men in the ranks of the officials. My work for the International Council of Women opened my eyes to the militaristic attitude of some of my German colleagues. There were certainly such women in all countries, but it distressed me that my own council should often threaten the peaceful atmosphere of an organization which had been formed on the premise that women are by nature pacifists. In the classical period of Greek history, Aristophanes' *Lysistrata* illustrated the absurdity of women bearing and raising children only to have them killed, or killing the sons of other mothers, paying so dearly for their lives yet knowing they are valued so lightly. This was the underlying motive of the [International] Council.

The years during which I worked as secretary of the International

Council were tense in world politics. I had to learn what supranational work actually implies. I had to understand national characteristics and peculiarities and that people have not only different languages but different ways of expressing their thoughts. After my first circular had been sent out, the complaints came in. The Latin Council wanted polite phraseology in business letters, the English, Scandinavian, and German wanted them short and matter-of-fact. If a circular satisfied one nation, it was considered inappropriate or even offensive by another. There was a good deal of mutual suspicion among the various nationals, even when they gathered for peaceful cooperation. Goodwill was not taken for granted. An embarrassing incident occurred at a formal introductory meeting in Stockholm in 1911 which I had arranged. The hall was decorated with the flags of the countries represented through affiliated national councils. They had to hang "in the order of affiliation." Cabinet ministers and local authorities received us and were answered by our president. After her, the council presidents—like the flags, in proper order—had three minutes each to say a few words exemplifying the special character of her nation. Before she began to speak, her country's national anthem was played. I had collected the scores of all the anthems, numbered them, and very carefully told the conductor what to do. But I did not speak Swedish, and probably he did not understand much German, French, or English. When the French speaker was announced and the German anthem broke forth from the orchestra, I nearly fainted, and actually some people were firmly convinced that I had arranged this as an anti-French demonstration.

The next disturbance proved how far we still were from our goal. While we were in Stockholm, world politics suddenly produced a crisis. Trouble arose over Morocco, where in 1906 France and Spain had been granted certain rights of domination. When they moved to extend their sphere, the German emperor, without warning, sent the battle cruiser *Panther* to Agadir, a Moroccan harbor. Excitement grew among the women in Stockholm.

The president of the German Church Women's League became hysterical—not because she feared a war, but because she was afraid there might not be one. Despairingly, this leader of Protestant women said to me, "If only the emperor does not give in again. It would be too humiliating for all of us." I had no idea to what previous compromises she referred. As far as I knew, the emperor had retreated only in cases where he had provoked some other power. She was the daughter of a general, brought up in the tradition of the military caste, and could not possibly reconcile this with the idea of universal brotherhood to which we were all pledged. Fortunately, no one wanted war over inner Morocco, and Germany was induced to "retreat," to withdraw the *Panther,* and as "compensation" she was given a slice of land near the Congo. The whole affair seemed incomprehensible in the cool air of Sweden, a country so rich in culture, without benefit of colonies or power politics.

Before the storm descended on the European nations, during the last days of July, I was hard hit in my personal life. After ten years of a normal, happy family life, my brother and both my sisters were married, and a third generation was growing up. I was alone with my mother, who was very content to have me with her in her old age. She had grown weak and dependent on me in most things and was longing for the end when my sister suddenly died. She and her husband had been advised to live in the mountains, since both had signs of tubercular infection. They had sold their estate, and after spending several years abroad and in a suburb of Berlin, had moved to a country home near Breslau in February 1914. They had a few mild, sunny days, and my sister sat in the garden to enjoy the prospect of her rural surroundings. Probably the ground was too cold. The following night she awakened her husband and told him that she had pneumonia. It was a violent case, and she died before we knew that she was ill.

The doctor had asked my brother-in-law whether he wanted him to give her camphor or morphine—to prolong the death struggle or to make the inevitable end as easy as possible. It was then my brother-in-law had first known that she was in danger, and he had said, "Fight for her life as long as there is one heartbeat in her." She had lasted only one hour longer. When he got me on the telephone, he was still benumbed. He asked, "Where is my eldest daughter?" She was studying at a horticultural college in England. He knew, of course—his asking was an automatic and unreasoned demand for what he most wanted. I wired her that her mother was ill and asked her to return instantly. Meanwhile, I had to break the news to my mother, and I thought she would die of it, but people can endure much grief and live on. A day later, I went to the station to meet my favorite niece. From the train she shouted, with tears in her eyes and anguish in her face, "Is Mother better?" I told her the truth in the taxi that drove us home. It was the hardest thing I have had to do in my life. She jumped up in her desperation, and I had to hold her very close and fast, or she would have thrown herself against the window or out of the car. She had been a passionate child, not entirely easy to manage. I could only try to love her more. I think she knows that I did and do until this very day.

This eldest niece of mine had often looked after my mother when I was away, and she did it with a selflessness and devotion beyond my own. She now took her mother's place, running the house, which included a park and a poultry farm, and caring for her father and the younger children. Mothers are supposed to love all their children equally, but it is the privilege of aunts that they need not. The others are sure enough of my love to forgive me if I say that this one is "the nearest of the near" to me. She has a heart of gold, and there is a warmth that flows from her like sunshine.

She stayed with my mother once more when, three months after her mother's death, I went to Rome for a meeting of the International Council. This was June 1914, such a brief time before all bonds were torn! To arrange a meeting in Rome was a hectic task anyway. We could only appeal to the few exceptional Italians who had kept pace with the women of other countries. Most of the women of the educated classes had been to convent schools and never dreamt of professions and rights, while the working women were largely illiterate and unprepared for organization. None had experience in the feminist cause, still less in international work, and they hardly ever sent more than one delegate, with a title but no foreign language, to International Council meetings. Their charming, cultured president, Contessa Spaletti, had never left the country and had not even been to the meeting we held at Innsbruck, not far from the Italian frontier. The Italians had made lavish promises for this conference, but they simply did not understand what we wanted. They had engaged the dining room of a hotel for the hours from ten to twelve and from three to six for our meetings. Between these times, it was a restaurant. Our schedule was much longer. I had to allot seats and provide the delegates with placards and flags. From past experience, I knew the consequences of overlooking the proper order of things. After what has happened since, it seems rather silly, but it was just as well that the meeting should not aggravate international susceptibilities. One of my German colleagues used to tell a story of a leading Italian who addressed a meeting on "Women in the Home." She claimed she saved more by washing her white gloves herself than she could earn by doing work outside her home. She cannot have saved very much, but it would be impolite to hazard a guess at her earning power.

We always come to know and love a place better when we live in it and move about not as tourists but in the interests of our work. I had been in Rome before, but never long and never in summer. We northern people, as the Italians tell us, go to Italy too early in the season. Later, the poppies seemed to shoot out of the walls of the Coliseum; the roses covered the houses like red, white, and yellow paint; the courtyards of the churches were full of purple irises. I had a delightful luncheon with Prince Bülow, the former German chancellor, and his wife in their beautiful palace. His lovely Italian wife was as cultured, witty, charming and vivacious as only Italians can be. The Queen Mother gave a garden party, where the officers of the International Council each received a present, a pretty gold medal which I sacrificed the year after on Germany's war altar.

Much more unforgettable than meeting the grandees, however, was a talk I had with Eleonora Duse, who came to one of our meetings.[8] I had often seen her on the stage; the people of Berlin always accorded her a reception of overwhelming enthusiasm. She not only acted: it was life itself, sorrow, suffering, agony, and despair. She stirred me as only reality ever had. In Rome, talking privately together, it struck me that in life, as on the stage, her voice expressed infinite hurt, like tears heard rather than seen.

With Rome in June 1914, our good times were over. Back in Berlin I worked feverishly to get out the records of this meeting, and I needed Lady Aberdeen's approval of the manuscript. If I did not catch her on the spot, she would be diverted by something else.

I arrived in Dublin one day before the Austrian ultimatum [to Serbia]—ten days before the war broke out. There had been riots in Dublin and some casualties. The Irish home-rulers had embarked on a campaign of violence. The Aberdeens were extremely pro-Irish and too absorbed in local affairs to evaluate the Austrian ultimatum properly. Until the last minute they were convinced that war would be averted, and after its outbreak they still believed, until the night of August 4, that Great Britain would keep out. I was no better judge of the situation. My own country had not been involved in a war since I was born.

I knew nothing of foreign politics, of wars. I did not even realize that war stops all communication, all travel, and that in case of war I might be prevented from going home!

When we became aware of the gravity of conditions, it was already too late. The Dutch frontier, among others, had been closed. Lord Aberdeen telegraphed the Home Office and the German ambassador, asking whether I could return with his staff should Great Britain become involved, but both answered that I must stay in Dublin for the time being. A day or two later a decree was issued forbidding any German to leave the country until further notice. That was how I learned my first lesson on war.

CHAPTER 9

# "The Evidence of Things Not Seen": 1914

Before plunging into the horrors of the war and the difficulties of my work during those years, I have to dwell on a personal problem that had always existed but was solved at the beginning of and through the spiritual upheaval caused by the war. For the life of the individual is not interrupted; it goes on with sorrow and grief but also with joy.

This is something my mother impressed upon me when I was very young by telling me of an aunt of mine who had lost a child. For weeks she had been dazed, as if she too had died. Then one day she again *saw* people in the street, in their various pursuits of business or pleasure, and she cried, "Look at these people—life goes on!" In the throes of her own grief, she had forgotten that other people meanwhile were living their lives with their own joys and sorrow. Unlike her, I am so deeply aware of the insignificance of the individual that I am reluctant to emphasize personal matters in time of war. Yet as a human document this story would not be honest if I did not refer to the most important decision I ever made, a decision in the matter of my faith.

Although I had wanted and discovered an independent life, independent thoughts and interests, ever since my childhood, I was more deeply rooted in the family than most of my friends—perhaps more than most career women who do not marry. Even in my old age, with my family scattered over the globe, the brightness of a day does not depend on the sun coming out but on whether I have news from one of my nephews or nieces in far-off places. This may be because I stayed in my mother's home, never went away to school or university, and never was away at all for any length of time. Or it may be the result of her dependence on me after all her other children had married. Our lives were closely interwoven. Sometimes my colleagues begrudged the time and thought I gave to my mother; relatives, on the other hand, felt that I should devote all of my life to her completely. But she understood. Such used to be the lot of a middle-aged daughter.

In December 1914 she passed away, aged seventy-six. She died of decrepitude, and the last weeks were terrible. One organ after another ceased to function, and she suffered very much. Life had not been good to her, and neither did death come gently. She had belonged to an era that was past, defending her ideas and traditions against the onrush of the storming, unruly members of her family. Now the sadness and incompleteness of her life was over and the peace complete. She did not have to suffer any more, nor endure the losses and hardships which the war was bound to bring. Her going seemed a blessing.

Although our relationship as mother and daughter had long been somewhat reversed, it was only after her death that I began to think of myself as a mature individual, a member of my own generation, an indication that we remain children not only in the eyes of our parents but also to ourselves as long as they are with us.

The religious conflict between my mother and me had started while I was in my adolescence. We had never celebrated any but the Christian festivals at home and knew nothing about Jewish laws and customs, the religion of our forbears, and neither did the families with whom we were acquainted.[1] But after the death of my younger sister in 1889, the habit of celebrating Christmas had come to an end. My mother could no longer reconcile herself to the idea of a candlelighted tree, and none of us felt festive. With the passing years, however, the younger family members missed the ritual. We belonged nowhere and wanted to return to our old custom. When we discussed this with my mother, she objected earnestly and said, "Christ was not born for you." I said that this depended on individual opinion, that I believed he was born for us all. My firm attitude was probably derived from the intensely religious aspect of the school I had attended. It might have been ineffectual if I had found spiritual nourishment elsewhere, or it might have weakened in time. There are many people who get along very well without religion—fine, honest, and unselfish people. But I had a genuine longing, a need that did not remain dormant but grew increasingly forceful. As a child, when I began to wonder about the meaning of life, the cui bono was with me all the time. Where did ultimate motives for action—the objectives and directions of life—originate, and was there no transcendental significance in the things of this world?

Similar problems must have arisen in the homes of thousands of young people who were brought up as I was, spiritually in a void, with an unsatisfied need. Like the rest, I had to find my way alone. Although I tried for years to avoid taking a definite stand, anxious to shun conflicts with my mother, Christianity took a new hold on me when I began to see it as the strongest motivating force of applied brotherhood, of charity and social reform. It drew me again into its orbit through some of the finest personalities active in the field, and still more when I studied the lives of the great reformers of the past who had all been stirred by religious emotion. It renewed its influence during my years at the university, when inquiring minds were confronted by opposite schools of thought. I found my spiritual teacher in Harnack, author of *The Essence of Christianity and A History of Creeds.*[2] He was a professor of the history of Christian religion and exercised a profound influence on his students as well as the general public. He was liberal, or modern, in his interpretation of the New Testament, representing the Gospels as inspired but historical documents. He united scholarship and implicit faith in a compelling synthesis. He won back for the Evangelical Church much of what it had lost through the "enlightened period." Many of my friends and I attended his courses in the Auditorium Maximum, at seven o'clock in the morning, after a forty-minute walk, where week after week, year in and year out, he wove the elements of faith into a spiritual unity. In the words of the Apostle Paul, "Faith is the substance of things hoped for, the evidence of things not seen."

Finally, I knew that I had to express my belief when destiny made me an educator and leader of young women. I could not have helped them to find precepts for life in my own had not been firm and unshakable; I could not have forcefully stirred in them the urge for service had I not been certain of values beyond those derived from reason and temporal wisdom.

My mother's attitude was not uncommon in Germany at that time. She said, "Believe in your heart what you like. Nobody prevents you." But there was something more I needed—the communion of prayer, the participation in ritual, the experience of living consciously and liturgically as a member of a congregation in the rhythm of the Christian year.

Long ago I had reached an age when I was entitled to follow my own conscience, the more so as my mother's loyalty to Judaism—like that of many liberal people—reflected primarily a bond with the past and was hardly more than a formality. She would not have objected if one of her children had married a Christian. There was more intermarriage in Germany than in any other country. Many liberal Jews believed in assimilation and had their children brought up as Christians, following the official state policy and the counsel of historians, both maintaining that unity within a nation cannot be complete without oneness of creed. Often these children grew up to be devout Christians, in the sense of people striving for a Christian way of life, who found in the church of Christ and in the strong simplicity of the teachings of Jesus a creed that enabled them positively to accept the struggles and defeats of living. Some of them became ministers, others trustees of their own churches, and, to make the German picture complete, the wealthy among them were politely asked to donate a window whenever the empress wanted to have a church built. I doubt if there was anything similar to this situation in other countries.

During the first week of the war, when the world seemed to lie in darkest ruin, when everything I had worked for had broken down and I was in deepest despair, something happened that decided me to put an end to a distorted and unworthy status. It was a small thing, a leaflet published by the "Society of Friends," that had been sent to me. It was an appeal, in the midst of war and chaos, to keep faith in a divine order and a divine purpose. There was a passage: "Some people may through this disaster lose their faith in the religion of Christ. Others will find it, and will proclaim it with a deeper conviction than ever before. They will testify to it as the only hope of mankind for restoring peace and goodwill." This was my call, and I followed it at once, before returning from Ireland to Berlin.

After some exploration, I found a church where—in spite of all the current hatred roused and often expressed in sermons—the minister prayed, "Lead us, if it is thy holy will, to victory and give grace that we prove ourselves as Christians also when dealing with the enemy." Even in reminiscences which aim at being essentially complete, there is no need to say more than this.

CHAPTER 10

# Patriotism Is Not Enough: 1914–1916

In view of the new cataclysm, the First World War has become remote. Yet no one is living today whose life has not been influenced by what it bred. Many of us had to reconstruct our political ideas. In my own case, there was less to be overcome, since I had learned to appreciate the culture of other countries and had spent the first six weeks of the war in an enemy country. Having friends in so many lands, I could not possibly be susceptible to chauvinistic feelings. I questioned the ideas which had been inculcated in Germans—that militarism, conquests, power politics, and expansion are justified, that they bring honor and glory. Our national festivals were not an armistice day but a day commemorating the victory of Sedan.[1] At the International Peace Conference at the Hague in 1899, the official German delegate, Professor von Stengel, had opposed and ridiculed the idea of a permanent peace. In 1907, at the second conference, Germany again held back, when a man like Admiral Tirpitz, father of the German fleet, must have constantly reckoned with the possibility of war.[2]

I was still in Ireland when I realized that few people in Germany shared my opinions. In the roundabout way in which news between belligerent countries traveled, a letter arrived from one of my students expressing her regret that I could not be with them through the beginning of "this great period"—an expression which I later learned was common. Then I knew that I could expect the additional hardship of differing with most of my friends.

I had believed in humanity, and humanity had collapsed. I had worked for world relations. They had gone. Nothing was left but nations attacking, hating, fighting each other. They had become either allies or enemies. It was frequently said at the beginning of the Second World War that there was now in England a much greater understanding of the gravity and risks of war. However, in 1914 I had the impression that the Allies were well aware that they were up against a life-and-death struggle. I associated with many officers in Ireland, and later my work for the German War Office kept me in close touch with military groups. One of the British officers told me, "The South African war was a picnic compared to this. It will be over in six weeks, or it must last six years." British army headquarters and the British press seriously taxed the confidence of the nation. They kept nothing back. Day after day for weeks, the papers reported "reverses of the Allies."

In Germany I met a different atmosphere: flags and banners, victory celebrations, outbursts of joy if an enemy ship was torpedoed. When more and more nations joined the Allies, the slogan went round, "Declarations of war are accepted here." When I returned from England, the defeat at the Marne was not yet known in Germany. It was admitted tardily and with reluctance.

A reporter of a liberal newspaper called me up at my home: "We want an interview with you, Miss Salomon. We want to know about your experience in Ireland." I told him, "It was embarrassing to be a guest in one of the royal houses of a country at war with us, and I know that I must have embarrassed my host, too. But everybody was most kind and did what they could to ease my difficult position." He shouted back, "In that case, we are not interested!"

No one can blame a newspaperman for wanting a sensational story. But what affected me most was that women were as chauvinistic and militaristic as men, and anyone who would not enter into their mood was considered a defeatist. My fellow workers, progressive women before the war, now seemed reactionary to me.

The president of the National Council of Women reproached me for not returning sooner.[3] She was very anxious to get at the British White Book that Lady Aberdeen had given me to take home but at the same time somewhat offended at this contraband.[4] She told me of a letter she had written to the council board asking them to keep my absence secret. "Perhaps she is without guilt," she had added. She brought me a copy of the letter—as a sort of welcome, I suppose. I should have noticed soon, anyway, that I was suspect.

The atmosphere at the headquarters of the newly organized Women's War Service League appalled me. It was exactly as though they were preparing for some joyful festival and carried victory in their hands. They were very proud of the conversion of German industry. One of them told me that factories which had manufactured hats were now producing caps for soldiers. She asked, "Are they just as quick about things in England?" I said, "There isn't a single stationery store that does not advertise 'What a soldier needs most in the trenches is a fountain pen.'" Another, younger woman remarked one day, "You look so sad. You spoil our gaiety!"

The one good thing my colleagues did for me was to give me work. So far I had been respected by all, admired and loved my many. No one had ever doubted that I could carry a heavy load. Therefore, when a new task arose, they called for me. But somehow I felt isolated, no longer "one of them."

I could not believe the atrocity stories—no more than those I heard after the war, which had been current in other nations. In other respects, too, it seemed to me that people on the home front were hysterical. A well-to-do widow was notified during the first months of the war that her only son and her only daughter's husband both had been killed in action. She took the next train to Berlin, locked herself in a hotel room, went home after three days, and refused to accept any expressions of sympathy or mention of her loss. The other women greatly admired her. I could not; for me, this was not human. A grief must be conquered, must become part of us, making us stronger as well as more humble. But my values had grown apart from those of my colleagues.

Was I less patriotic than they, corrupted by my international contacts? Recently, when I met a very famous physicist whom I knew well in the old country,[5] he said, referring to my expulsion from Germany, "And you were always so very German!" Of course I was. What else should I have been? Germany had been my father's land, German my mother's tongue. I had been reared on the German poets and philosophers, and every morning at school I had sung one of Martin Luther's or Paul Gerhardt's beautiful hymns.[6] I had worked first of all for Germany's underprivileged people, then for her working women and for her younger generation. The landscape of Germany in spring, with the young green of the trees and the white and pink petals of fruit blossoms blown on the meadows, means more to me than the richest scenery of any southern country. Truly, what else could I have been?

It was natural that war enthusiasm gradually weakened. People were less inclined to hang out their flags. Women were no longer so eager to leave their jobs to nurse the wounded. The working-class women became ardently concerned about their husbands being drafted. Who could blame them? Many families could not exist without the husbands' wages, and for many soldiers' wives the next all-absorbing question became the subsidy they got from the state. One woman threw up a part-time job, believing she would be entitled to a larger subsidy if she had no earnings of her own. These women had always been subjected, without rights, even within the family. They had been brought up to obey their husbands and even more to respect the authority of the state. Of course, when their husbands had to fight, they did not doubt that they had a claim to public maintenance. Only a small fraction of the women active in the labor movement had a wider view. Later, the food problem became the primary interest, and in the end women were accused of having caused, by their complaints, the defeat of the army.

The Women's War Service League, on which I concentrated during the first years of the war, until I had to join the War Office, was similar to women's war organizations everywhere. It raised and distributed additional relief for the families of soldiers, provided opportunities for work during an early period of unemployment, organized public kitchens when women taking the place of men in industry and agriculture had no time to prepare meals. It taught people how to economize on food and raw materials and organized metal and textile drives.

In Germany, where class war had divided not only men but women into antagonistic groups, the Socialist women had kept aloof from women's clubs and councils aiming at social improvements. They had, rather, attacked us and remained suspicious of cooperation. But this changed at the outbreak of the war. The emperor had proclaimed, "Political parties have disappeared. We are all exclusively Germans." The Socialist women joined hands with us in the Women's War Service League, although prejudices implanted in all of us through political propaganda made it difficult to sustain complete unity.

One of my first projects had been a campaign for economizing on foodstuffs. The Germans are a nation of bread eaters, and they never produced enough wheat for their needs.[7] When the Women's War Service League asked me to write an educational leaflet on this immediate problem, I began with the words "Give us this day our daily bread!" The Socialist members on our board turned down my draft. Their party doctrine was antireligious, and they considered this "religious propaganda." The leaflet was then issued by the National Council of Women. Such superfluous wranglings did not simplify our work.

We hardly anticipated that later we should have to do without practically everything: the ration cards and endless queues, the turnip plague—turnips as vegetables, turnips as meat, jam made of turnips, bread made of turnips, and even tarts, attempted by some daring pastry cooks. In one of the cooking schools, it was a common joke to quote the teacher giving a recipe: "This pudding should be made with cream. You can, however, use milk instead. We use water."

Those of us who would not buy on the black market have been permanently injured by lack of nourishment, and many of us would not have survived if we had not worked in the "occupied" districts, where food was abundant. At Berlin University I had been taught by an advocate of free trade that a Germany encircled on all frontiers could not hold out even for a few weeks. And truly, without the food and raw materials of the sections occupied by the Germans, it would have been impossible to feed and clothe even the army. While I was working in the War Office, I rejected a girl who applied for a job in the Women's Army Auxiliary Corps in Russia because she was only sixteen. She began to cry. There were ten children at home, and they had nothing to eat. If she got the job, she could economize on her soldier's ration and also buy food to send home. To those who lived in Germany during the "old war," it remains inconceivable how the people of Europe now exist. And the effect of years of starvation on mental balance is well known.

One of my early jobs in the War Service League was to organize a department for assisting professional people—artists and writers—whose jobs had been liquidated by the war. Newspapers hired war correspondents instead of literary writers, and the money of the wealthy class went into war loans and speculations rather than pictures for their art galleries. Our clients were a peculiar sort. One singer drew considerable money from us when she was destitute. Later, when she had a job, I met her on a streetcar. "Do you still dabble in charities?" she asked me. Years later, before I left Germany, I heard a noted Swiss novelist glorify Hitler's policy, including his brutal anti-Semitism, and remembered that he had allowed my department to support him and his two wives (!) very generously. His eulogy was made in the home of one of the many Jewish families who also had helped him. I could not refrain from asking him whether he had not chosen a strange place for his confession of faith. Afterward I read that he had received high honors from the Nazi government.

Early in the war, I suggested to one of our women's associations that we ask permission to visit the civilian and military prisoners' camps. One day, I thought, the women of all nations who had worked together for so long would ask each other what had been done for their respective imprisoned countrymen. The military authorities refused our request, one after another. Finally, an influential woman in our group promised to talk about it to the empress. I begged her to remind the empress of the words of St. Matthew: that we shall be judged not according to our negative virtues, that the test will be rather whether we received the stranger, visited the sick, and helped those who were in prison. My friend returned, downcast. The empress, although a deeply religious woman, had replied that she had six sons at the front, that for the time being she could only think in terms of "an eye for an eye."

My foreboding was not unjustified. Women of different nations did hold one another responsible. Some of our leading women drafted a document refuting the charge that our husbands, sons, and brothers committed atrocities, defending the integrity of our men. They sent it to women in neutral countries to be forwarded to those among the Allied nations. The answer came: "Have you forgotten that not only your highly educated husbands and sons are in your army, but that the prisons have been opened and that criminals, procurers from the Friedrichstrasse (the red-light district) are enlisted with the others?"

The refusal to let us visit prison camps had its consequences. After the armistice, when prisoners returned to their own countries, there was an outcry in the British press: some of the wives of British consuls overtaken by the war in Russia had complained that after the German invasion they had been imprisoned in camps together with criminals and harlots. Someone from the German Foreign Office called me on the telephone. They knew I had many friends abroad and wanted me to testify that Germany had treated the Allied prisoners fairly. They were quite surprised to hear that I could not possibly testify, that none of us had ever been inside a prison camp, and that we had been refused admittance.

After nearly a year of war, the courage of women was challenged in taking a most unpopular stand. Some who had always been more advanced than council women openly declared themselves pacifists and called an international meeting at the Hague late in April 1915. In belligerent countries, people with an active pacifist policy were outcasts, so it was only a handful of various nationals who gathered in the midst of war to discuss mediation for peace. Jane Addams, beloved and respected by so many, came as the leader, and her American group suggested a conference of men and women from neutral countries who would deliberate continually, repeating offers of mediation to bring about the settlement of the war. The plan was accepted at the Hague, and it was decided to send a delegation to confer with the heads of the belligerent governments.

When the meeting was convened, some of my friends in the National Council thought of going. But we received a letter from our president (the same who had written about me, "Perhaps she is not guilty") stating that women who went to the Hague could no longer hold office in the German Council. There we were faced with the crucial question which public servants have had to answer for themselves in every age: Is it better to keep an office in order to use its influence from within or to resign and accept open opposition? I am certain that those who submitted to the German Council's order, as I did, were wrong. As usual in such situations, it proved that nothing could be done inside the Council.

The affair did not run smoothly in other countries, either. The British delegation could not get a permit to leave the country. Yet the meeting was held, and the American plan was accepted. The result was the International League for Peace and Freedom, and two delegations started on their mission.[8]

Jane Addams and Aletta Jacobs, the Dutch physician, came to Berlin, while others went to the Scandinavian countries. The only thing I could do for Jane Addams was to help her get an audience with the German chancellor, Bethmann Hollweg.[9]

From what they reported, the statesmen regretted that military authorities made it impossible to stage a mass movement for peace and, moreover, that the masses were not ready for it.

How much disaster could have been prevented if, at that stage, the influence of these women had prevailed!

CHAPTER 11

# In the War Office: 1917–1919

The first two years of the war, the German people were patient and docile. They believed, like the other belligerents, in the propaganda organized for their benefit. Even the Socialists, in spite of their "International" and the fraternity of the workers of the world, supported the government and, with the exception of the Independents,[1] voted for the war credits. The founder of the party and its leader until his death in 1913, August Bebel, had always stated that they would fight if Germany were attacked. Now the Socialists, like practically all Germans, believed this was actually the case. They had always felt as Germans, but under the influence of party slogans, they were simply unaware of it.

By the end of 1916, the people grew restive, the troops were decimated, and the replacements far from fit. The "Ludendorff program"[2] was issued with an order to form a Women's Auxiliary Corps, and the conscription of women was given serious consideration. I was appointed head of the women's department of the War Office for my home province, the area raising the Garde Corps and the Third Army Corps, and for all occupied districts behind the front where they were stationed.

I was most reluctant to accept this post. There was not a grain of nationalistic enthusiasm in me. So far, my war work had been confined to helping people who were in difficulties, but this new job meant actual service in the war machine. After much discussion, I surrendered to pressure, to the argument that everyone who refused to serve weakened the ranks of our soldiers and increased the danger of defeat, and because I would probably soon be conscripted anyway, but also because the war seemed easier to bear if I drowned myself in work, if I shared the common lot, if I became a part of the masses.

My department organized the work and working conditions of women in my province and, insofar as possible, living conditions as well—everything, in fact, from waking to sleeping. I had to direct the labor exchanges in giving preference to war industries and to arrange for the supervision of children in industrial and rural districts so that the mothers could be induced to go to work. In munitions factories, where working conditions were especially unsuitable for women, we persuaded the authorities to make it compulsory for management to appoint a personnel of welfare workers.

I began without any help except occasionally that of a typist from another section, but as the work expanded, my department did too, as is usual in government offices. Toward the end, I had required a large staff of about seventy social workers and secretaries. If this had not been wartime, the unlimited power given to women would have fulfilled our highest aspirations. Under these conditions, the scope for our humanizing efforts was insignificant.

What we were doing seemed quite unintelligible to the officers who were our chiefs. For more than two years, my immediate superior sent for me only whenever his wife or one of his cousins needed a servant. He was convinced that I had some mysterious method of producing these rare human beings and that it was my job to do so.

Serious responsibilities began when we had to send women into the occupied districts and communication lines behind the fighting front to replace men in work ranging from kitchen service to administration. It was something of a desperate undertaking; time and again, we asked ourselves whether we should lend a hand in this business. In earlier ages, an army was frankly accompanied by prostitutes. With our modern standards of a womanhood more conscious of its dignity and value, we could not overlook the danger of sending respectable girls of varied backgrounds to supplement the army. They had been deprived for years of any pleasure, any social stimulus and friendly association with men. The soldiers, too, had been cut off from all this. Some of the women we dispatched were idealistic and patriotic, but they worked under adverse conditions.

I had to provide the auxiliaries for vast regions in Poland, Russian, and the Ukraine, where diseases such as typhoid and spotted fever were endemic. After choosing and engaging the women, we arranged for medical examination and vaccination against smallpox and cholera. They traveled in fairly large groups with an escort, since they had no experience of travel in foreign countries. We secured hostelries for them and regulated their wages, working hours, and discipline.

Choosing the women sounds simple enough. But there was a labor shortage, and the War Office did not pay for this "voluntary service" what individual employers were only too glad to give. Sometimes the army sent us urgent telegrams asking for twenty or sixty clerical workers, telephone operators, telegraphists, cooks, seamstresses, "to be sent at once!" Rarely did the military authorities understand that these people could not be produced like soldiers requisitioned from the barracks. We had to engage many whom we would much rather have rejected.

Oh, those mornings when the heterogeneous crowd of women was herded together in our inadequate office quarters to be vaccinated wholesale; the degrees of cleanliness, demeanor, and attitude toward this summary treatment!

On the other hand, we failed to make it clear to the commanders—and still less to the subordinate officers—that women did not serve under compulsion like soldiers, that they were less willing to accept hardships, and that more consideration had to be given to their housing and sanitary arrangements. Most houses in the small Polish and Russian towns or villages were infested with vermin, and no one of us was allowed to board a train back to Germany without a document attesting that we were free of lice.

Once I was urgently summoned by telegram to headquarters in a small Polish town. Why the alarm? Something must have gone wrong. On my arrival, the commander told me that two girls had been transferred, in punishment for misconduct, to a remote village in the dense forests of the Ukraine. After a few days, they had run away. It was, in fact, contrary to all regulations to shift them like this; if their deportment was not satisfactory, they should have been sent home. The girls had complained at headquarters that the lodging was bad, the food was bad, the village was bad, and the major in command of the district none too good either. Therefore, I was asked to investigate the Ukrainian village, the major, and everything else before a new unit was called in.

It was a most unpleasant journey from my Polish headquarters on a cold, wet November day. I traveled on an army train and was met at the last station by a lieutenant from the automobile corps with an open car. He gave me a Russian sheepskin coat to put over my own fur coat in the fierce, biting wind. We drove at full speed through the forest, but before we got there it was pitch dark. In the East, the winter sun, if it rises at all, sets early. When we got out, I thought we were in the desert. The only glimmer of light came from the ground. It might have been snow, but it was only sand—soft, light sand. I said, "But I am to see the commander! Where is the building?" My escort pointed to tiny wooden hut right before us and opened the door. There was one small room, lighted by a candle inside a lantern, such as we used in cellars and stables before the era of gas and electricity. Behind a partition was a tall, heavyset, fair-haired man who talked in a broad Bavarian dialect. He was, I heard later, a professional officer, of the nobility, and had been put in command of his district with its important agricultural hinterland after having been severely wounded and disabled.

I showed him my credentials and explained my errand as politely as possible. He seized his lantern. "Come along, Madam. I'll let you see for yourself. If the 'ladies' are not satisfied here, send them to hell. I built a house for them specially—yes, for them and for the parson who is sent to us once in a fortnight—a house with two separate doors, and even keys. Look at this." By the light of his lantern I saw a kind of garden, with a heart-shaped flower bed. "What more can they want? A heart! But they ran away. They said it was 'all no good.'"

The house was a wooden bungalow, Russian peasant style, with one big room for the girls. In the center was a huge stove built of bricks. Apart from this and eight planks which served as beds, there was not a thing—no washstand, no cupboard, nothing on which to hang clothes. I believe there were not even blankets, and certainly there were no sheets. Nothing at all. He said the soldiers had no cupboards—and where would he get such things? He did not have them. I pointed out that they would be supplied by provincial headquarters if he sent an order. I inquired whether the girls received fare from the "second table" (the second-best of three kinds of food, served to noncommissioned officers, to which the girls, since they were not conscripts, were entitled). The major replied that in so small a garrison, there was no second table. I explained that then they should be given the same food as the officers and that the difference in cost should be taken from their wages.

He invited me to his mess room to talk things over and to give me some hot tea. He hated the girls, who were pretentious and critical. I saw his own Spartan room—an iron bedstead set in jars of water to keep off the bugs and a few planks nailed together for his belongings, including a cardboard box filled with nuts and dried apples. Into this he dipped both hands and emptied the contents into my lap.

I suggested that it had been wrong to send the girls to this forsaken place. It was bound to make them more rebellious. I added that the conveniences furnished to girls in other army posts was a factor not negligible in keeping the war machinery going. We talked for a long while. He said something that helped me very much to understand the unnatural conditions under which we all lived. He expressed it quite simply: "What we miss here most, Madam, is a woman's voice."

I promised to send him a carefully selected unit of educated girls who would come for service, not flirtations. This I did. Some were chosen from among my own students, some were university women, some teachers of home economics. The major followed my suggestions, and it worked marvelously well. The girls carried on the administration of the county. Two of them were sent out to count the cattle and raise taxes, and when I came again, they told me of having eaten twelve eggs in one day, since they had been offered four by each peasant. They enjoyed it after those lean and hungry years. On Sundays they dined with the officers, and they liked their work.

I traveled a great deal during the last two years of the war. In Kiev I had to straighten out a difficult situation which had arisen soon after the Germans conquered the Ukraine. Kiev, though it was anything but comfortable, is a wonderful place to remember—a city built on many hills, like San Francisco, with the gilded cupolas of many churches, ancient convents with sacred shrines, long-haired bearded priests in exotic robes, and a population of Slav and Tatar tribes.

The city was packed when I arrived. It had a normal population of five hundred thousand, but with the Russian refugees and the army of occupation, it numbered one million. With the chief matron attached to our eastern district, who accompanied me, I went to the commandant's headquarters and received a billet for a hotel. Because of the housing shortage, hotels were allowed to accommodate natives only so long as the rooms were not requisitioned. I presented my billet, we were taken to a double room, and before our very eyes a couple were torn from their beds and thrown with all their belongings into the corridor, like some low species of animal. Their bedsheets followed.

This was not a very pleasant beginning. No attempt was made to clean the room. I thought, "Well, this is war." I asked for sheets and was told they were not provided before seven in the evening. I was tired and dirty, so I decided to wash and lie down on the mattress. There was a small basin with running water and a pail underneath to catch it, now full. I asked for a plug, but was told there was none and advised to let the water flow over my hands. Apparently they had not heard of more elaborate methods of washing. While we harangued, a German officer came in to advise us not to stay here. The house was full of vermin. Also, there was only one key to all the doors. Returning to headquarters, we were told there was absolutely nothing else, not even for a general. Then I remembered that a member of the YWCA who worked in my department had asked me to look up a small hostel for servant girls, run by the Y. There we found not only a bed but people who were kind and enjoyed having us.

If these were our troubles, what shall I say about those of the girls? The situation was complicated. Before the military administration was duly organized, the War Ministry had sent out a large economic staff. For a country completely isolated and depending on imports, the conquest of a rich province is of the highest economic importance. The Ukraine was literally the land where milk and honey flowed, not to speak of other nutriment and urgently needed raw materials. Many of the leading industrialists were on the spot, and with them their secretaries, who were well paid, housed in the best hotels, and wined and dined with the high and mighty.

When the army girls arrived, they were paid and boarded according to army regulations, and as soon as they heard of the other group, the devil broke loose. How the civilian administrations ever got their girls into the Ukraine, I never found out. It was against law and order to enter an occupied area without military papers, but economic considerations were paramount for Germany, and these gentlemen could do as they liked.

I did not succeed in placing the different groups under the same rules and supervision. However, we did acquire a beautiful building, a former convent, where our army women could be well housed and provided for.

By direct order of the general quartermaster, Ludendorff, I went on another tour all along the Western Front, from Sedan into Belgium as far as Bruges.

The object here, too, was to bring about uniformity of regulations for the employment of women. Prussian, Saxon, and Bavarian armies were massed together, and as each army had its own rules concerning salaries, hours, and discipline for women auxiliaries, there was much friction. This was at the time when tremendous efforts were being made to end the war through a decisive battle. Fighting was fierce, the women were hard on the heels of the fighting front and advanced and retreated with the army. Bombing was continuous; our windows vibrated steadily and were often shattered. I saw a village which had been taken and lost four times, and there was very little left.

If a girl applied for service on the Western Front, it was like buying a ticket in a lottery. There was a world of difference between a dismal little town like Hirzon ("pronounced," they said, "Irrsinn," which means insanity) and Charleville, where the crown prince had his headquarters. In Tournay and Valenciennes, Ghent and Bruges, the architecture was beautiful and the climate mild. We picked snowdrops in the Belgian woods in January until the fighting increased and curfew was rigidly enforced. But Sedan, where my tour began, was dark and muddy, with partly frozen streets impossible for driving, even with heavy chains on the wheels.

Nothing offered a greater contrast to such a dreary place than Brussels. There the fighting had nearly come to an end; it was the capital of a prosperous country annexed for the time being. There was a large military staff, an important industrial administration, and a "cultural" department for propaganda purposes. There were also brothels under German control, and pressure was exerted on the native women to keep them filled. The best hotels, in which the officers were billeted, were not unlike these institutions.

The wealthier families of Brussels retired into their attics, while the other rooms were occupied by German officers. Many who had been promoted from the ranks and had never before set foot in a luxurious home handled family treasures with less consideration than would be expected in the cheapest rooming house. Hatred festered all around, as it did later among the Germans when the Allies sent their troops into the Rhineland. There were the brutal traits that are bound to develop when unlimited power is given to one group over another with no possibility of striking back. The emperor's birthday was celebrated with a military parade on the famous "Grande Place," and all people of rank in the army and civil administrations had seats in the "Hotel de Ville"—that jewel of Brussels architecture. As I looked down on the pageant, I could not help thinking of the sentiments of the Belgians who saw us there in possession. This was an impossible attitude for someone in office, but from the beginning of my conscious life I had always felt a compulsion to take sides with the underdog. Was it a curse or a blessing? It meant conflict, without end, during the war.

Even after the United States had entered the war in the spring of 1917, the Germans were cocksure of ultimate victory. "The Americans cannot swim the Atlantic," was a new slogan. The military concentrated on a victorious not a negotiated peace. The Press Department of the War Office for Berlin and Brandenburg, to which I was assigned, published leaflets on this subject and wanted me to have them distributed among the women working in factories. I refused, and we went to the highest authorities over this divergence of opinion. I felt that until now the people had accepted hard work and privation, believing that they must help defend Germany. But for conquest, they would not go on. When I declared I could not guarantee the reactions of the people, I won my case.

But the generals were not alone in striving for conquest. Even a liberal professor of economics writing in a liberal newspaper proposed that Germany should not merely claim from Russia the Baltic provinces of Estonia, Latvia, and Lithuania but also a big slice of Russia proper.[3] Amid the general and firm assurance of a victorious peace, some of the old liberals even feared the consequences of too much victory—those liberals who knew this would be followed inevitably by a new wave of chauvinistic reaction.

Not until September 1918 did I hear that Germany was endangered. I had been summoned to Udine, in Italy, to discuss sending out a unit of women. The German army shared the administration of this Italian district with the Austrians. I had been in a mixed garrison before. It was never easy when the two nations, whose fate was so closely knit and which differed so much in temperament, were thrown together. They usually divided the town into two sections. In the Austrian zone there was invariably a café that served cake and whipped cream. Now and then, when the temptation proved too strong, we invaded this stronghold. Austrian officers were allowed to bring their wives into the occupied districts on pleasure trips, and in Udine the military orchestra held a concert in the square every day at noon. The officers and their ladies promenaded about as at a summer resort or a spa, and the Germans resented this sort of life in the midst of deadly danger. German officers frankly confessed what no one would have dared to utter at home: that we could not hold out much longer, that our resources in human and other war materials were exhausted—that we were defeated.

The last years of the war, when so many lives were lost, so many of those surviving physically impaired, I too had my share of suffering. Apart from personal losses, I had contracted bronchitis, and a resulting emphysema of the lungs did not leave me for years. One attack followed another. I had to travel in all kinds of weather, and I had never been strong. Often I literally had to fight my way into army trains, for we had no uniforms because of the shortage of textiles, and the army personnel on trains would not believe our military status.

But there was something else—a mental and spiritual burden which was with me all the time. Ever since I had chosen my work, I had tried to build safeguards against poverty, disease, demoralization, and here I was up against a dehumanized world. War is waged against everything and everyone. It is waged even against the unborn child. It impoverishes the world, it stops production or diverts it into wasteful channels.

But above all, war fosters attitudes which are the source of social injustice and distress. It annihilates respect for property, it drills men to requisition, loot, and steal. It instills hatred in the population. It paves the way for cruelty, for domination, for a belief in the superiority of one nation over another. It is an all-around violation of the idea of universal brotherhood.

Patriotism is not enough. Natural and valuable as it often is, it is not enough for the welfare of mankind.

CHAPTER 12

# Fourteen Years of Democracy

## I: Years of Chaos, 1919–1924

The fourteen years of German democracy were fertile in a new conception of the social state, with emphasis on the rights of the individual. But below the surface, constantly threatening, was a volcano. During the period from 1919 to 1923, the young republic was in danger of being smothered both by the Allies and from within. It was weeks before the armistice was concluded. The blockade went on for another eight months after that, and the government could not feed a nation that had been hungry for years. The people were bitter that peace was delayed for so long. When at last the terms dictated by the Allies became known, Germany felt doomed. Only one thing was clear—that the obligations could not be met.[1]

For us in Berlin, on November 9, 1918, the republic began with shooting in the streets, barbed wire, and recurring strikes which left houses and streets in darkness and kept doctors in hospitals from operating. There were, of course, no newspapers, and no one knew what was happening. Only after many days was it established that the emperor had fled on November 7, gone to safety without glory. The soldiers, streaming back from the front, tore the stars and braid from the officers' uniforms, and in public departments under military control, many officers sent for their civilian clothes and left by the back door.

For fifty-one long months the people had been promised a glorious future, for which they had paid in advance with the lives of their young men and of many old men too. Now disaster, sprung on them suddenly, was the result. It was beyond understanding. They said over and over again, "We have been betrayed."

The former ruling classes, the militarists, and power politicians could not believe in their defeat. The Germans have never been good at facing realities. They were educated for fierce competition. Their pride was deeply wounded, and many of them went under cover to prepare for the overthrow of the republic. It is characteristic of their illusions that Ludendorff, who had telegraphed the chancellor in November 1918 to rush an armistice because the army could hold out no longer, later accused the people at home of the "stab in the back."

There were many who talked as if Germany were in a position to defy the armistice. A well-known and witty author who had lived in Switzerland for twenty years came to Berlin for a visit and said after looking around, "The Germans have lost the war, but in Berlin they are not yet aware of it."

The radicals who had launched the revolution—and who were quickly overcome by the "constitutional" moderates in the Socialist Party—also felt that they had been cheated. So the nation was split and the new regime endangered, although the bulk of the working class yielded to discipline, even after mutiny and revolt.

The average German was not much concerned about the form of government. Even middle-class people, always an uncertain element in Germany, hung up the red flags of international socialism and accepted the new situation.

A provisional government was formed and called elections for a National Assembly on January 19, 1919. All this was done according to the good old Prussian pattern of command and obedience, under the direction of the old bureaucracy, since the new leaders, aside from those who had been on municipal councils, had no experience in administration.

If there was ill will among the dissenting and dispossessed groups, there was considerable goodwill among those who had suddenly risen to power. But their capacity for leadership and reconstruction was limited and did not reach beyond the range of social and industrial reforms.

After the elections, the Socialists no longer held a decisive position; they had to share the government with the Catholic Center Party and the Democratic Party. This instituted a policy of bargaining.

Women were the ones who profited from the revolution. Almost the first thing we heard from the provisional government was that women were enfranchised. The Socialists lived up to this point of their program. Most women got suffrage without ever having shown the slightest interest in it. Now that they were voters, all parties tried to win them, and so it came about that women actually voted in higher percentages than men. Some leading women chose a party not for its program—in fact, the printed programs did not differ much at that time—but according to their chances of becoming a candidate for Parliament. This may not have been honorable, but it was in keeping with political tradition in all countries.

There was naturally much excitement over canvassing. Under proportional representation, which had been introduced by the republic, the voters cast their ballots not for an individual but for a party list. This system transferred the struggle for a seat in Parliament from the constituency to the party machine and bosses, who chose the party candidate. They were rarely willing to give a woman first place; women were almost always put second or third. As a result, the Liberal Democratic Party, which had few reliable districts, listed its old party warhorses except for a handful of fine younger men and two or three women. The Socialists, however, with an uncontested majority in many industrial areas, got twenty-two women in. Some of the Socialist women were very able, but altogether the party had a deficiency of competent candidates. There were women who came in on the merit of having distributed party leaflets from house to house for the greatest number of years.

There was, for example, one woman with a dozen children whom we had put in charge of a soup kitchen at the time of our war-relief work. She was small and plump, good-natured and kindly, with little intelligence and scant knowledge of political issues. Her children all looked like her, and she always fed them from the public kettle before the place opened. We were amused, but there was nothing to be said against it. A workingman's family of twelve would have been fed at least, and it was certainly commendable of the mother to look after them first instead of later. When she got into Parliament and received the customary remuneration, it was probably more money than she had ever seen before. However, she did not add to the scene of government.

Such were the contingencies of political life.

I had been recommended for the Reichstag as one of the Liberal Party candidates in the Berlin district but declined, unwilling to give up my school and convinced that people who want to lead the younger generation in social work should stay outside the arena of party politics. Most of all, I knew I was not fit for party warfare. I was born to conciliate, not to fight.

Nevertheless, I had promised to help Friedrich Naumann, one of the outstanding Liberal candidates, in this campaign. I have mentioned his position as a former minister and his decision to go into politics in the interests of greater social justice. For the National Assembly elections, the Democratic Party had offered him the best and safest constituency on the Berlin list. At a packed meeting in one of the largest halls, before an audience of small tradesmen, employees, and lower officials, I made in his behalf my one and only speech on party politics. The only other speaker was Hjalmar Schacht.[2] Schacht was then a Liberal and Democrat, long before he became an intermittent member of the Nazi cabinet with varying political convictions. When he entered the hall, very conspicuously, he seemed to tower above me, though I am a tall woman. He made an excellent political speech and pledged that his party would mend all ills. At the end he roused the audience to such a fervor that everyone rose, and Schacht shouted rhythmically, "Three cheers for the German Democratic Party . . . !" After all this time, they still ring in my ears when I think of him in connection with his Nazi sponsors.

My talk was a complete failure. My argument was: the common weal is more important than that of the individual and that this is the essence of democracy. The audience, hungry as they had been for years, expected me to disparage the other parties and to guarantee that democracy would lower the price of butter—at that time not yet associated with the guns of Goering's jargon. They behaved quite well. They were just bored. Party politics was obviously not my domain, for I could and would not promise to bring down the moon.

Strange to say, the very words I used about "the common weal and our own" later became one of the slogans of the National Socialist Party. Perhaps their later appeal was tied up—not with cheap butter, certainly—but with flags, uniforms, badges, festivals, holidays, employment for all, and cancellation of the Treaty of Versailles. What would follow they could not guess, and nobody would have predicted it.

The constitution was approved on August 11, 1919, a few weeks after the terms of the Versailles Treaty had become known.[3] It was a queer sort of constitution, rather like a charter of hopes and promises toward a perfect state. All the reformers and idealists managed to get their favorite theories into it. It contained extensive clauses on marriage and the family and the education of children, on land settlement and principles of labor legislation. It was the first constitution in Europe—and probably in the realm of what we call civilization—drawn up by men and women acting in collaboration.

Progressive women had long ago widened their interests beyond the traditional three: kitchen, church, and children. They had won, after a long, fierce struggle, entrance to the universities, the professions, and influence in the field of social reform. Now that they had the franchise, they fought energetically for adequate representation in all public and parliamentary bodies.

They could well be proud of the election results. Women voters were in the majority, and women won over forty seats in the Reichstag.

An English financier who had come to Berlin with one of the reparations committees was once introduced to me as a relative of Lady Astor, the American-born first woman member of the House of Commons. I made some complimentary remarks about her. Looking down on me from his height, he said, condescendingly, "How long will it take you German women to get in?"

"But we are in," I said, "forty-two of us."

He said, "Not in the Reichstag!"

"Yes, in the Reichstag. Seven percent of its members are women, and we are just as fully represented in the state diets and municipal councils."

That was in 1920, when women as yet were scarcely to be found in government bodies in England and the United States.

Friedrich Ebert was made the first president of the republic.[4] A former saddler, he had been the leader of the Socialist Party and had presided over its congresses with impartiality, authority, and some success in keeping the many factions together. But as president of the republic he was surrounded by the old camarilla of officials, which could not be suddenly replaced. Germany had always prided herself on being a state run by officials (*Beamtenstaat*) and had developed a complicated hierarchy with an intricate system of rank and training. These men must have made Ebert's position exceedingly difficult. His aide-de-camp, [Otto] Meissner, the secretary of state for the president's chancellery, was one of these. He served later under Hindenburg[5] and kept on when Hitler seized power, swimming on the wave which had drowned so many honest men.

Ebert had refused to live in one of the royal palaces and had chosen the less luxurious, less pretentious chancellery, where I first met him at a reception. Under his auspices, in the presidential residence, I spoke several times for charities. He had natural dignity and courtesy and moved about with ease, as would a man who had presided over many such functions before. With the officials of the old regime he was patient and understanding, displaying remarkable tact and a sense of humor that was apparent even in his voice. He gave a fine example of how this unprecedented position should be filled—if only there had been followers to let it grow into a tradition. But the upper middle classes remained monarchic at heart and critical of a man of the people. In Germany, obstruction and the spirit of class antagonism kept large groups from appreciating such men when they rose to high office.

Ebert's wife also lived up to her position. She was tall and handsome, with genuine simplicity and lovely manners. She had no education beyond that of grade school, but she understood the art of conversation. At a party given by a secretary of state, Frau Ebert told me of having worked as a servant in her youth because her parents were prejudiced against work in a factory, which would have been easier. Her brother had finally intervened. She spoke of this without reticence or pretense. Those of us who were democrats at heart loved and respected her sincerely. A high official of the old regime who had become a loyal adherent to the republic once told me that he had never known a queen who filled her place better than did Frau Ebert.

Walter Rathenau,[6] another high dignitary of the republic, had been one of the first to detect the absence of economic preparation for the war. He had drawn attention to the fact that soldiers cannot fight if there is no leather for shoes, no wool for uniforms . . . and that an army needs great reserves of food, not only ammunition. As president of the German General Electric Company, he lent his experience and organizing ability to his country. He and his friend Wichard von Moellendorf, an electrical engineer, had devised a system of national self-sufficiency—during the national emergency, when Germany was a besieged fortress—bringing all economic forces under central control. They called this "planned economy," a term now in general use. Rathenau was a patriot, not a blind follower but a leader, with an almost mystical belief in Germany's cultural mission. It was a moral bent that prompted him to demand a more equal distribution of wealth and a curb on monopolies. As soon as the republic was established, he was made minister of reconstruction, and in 1921, as minister of foreign affairs, he brought about the first successful diplomatic move for republican Germany—the Rapallo agreement, with the reestablishment of diplomatic relations with Russia.

Quite apart from his industrial and political achievements, Rathenau represented the best of German culture. He was definitely more interested in writing on philosophical subjects than in his business career. His summer residence, the little castle at Freienwalde, once the abode of Queen Louise, was restored and decorated with reverence. I once visited him there as chaperone of a young girl who was very fond of him. He took us into the garden and remarked, "I doubt if you know these flowers, they belong to a long forgotten period." But I, who had grown up in an old-fashioned garden and who loved growing things, I knew and said, "They are verbena and zinnia." He, the great industrialist and statesman, was immensely proud of having chosen flowers from the period in which the little treasure house was built.

He could have had all the money he wanted as a young man but preferred to live independently. He was very friendly toward women and corresponded with some on problems of philosophy. But he was most charming with young people, with whom he behaved exactly like an amusing uncle, witty, teasing, protective, and discreet. He said he did not marry because he was too absorbed in his work and that it would be unfair to take a wife only to neglect her. It seemed to me that his vitality was intellectual and spiritual rather than physical. He was very much *fin de race:* too refined and aloof for family life. He seemed like one of those rare exquisite flowers that grow from the heart of the plant but bloom only once, since the plant withers with the flower and does not propagate.

He lived for Germany and died for her. When, during the chaotic postwar years, he faced the possibility of assassination, he refused to be guarded. On June 24, 1922, while driving to the Foreign Office, he was shot near his home by Techow and Fischer, members of one of those pre-Hitler revolutionary gangster groups which resented a Jew in a prominent position. It was an act of blind abstract hate, of something like insanity. No one who knew anything about Rathenau could have harmed him. It was one of the first evidences of the delirium to come. Ten years later, the Nazis removed the memorial tablet to Rathenau placed on a tree in the suburb where he had lived and where he was shot. By order of Hitler, the names of the murderers, who were caught by the police and committed suicide, were entered on the list of "National Heroes" of the Third Reich.

The three political parties which had to cooperate during those years, Socialist, Catholic, and Democratic (Liberal), were united in their desire to do constructive work in the only field in which this was possible, in that of social policy, thereby carrying out the promises of the constitution. The newly formed Ministry of Labor was given far-reaching authority.

Immediately after the war, a Central Joint Committee (Zentralarbeitsgemeinschaft) of employers and trade unions had been formed, for cooperation and arbitration in industrial disputes, for the administration of labor exchanges, and for collective bargaining. This was an outstanding accomplishment, a courageous step toward self-government, toward industrial democracy based on the idea of a free relationship and the cooperation of employers and employees. It never received the acclaim it deserved because people were concentrating on the problems of armistice and peace.

The Ministry of Labor took over this structure for the management of industry and added the eight-hour day. It was a Magna Carta of labor, a triumph of social reform. Committees of "workers' representatives" were elected in factories and shops. A law for collective bargaining and for introducing minimum-wage schedules was passed, and up to 1928 the wages of nearly thirteen million people in about nine hundred thousand factories had become tariff wages.[7] A complete set of protective laws went through.

Even the stepchildren of politics—agricultural laborers—were protected by law. The trade unions increased their membership to six and seven million. Trade-union leaders were members of the cabinet. For a time one of them, [Gustav Adolf] Bauer, was chancellor. Surplus workers were transferred to districts with a scarcity of labor; home colonization was carried out on a large scale; marginal settlements were annexed to cities; and the slum problem was practically solved by public building schemes.

Social reformers were acknowledged—we had influence. There was a new will for economic and social justice. The republic had assumed responsibility for the rights and needs of the people, and if these were not expressed in the terms of "life, liberty, and the pursuit of happiness," they were endorsed in universal suffrage, industrial democracy, unemployment insurance, and in the right of all children to be brought up to physical, mental, and social efficiency.

Yet what good were all the laws for social regeneration when economic recovery was impossible? Inflation, which had begun stealthily during the war, suddenly wrecked the monetary system. As soon as the republic had come into existence, an avalanche sent the whole nation down into a financial abyss. Where we used to spend one mark, we had to pay ten, then a hundred, a thousand, a million, a billion. . . . Budgeting became impossible for the individual, for institutions, and for public bodies. We raced to get bread the moment we were paid, since the value of our money decreased every few hours.

On January 11, 1923, the Allied army of occupation marched into the Ruhr District in answer to German default in the payment of reparations. The Ruhr is the most important of Germany's industrial centers, and everything broke down before the Allies realized that the economic clauses of the Versailles Treaty had to be changed. The currency collapsed utterly. The workers' wages could not even buy bread. The mark vanished into a void. At the end of 1923 the established system of property was destroyed, and the middle class expropriated. Now the radicals, nationalist and communist groups, believed their hour had come and attempted "putsches." They were suppressed for the time being, only to prepare for new revolts with intensified force.

The phenomenon of inflation had become apparent to me in 1919 when my physician urged me to try a cure for the lung emphysema contracted during the war. Before I started, I had bought enough Swiss money to last for the summer. In the fall when I came back, I received for the little left over in Swiss currency more German marks than I had originally paid for the whole sum. This is, so far as I remember, the only business transaction in which I ever gained anything—if only in appearance. A few years later, I realized, like so many others, that my property was gone and that I would have to work for a living. I was then fifty years old, but since I had already experienced various shades and degrees of wealth and poverty, I took it as the natural swing from the seven fat to the seven lean years and was thankful that I had always worked, anyway.

One of the ghastly aspects of political dissolution and inflation was the complete collapse of sex morale. The younger war generation had already been more sex conscious than Germans habitually are. After the war, all discipline was gone, and an equal moral standard for men and women, for which we had striven, was now accomplished—but in an inverted sense. The marriage bond seemed to have lost its validity. Men divorced their wives after twenty or more years of married life to take a young one, and married women had their "boyfriends." The "gigolo" was symbolic for these years. A similar situation occurred in many countries where moral standards had been high, and everywhere the very young, barely of high school age, were the most deplorable victims. Judge Lindsey would not have written his *Companionate Marriage* otherwise.[8] The foreigners who flooded into Germany, some on business, some with the occupation forces and reparations committees, spent on a gay evening what seemed like unheard-of wealth in the midst of our abject poverty. The Germans had been hungry for so long that even reputable girls sold their bodies—and might have sold their souls—for a good meal.

A group of women once met in my private study in the school to discuss what could be done about this. There was not one physician or teacher among them who did not tell about a child of fifteen or sixteen who was either expecting a child or had tried abortion. There was a good deal of talk about the principal of one school who was not above attempting to seduce his students. One of the women broke out: "All this comes from having male teachers in the higher grades of our girls' schools. We should petition that these responsible jobs be reserved for women." This had always been a contention of the women teachers' unions. But would it have cured the evil? Many of them were shriveled and spinsterish and affected the sort of clothes that I called "bodice checked and skirt striped." One of the younger teachers retorted, "For heaven's sake, let's not put the girls in schools where they never see a man! Let's make school as attractive as possible and show the girls that we're alive, or else they'll think, 'We don't want to be like them—teacherish!' These girls belong to a lost and betrayed generation. It is the lack of hope and ideals for the future that drives them into adventures."

All my life I had tried to live with them, to remain young in mind and spirit and to let them realize that a woman can have a full and worthy life. I had helped them to meet their beaux if for some reason they could not have them at home. One of my secretaries used to joke about it: "Wouldn't it be a good plan to advertise in the Junior League Monthly Bulletin: The president offers her services to young men and women who intend to enter the honorable estate of marriage?" But now the situation was more difficult. The moral upheaval was a side issue of the political and economic chaos in which we lived. It would only quiet down if chaos came to an end. Regeneration could not come before the inflation was over.

Before this could happen, Hitler and Ludendorff had made their first attempt to overthrow the republic, in November 1923.[9] Hitler was sentenced to five years of mild detention. A weak government released him after nine months, which gave him time to write the book that became the Nazi bible, but at that time no one, apart from the disinherited sons of the lower middle class, took him seriously. Meanwhile, the republican leaders had spent their physical strength, and under duress of constant struggle some of them did not live to see the years of convalescence and hopefulness.

Ebert died prematurely on February 28, 1925, of a disease aggravated by grief, sorrow, and despair. He was only fifty-four years old. Stresemann, chancellor in 1923 and then minister of foreign affairs—who succeeded in liberating the Rhineland from the army of occupation and having Germany accepted into the League of Nations—also died, aged fifty-one, in 1929.[10] He might have been cured but for the strain of working under such desperate political conditions. Ebert's death, like Stresemann's, was more than a terrible loss for the country—it was a disaster. Other leaders like Erzberger and Rathenau had been murdered, along with radicals like Rosa Luxemburg, Karl Liebknecht, and Kurt Eisner, the Bavarian minister.[11]

Erzberger, a Catholic and an astute politician, had become the deadliest enemy of militarism. During the last years of the war he was prominent among those who wanted peace without conquest. He had conducted the armistice negotiations, which made him a target for the reactionaries. He was the first to be killed, on August 20, 1921, aged forty-six. Rathenau was fifty-five when he was shot.

The murderers were war veterans, who, like Hitler, could not adjust themselves to normal existence and grouped themselves into "free corps," "brigades," and similar gangs—the predecessors of the Nazis.

There was hardly any outstanding candidate for the presidency after Ebert's death, no one who towered above the others. However, some good names had been proposed. On the evening of the election, April 26, 1925, my maid came in and burst out, "Hindenburg has been elected president!" I would not believe it. In other countries, generals who lose a war retire in disgrace. I said, "Oh, nonsense. It's just a hoax of one of the boulevard newspapers." But no, it proved true. The German nation, by universal suffrage, including a majority of women voters, had given all power to a man seventy-eight years old, a defeated general with no knowledge of statecraft.

The period of intrigue and camarilla began. It was the beginning of the end.

CHAPTER 13

# Fourteen Years of Democracy

## II: My Foreign Affairs, 1920–1933

In the midst of Germany's deepest despair, we received an expression of international solidarity, of *caritas inter arma.* Members of the Society of Friends, who had helped the French rebuild their homes in devastated areas while the war still raged, were again aroused by their Christian and humanitarian conscience. Immediately after the armistice, they sent cod liver oil for the starving children in Germany and Austria. Dorothy Buxton, and her sister, Eglantine Jebb, in England started the "Fight the Famine Council."[1] Herbert Hoover's plan for an emergency committee to feed the innocent children got under way.[2]

Jane Addams, who had been in Switzerland for a meeting of the International League for Peace and Freedom, came to Berlin, accompanied by Carolena Wood.[3] Hoover had asked her to investigate the condition of the German and Austrian children. No one could have been better qualified for a mission of goodwill, kindness, and generosity. In 1915, on her mission to the statesmen of Europe, everyone had been glad of the opportunity to meet her in my home. Now, when she came into our shadow-haunted country in 1919, the Americans had become "enemies," Germany had been excluded from the peace deliberations currently held in Paris, and German nerves were tense and raw. The wound of hurt pride would not heal, and people who believed in reestablishing bonds with foreign nations and individuals were regarded with more than suspicion—with contempt. I had to learn that the women who had been chauvinistic during the war now had a tendency to hysteria that amounted to a persecution mania. They took every attempt at conciliation on as an offense.

Alice Salomon, 1925. (Photograph courtesy of the Alice-Salomon-Archiv Berlin.)

I thought I had been very careful in preparing the reception to be given in honor of Jane Addams by the league of social work. We decided to ask each person on the list whether she would like to receive an invitation, in order to save her the embarrassment of a formal refusal. One American woman, married to a German high official, wrote me a very courteous letter. She said, "I feel I cannot yet meet people from the country of my birth, that rose up against the country which is now my home." I considered this a question of sentiment and beyond criticism.

The reception, in the assembly hall of my schoolhouse, was very informal, and we served a substitute tea made of bramble leaves, which we had been drinking for years. Jane Addams was as natural and simple, full of warm sentiment without sentimentality, as I had always known her to be. She looked rather ascetic, perhaps the result of much illness in her childhood, but Carolena Wood, with her good nature and look of well-fed, rosy contentment, seemed quite a novelty. In a short speech I explained the purpose of the meeting, and I asked their permission to welcome our two guests, who did not understand German, with a few words in their own language. Jane Addams and Carolena Wood then spoke of the goodwill that had prompted them and the "Friends," whose emissaries they were, and about Hoover's plans.

The evening seemed quite harmonious. Of course we were all deeply moved at meeting the Americans after years of isolation, the more so since it was our national tragedy that had brought them to us. But the next day a board member, one of my former students, resigned. She had "never dreamt of hearing English words spoken by a German woman." Apparently she thought it proper to invite Americans but not to communicate with them.

Aside from this outburst, she was and has remained a fine, sensible woman. She was a tower of strength and sanity when the Nazis came into power. When we again became friendly, there was no grievance left in me. But the incident left no doubt as to the difficulty of restoring a spirit of understanding among individuals of former enemy countries.

Jane Addams did not have a much better time. Her efforts to keep the United States out of war and her pacifist attitude later had injured her popularity at home. Her propaganda for the German children killed it, for the time being.

Up to the end of the war I had never personally come across any manifestation of anti-Semitism. In the group in which I lived such a thing did not exist. It was toward the end of the war and during the years of the republic, when "officially" religion had become a "private affair," that the poison gas of discrimination began to spread. For the first time impediments barred me from certain fields of action. Gertrud Bäumer, who was president of the German National Council of Women, had told me during the first years of the war that I was to be her successor. She made it clear that since I had worked as a prominent officer longer than any other woman, it was my duty to take over. At that time a fairly unanimous vote would have been assured. But we postponed elections until the war ended, when my colleagues informed me that the members hesitated to make anyone of Jewish name and ancestry president since the attitude of the population was no longer reliable in this respect. I had not been anxious for more work. I would have accepted merely out of a sense of obligation, but this news implied danger for the nation.

Real trouble came for me in the aftermath of the war, in 1920. The International Council of Women was to have its first postwar meeting in Oslo, Norway. As president, Lady Aberdeen maintained that the Council was an unbroken family, since none of the national councils had withdrawn. The German Council had advised me to keep my office as corresponding secretary of the "international" in the interests of German prestige. Mine was a personal appointment, not made by the Germans but a result of the elections of the International Council. But now the Germans ruled that none of us might attend the conferences and included me in the ban. Some resolutions on the agenda, proposed by one of the Latin councils, dealt with the League of Nations, and the League had been set up in connection with the Treaty of Versailles, to the exclusion of Germany. This decided the Germans to keep away from the Oslo conference. I was certain that the resolutions were not meant as a slight to German women and that they would not be accepted. But the ruling was so definite that I submitted once more. I had always suffered severely from personal conflict. After working with the leading women of Germany for so many years, I felt I could not go to Oslo without their backing.

Long before the conference, I had promised the president of the Norwegian Council, one of the staunchest friends I ever had—Betsy Kjelsberg[4]—to spend the summer as a guest of the council in the hills of Norway, partly to recuperate from the strain of war, partly to advise them on local arrangements for the coming sessions. Now I wrote her that I must decline. She was shocked and bewildered. She replied that I should at least come for a holiday, even if I had to return before the September meetings took place. I saw no earthly reason why I should turn down this kind and loving offer. Norway had been a neutral country—and what did it matter where I spent my vacation!

The German Council differed. They must have had misgivings about their step, for they sent a personal friend of mine—a liberal woman—instead of a power politician to tell me that I must not go. We argued. She said, "Even if you return before the international meetings start, you might meet women of other nations who are there for the conference we refuse to attend. If the Norwegians want your advice about files and archives, they can come to Berlin." This was the last straw. A year before, I had met this same friend upon my return from Switzerland, and after answering her inquiries about the trip and my health, I mentioned the intense pleasure of a reunion with Lady

Aberdeen, after the long years of war. She had come from the north of Scotland to Geneva—with considerable inconvenience during the English railway strike—to see me. My German friend had remarked with disfavor, "You know, Alice, that I do not approve if Germans make themselves cheap." I had begun to wonder whether I still belonged in this group. But now, having been strictly *ordered* to stay out of Norway and reproached that I had not consulted my fellow workers about this invitation, I rebelled. I left for my Norwegian summer and wrote a letter of resignation to the German Council of Women after twenty years of devoted work.

Several months later my "case" was on the agenda of the German Council meeting. I had the choice of staying away and letting them accuse me as a "traitor" or of appearing to defend myself. I decided to go. The leading women tried passionately to sway the others, but some of the younger members came forward to testify in favor of international reconciliation and the right to individual decisions—perhaps also to show their confidence in me. I do not remember if a vote of nonconfidence was suggested and passed. It was immaterial, since I had resigned from office. This was the end of my career in the German Council, and it only strengthened me in my belief that patriotism is not enough.

The resolutions which had originally caused the commotion were adopted in Oslo in a form that proved satisfactory to the German Council after all, and when a telegram informed them of my election as vice president of the International Council of Women, the Germans did not only endorse it but asked me to accept. Two years later, a full German delegation attended the executive meeting of the International Council at the Hague. "Life is a comedy to him who thinks, and a tragedy to him who feels" (Horace Walpole). Years later, after Agnes von Zahn-Harnack[5]—a true liberal—was elected president, I was invited regularly to the meetings of the German Council as a guest of honor.

I must say once more that all these women were intelligent and well-meaning, and later, when they could see more clearly, they did not hesitate to try and make amends. They should not be judged according to their actions right after the German defeat, steeped in the bitterness of that wound. I became rather sorry for them later when they were among Hitler's victims. Although they were in Nazi terminology pure Aryans and were not thrown out, they share in the collective guilt of the German people and must atone for it.

Long before this fray, some of my colleagues had found important jobs in the administration. Through pressure from organized women and from their political parties, they had been made counselors of state and even heads of government departments. I had been asked whether I would accept some post in the Foreign Office if it came up. I declined for more or less the same reason I had stayed out of party politics—feeling that I had more influence as an educator and reformer, an international freelance. Furthermore, the idea of being an official in a government department where even doorkeepers moved about with a stiffness reminiscent of bundled documents, where one spoke only in half tones, did not attract me, although the Foreign Office was now less conventional than formerly.

The time had come when official circles knew what my friends were slow to learn, that honest acceptance of defeat and unofficial relations of Germans with other countries could be of diplomatic value. The minister of foreign affairs in the early years of the republic, [Ulrich Graf von] Brockdorff-Rantzau, appreciated my point of view, and so did some of the undersecretaries. They welcomed my opportunities to lecture on what we then believed to be "the New Germany" in the Allied countries, where official emissaries could not get a hearing. George P. Gooch, the British historian who had long been a friend of mine, had me speak in London before the Institute of International Affairs, as the first German and the first woman to lecture there. I could not have done this sort of thing if I had been part of the official machinery. The Foreign Office people did everything they could to help me when I was abroad, and for years I traveled with a Foreign Office passport.

After the London lecture, one of the power politicians among my former colleagues who had driven me out of the German Council sent me a letter she had received from a woman of British nationality but German by birth. She accompanied it with a few personal words only, but they implied regret for the way I had been abused. The English woman's letter said, "Nothing could help the British so much to appreciate the best of German culture and the high moral spirit existing among Germans as the appearance of Alice Salomon before these men, with dignity, modesty, and a scholar's knowledge of the international situation."

When the war restrictions had ended, invitations to lecture abroad were frequent. I had hardly returned from London when Jane Addams asked me to go to the Hague and address a meeting of those unwavering and courageous pacifists, the Women's International League for Peace and Freedom. Among the German members—radical pacifists—there was no social worker or anyone sufficiently informed about the social needs of the time.

I remember this conference with particular pleasure because there I met Eglantine Jebb and because a lasting friendship with her sister, Dorothy Buxton, began there. After my solitary stand in recent years, the Jebbs seemed like kindred souls. The sisters had been born into the Society of Friends and had started the "Fight the Famine Council" in England to stop the blockade after the armistice. When they realized that a political move did not lead to immediate action, they organized, on a purely humanitarian basis, the "Save the Children Fund," which later developed into the "International Save the Children Union."

Eglantine began her campaign in 1918 with fifty dollars, although her friends warned her that all an individual could collect would be no more than a drop in the bucket. Nonetheless, she sent out an appeal. The first to respond was French governess who had been in charge of German children. A little English boy sent 2/6 d. and wrote he hoped it would be enough to help all the children in Germany. In the next six years, Eglantine collected twenty million dollars. In one of her appeals she deliberately infringed the censorship rules, and during a pause in the ensuing court proceedings her friends were puzzled to see her talking animatedly with the prosecutor. "He insists he can't contribute anything to my fund till after the sentence is passed," she told them.

The fortress she built for the children of all countries was also meant to further the cause of peace. Children of all nations were to help one another. Each national body of her union was pledged to help the other in their time of need. Eglantine felt distress even when she did not see it, she could rouse a will in people and turn it into action. The League of Nations accepted her relentless proposal for a children's charter, stating as one of its principles, "The child must be the first to receive relief in times of distress." She was internationally minded, and in this we felt affinity. In her relations with foreign fellow workers and in her devotion to the children of all continents, she experienced a widening of her own life. "Already we realize to a certain extent that the men and women whose memory is most dear to us belong to the whole world rather than to any one nation, and when we can feel that we have our part and lot in every good thing which every nation possesses, we are dazzled by the grandeur of our inheritance."

Eglantine made a striking appearance. She dressed in gray, Quaker fashion, and wrapped herself picturesquely in gray veils; a dark ribbon holding a cross was wound twice around her neck, reaching to her waist. She must have been ill long before I met her at the Hague. Speaking was difficult for her, since she could not breathe without pain, and her heart was failing. She spent herself and died at the peak of her life, in 1928. But her challenge is still very much with us and will remain with the generations to come.

During the years following the war, many Americans visited Germany, and those who were interested in social conditions found their way to my home. The tale must have spread that I was reliable. Judging by another woman with international contacts, not all were. To determine the extent of undernourishment among German children, she had used the figures on children in an industrial city as a basis for conditions prevailing throughout the country. Of course, the situation was actually much better in rural districts and other regions of Germany. When this miscalculation was established, we were so struck by her "facts" that a more thorough investigation seemed advisable.

Among my American visitors was Julia Lathrop, one of the early Hull House group who had been on the Illinois State Board for Charities and later became the first chief of Children's Bureau in Washington, D.C.[6] We had much in common: both of us had been led from neighborhood and community social work toward the wider perspectives of the peace and well-being of mankind. Neither of us had become a "professional pacifist," and we had not taken a conspicuous stand against the war, although we responded energetically when challenged. Both of us were full of stories, and we enjoyed knowing each other. A year later, in April 1923, I received the longest cable I had ever seen—worded with American extravagance—inviting me to attend the fiftieth anniversary of the National Conference of Social Work in Washington, D.C. It was Julia Lathrop who had suggested me as one of five European guests, with some difficulty in getting approval from her fellow workers for a German. It was also Julia Lathrop who honored me with the unmerited title of "the Jane Addams of Germany." There never was anyone like Jane Addams in Germany, and had there been someone of similar talent and character, the reactionaries would have seen to it that she could not freely unfold.

This invitation was an exceedingly lucky one for me. It was then practically impossible for Germans to travel to the United States, partly because of lingering animosity against the Germans and still more because no one could raise the money for a transatlantic trip during the inflation. My expenses were paid, and I could accept. New York was immensely changed since 1909. More and higher skyscrapers had been built, meanwhile, and I was fascinated. The mixture of architectural styles which had been characteristic of the earlier period had given way to one of new and more homogeneous character. Washington was new to me, with its gleaming office buildings, wide avenues, and overpowering national monuments. Everywhere I noticed that interest in art and music had grown. I was aware of a typically American effort to let everyone have his share of the good things—education, health, the joy of beauty. There seemed to be money for everything. The country's wealth was then enormous—beyond anything I had ever seen in European countries, where even the richest display had become a little shabby after the war—and the waste I saw appalled me.

The conference was a stimulating affair. I was given opportunity to address sectional meetings and to speak at one of the public meetings, in a hall packed with thousands of people, and this had ticklish implications. The topic of the evening was "The Church and Social Work," and the other speakers were a French priest and an American professor of divinity. They dealt, as theologians, with the conviction that the concept of charity and of "a love that seeketh not its own" has its origin in the teachings of the Old and New Testament. As a laywoman, I had to present the motives of the social worker, who serves outside the church, who is drawn into the profession by patriotic ideals, humanitarian impulses, or by the solidarity of class or other sociological groups. I talked about "Mutual Aid as a Law of Life," as expressed in Kropotkin's beautiful book—a law that links all social workers together as servants of mankind.[7] "No life is complete unless we make it full with sympathy, friendship, and love, unless we cross the threshold which separates the 'I' from the 'You.' Either we live to do or achieve something for others, or we are not really alive; we merely exist."

Alluding to my social philosophy, I said, "It was the most dismal period in history that created a doctrine of merciless struggle among individuals, that launched the belief that a better-equipped race would result from this struggle. The result, instead, was competition and antagonism between classes, between employer and employee, between urban and rural communities, among races and creeds, and ultimately the most terrible war, that among the nations. The result of this doctrine of individualism has been engraved with letters of blood and fire in the history of the human race. And here we stand and mourn for the millions of lives sacrificed.

"We know that we must atone for their deaths, we who are still of the world which belonged to them as well, who see the light of the sun that was taken from them at the age when they loved life most. We are bound and pledged to overcome the theory of the struggle for life and the survival of the fittest as a principle for human behavior—which it was never meant to be—and to uphold the law and the gospel of mutual aid as the first rule of conduct."

I quoted Carlyle's story of the Irish widow who lived with her children in Scotland in dire poverty and who appealed for help to her neighbors and the welfare agencies. "I am your sister, you must help me," she said. But they repudiated her sisterhood because she, being Irish, did not belong to Scotland. However, she proved her sisterhood. She contracted typhoid fever, many of the people in the neighborhood caught it from her, and seventeen of them died.[8] Service for the weak, as this story illustrates, is not a sentimental ideal but a law of life and self-preservation.

I then spoke of the imperative need to implant this new-old gospel of mutual aid into the souls of our nations, bringing up the children in a spirit of cooperation. "As social workers, we must impress it upon all with whom we have work or neighborhood contacts—by the very conduct of our lives, by the character of our work, by rendering our services not as a profession but as a privilege, not because we like our job but because the spirit leads us."

After my talk, I was surrounded by old and new friends and by people who wanted to take me across the continent for lectures. I had to be home for state examinations at my school, but I arranged to come back in January 1924 for a longer period and tour for a lecture agency which booked me as far as California.

Again I crossed the vast American plains, the mountain ranges in winter, the wide torrential rivers, and again I was struck by the immensity of everything in the American scene. Here so much land awaited cultivation, and Germany with its dense population and intensive agriculture seemed very small and economically limited.

For a born traveler willing to bear considerable strain for the compensation of learning new things and gathering new impressions, there is no more delightful experience than an American lecture trip and American hospitality. The tour began with a talk at the home of Mrs. Francis Conkling Huyck in Albany, who, with her husband, unhesitatingly gave me an affidavit of support years later when I had to leave Germany.

My agent took me south and north on a sort of zig-zag course. Sometimes in the Middle West, where I had many engagements, I thought there simply could not be any more cities. But there were always more. Everywhere I went I had to talk on some aspect of what we then believed to be the "New Germany."

I suppose I was never fit for such exertions, certainly not so soon after the hungry years. In Cincinnati I broke down with a gall bladder attack. I did not know what it was, only that I had terrific, tearing pains. I got through a midday lecture, but after that I had to submit to the doctor under the hospitable roof and kind care of Mrs. Ferdinand Kuhn and miss the receptions arranged for me.

The worst of the affair was a telegram from a Detroit committee which was collecting money for the German children, insisting that I give my one and only free day in many months to lecture there. It meant returning northeast the second day after my collapse, and I refused. Another telegram followed, informing me that I had been advertised as "the Jane Addams of Germany" and that someone was on her way to Cincinnati with the order either to bring me or get Jane Addams as a substitute! This was, of course, quite impossible. The messenger had engaged a drawing room on the train, and I had to go.

Perhaps the most fascinating experience of all was the trip across the desert. I stopped to see the Grand Canyon, and it seemed a wilderness inhabited by God, indescribable except in the language of titans. In California, people were still very hostile to the Germans. The West is so far away from Europe that it is difficult to create excitement over things that happen on the other side of the Atlantic; but once it is aroused, antagonism persists longer, and this somewhat dimmed for me the beauty of some Californian cities.

At a dinner party and reception in a university city in Wisconsin, I asked my hostess a question that had occurred to me before: "Why are you, who do not know me at all, so very kind to me—even before my lecture? You don't even know if you will like it." Her answer was candid and, I think, typically American: "We like people who are successful, and for us people who talk in public and are well paid for it *are* successful." I have since thought how very true this is, perhaps not only for Americans.

I have never forgotten the remark of a very wise elderly man related by marriage to Felix Adler, the founder of the Society of Ethical Culture. He said to me one day, "Miss Salomon, you go about this country telling people that your friends are proud of having seized power without violence toward the former ruling caste, without killing a single person who was prominent in the imperial government, without hurting a hair of anyone. You and they are all wrong. Germany will never be a liberal and democratic country until tens of thousands of your reactionary bureaucrats and Junkers[9] have been killed off." I regret that history has proved him right. Now tens and hundreds of thousands have been killed off and millions ruined on the democratic side. Yet I cannot help being glad, in spite of everything, that the republic kept humane standards.

During the first of my American trips, I met Lillian Wald, who took me into the Henry Street Settlement like a sister and looked after me better than any manager, as if she had no other concern in the world. I observed her moving among old people, babies and children, men and women, directing a hundred different activities, radiant, joyful and laughing, asking for impossible things and getting them, making everyone love and many worship her. She had the most victorious personality of any social worker I have known. There was an aura about her, whether she was in her own home, in the country, or in the darkest slum. In Chicago I stayed at Hull House as Jane Addams' guest, and during the period of Germany's deepest political and inflationary disasters I learned to regard the United States as the land of many friends. When I left, one of them gave me Mary Antin's book, *The Promised Land,* as a farewell present.[10] But I had realized even before I opened it that America really is "the land of promise" for children. Children are treated not as inferiors or subordinates in the schools but as personalities; they grow up less fettered by class distinctions and class-consciousness.

In time I published a collection of essays—impressions of the United States. It was not an uncommon thing for European visitors to do. On my second day in New York, an Englishman asked me, "Have you already written your book on America?" I said, "But I have just arrived!" "That's just it," he remarked. "If you don't write it today, you never will." Perhaps this prompted me, but I actually wrote it much later, after my third visit.[11] In the preface, I said that every comment on the United States is both right and wrong, that the diversity of this continent-country is so great as to belie for one part what is true for another. I also claimed that if any country ever solved the capital-labor problem, it would be done here. This too I still maintain, in spite of periods of strikes and unemployment and "poverty in the midst of plenty."

Some time ago I met a former student of mine who had gone socialist and had attacked me frequently, according to party doctrine. She said, "Look here—years ago I read your little book on America and thought that all you said about social conditions there was just your bourgeois outlook—and therefore not to be taken seriously. Now I came across it accidentally and read it again. I do confess, you gave a very good, unbiased picture."

During the time between my American visit in 1923 and the longer one in 1924, a new monetary system, an ingenious method to stop the avalanche of inflation, had been created in Germany. In 1923 I could not have paid for a cup of tea with the German millions I took with me, and on my return only the few American dollars I had could have got me home from Bremen. But in 1924 the miracle of stabilization had been accomplished. We had lost much, but now we gained hope. It seemed as if we could return to a well-ordered, undisturbed life, as if the volcano were almost extinct. However, this was merely on the surface. The enemies within and the industrial crisis were not yet beaten.

My life job in the International Council also kept me busy throughout these years. I went to meetings in the great capitals—Vienna, London, Paris, Rome, in the Hague and Oslo, and in Brussels, Copenhagen, and Stockholm. Like many Americans, I had questioned the validity of so many frontiers, so many governments, languages, and customs within small areas, but when I came to know the small countries better, I realized that they were guardians of great traditions of liberty, of an independent spirit, and models, in a way, of the perfect state, combining reverence for the past with progressive action. Their contributions to the solution of social needs were original and effective. Holland had practically solved the housing problem, Norway led in protecting the illegitimate child, Denmark in higher education of the rural populace, Sweden in the centralization of all social services. They have cultures of their own, and the world would be poorer if they should cease to exist.

I went to Geneva every fall, when all international women's organizations met there during the assembly of the League of Nations.[12] We considered the opportunity of meeting the statesmen of so many countries advantageous to the advancement of women and the causes in which they were particularly concerned. We took part in meetings of League committees, some of which had been especially organized under pressure from the women. Our members who had been appointed to the "Advisory Committee on Traffic in Women and Children" and to the "Child Welfare Committee" gained influence for the women's point of view. We also went to meetings of the League assembly and its Council. I was present when Russia was admitted to the League to hear Monsieur [Giuseppe] Motta's warning and notice the amusing incident when Litvinov and his delegation came in a little too early, before being called.[13] Their hurry to come in may have been a forecast of their equally hurried exit. It was quite a game of chess that the "great powers" played with one another before the Nazis made all diplomacy futile for the time being.

When Germany became a member of the League,[14] the Labor Office appointed me to one of its advisory committees. A few years later, when Germany resigned from the League under the Nazi regime, I received a letter from the German Ministry of Labor to the effect that it was no longer appropriate for a German to hold any position in the League or the Labor Office. The letter asked me to resign "without expressing any regret or gratitude." As this was apparently not considered enough for my guidance, a draft of a letter to the International Labor Office was enclosed.

Unfortunately, the League did not break quickly and definitely with the spirit of Versailles. It perpetuated the policy which it had intended to abolish, and where it failed in the sphere of politics it had to withdraw into social and humanitarian activities to justify its existence.

From 1921 on, I spent many summers with the Aberdeens in Scotland. They had handed over the Haddo House estate to their eldest son and heir and lived in the smaller, more modern House of Cromar, nearer the hills and right in the moors. Aside from continual work for the council, our days there were filled with many lighter and happy activities. On my first visit I said that I would go and search for white heather—that symbol of luck and indispensable requisite of all novels with a Scottish background—and came back with some, to the amazement of the skeptics.

I also made one trip that had nothing to do with "the cause" but for friendship's sake only. In November 1927 I went to London for the golden wedding [anniversary] of Lord and Lady Aberdeen. This was no brilliant festival—just a luncheon for the Aberdeen children, the in-laws, and seven grandchildren, and those who had attended the wedding fifty years before: Lord Balfour, who had been "best man"; a bishop who had assisted in the wedding service as a curate; and seven of the eight bridesmaids. This, I thought, could only happen in England and Scotland, where the climate is rough and the houses unheated, where people go out golfing when the grass is wet enough for a bath. If they survive this regime until they are twenty, they have a good chance of continuing strong, sturdy, and weather-beaten into the nineties. After the luncheon, a reception was held, and all of us who had been close to the lovable couple came to express our delight and gratitude for the friendship they had given us.

Still, after a golden wedding no one remains as agile and physically fit as in his younger days, particularly if his financial situation is insecure and compels him to give up lifelong habits and comforts.

This was to present a problem in which I was involved several years later. Elections for the board of officers of the International Council of Women were to be held in 1930. Lady Aberdeen was growing very old. The younger generation, not having known her in her great period, was critical, impatient, even aggressive, and her friends felt that she should not go on any longer. There were other, personal complications. As vicereine she had traveled with an aide-de-camp, a manservant, a maid, and her secretary. Now she often traveled alone to save expenses, and she did not really know how to do it. When a railroad porter brought her expensive luggage to a hotel—crammed with records, leaflets, and papers of course dear to her heart—she would, after tipping him, shake hands and smile engagingly. This would certainly have been proper in Ireland and Scotland, where she was known. In Brussels or Paris it was not. Moreover, everyone close to the Aberdeens feared that Lord Aberdeen, who looked very frail in his eighties, might fall ill or die in her absence.

But she would not resign unless a "suitable successor" were found.

The Board of Officers of the International Council of Women, 1928. Lord and Lady Aberdeen are in the front row, left. Alice Salomon is in the front row, right. (Photograph courtesy of Aberdeen Bon-Accord and Northern Pictorial; copy in the Alice-Salomon-Archiv Berlin.)

Suitable to her meant imbued with the "ICW Spirit." She had hoped that I could succeed her. In 1928 I was proposed by some of the national councils. Then the president of the German Council, Frau Eder, told Lady Aberdeen that this would be impossible—that intolerance was spreading in Germany and that the German Council could not back one of my "race." Lady Aberdeen was so shocked and offended that she would not even speak of it for a long time. I was very sorry for my German colleagues. I cannot believe that they were poisoned themselves after so many years of friendly cooperation. It must have been distasteful to them to express this attitude in an organization which existed primarily to combat such prejudices. However, I cannot deceive myself that, with my insistence on the principles of the International Council, I must have been a constant thorn in their side. It was extraordinary luck for me; no one knows what the Nazis would have done to me later if I had held a coveted position. They would certainly not have given me the choice, as they did, between expatriation and a concentration camp.

The election of a new president of the International Council was postponed for another five years. Meanwhile, Lord Aberdeen died in 1934, at eighty-seven. His wife firmly believed that she would meet him in the "great beyond." Her last years were not easy; she had to leave the House of Cromar and lived in a furnished house for two years. I felt her love and care for the last time when I was on my way to exile or, as I prefer to call it, my new home. She died in March 1939 with "the sense of the enormous privilege," as she expressed it, "which has been mine in being given some amazing power outside myself to win the love and confidence showered upon me by so many wonderful people."

During these years, the poison had covered Germany, and Hitler had seized power. I was out of the [German] Council, out of German and foreign affairs, out of social work and education for social work, out of everything that had filled sixty-five years of my life, or at least all the years of my conscious existence.

CHAPTER 14

# Fourteen Years of Democracy

## III: Social Reconstruction, 1924–1929

When inflation was over, hope was reborn, and a propitious period began in economic and social spheres. Everyone with hands or a mind and the will to do it could find work and earn a living. There were, of course, many people who could not find their way back to an orderly life, and the war had made some newly rich and many newly poor. Some of the newly rich displayed their wealth ostentatiously. Of the palatial residence of one of these profiteers, popular wit observed, "Like the inscription on the lintels of public buildings, 'For the German People,' this house should have the inscription, 'From the German People.'"

The newly poor were more interesting for the socially conscious. We had urged the government to make provisions for them, and laws had been enacted for every kind of war and inflation victim. Now, in 1924, when it was possible once more to gauge needs and to plan a budget, all the various branches of public assistance were combined in a comprehensive system which threw the customary poor-law attitudes and practices overboard. Similarly, a law was passed coordinating all branches of social work for children and young people, pledging the nation to give every German child the means necessary for normal development. The women in the Reichstag had been united, irrespective of party interests, in bringing pressure to bear toward this end, reaffirming the age-old verity that women are more interested in human aspects than in politics.

This social reconstruction was clearly reflected in my first life job: education for social work. Some of my former students had been

The opening of the Sonnenhaus Day Care Center for Children, ca. late 1920s, for which Salomon's school helped to provide trained workers. (Photograph courtesy of the Alice-Salomon-Archiv Berlin.)

appointed to influential positions on the merit of their abilities. Probably in consequence, similar schools had been established in all parts of the country, some without adequate means and equipment and with teachers insufficiently prepared for this particular field of teaching. A number of these schools were denominational or had party affiliations; others were municipal or state schools, or directed by social agencies, or like ours by an independent committee.

All the newly organized city and district welfare boards needed social workers, and the great demand that had necessitated emergency courses during the years of the war grew rapidly. Now it seemed essential to have uniform requirements for the schools, whose standards differed widely, and a generally recognized status for the young profession.

I had decided, therefore, toward the end of 1916, to invite representatives of the schools to a conference to discuss the matter. When the meeting took place in January 1917, we met with fierce opposition, not from within our own ranks but from the representatives of the Ministry of the Interior and of Education, whom I had invited. A recognized professional status was impossible in Germany without state approval, and the reactionary officials again struck against progress and progressive women. They came to the meeting; they listened all morning. They were silent as Trappist monks. Then the head of the public health section of the ministry, a very stiff and worthy gentleman, finally broke out: "You talk about a number of different things, about training for health work—for educational activities—for relief—for protection of labor—and all this you call a profession of social workers. What you talk about does not exist." To my amusement, many years later, while looking through French archives, I found that exactly the same thing had happened in France. When the first five schools of social work in France, together with the director of the public relief and hygiene board in Paris, petitioned the minister of health asking for state regulations for schools of social work, the reply was that "the petition deals with a profession which cannot be defined, which hardly exists in France, and the character of which makes regulations impossible."

Nevertheless, at the close of the meeting in 1917 in Berlin, we resolved to make this "German Conference of Schools of Social Work" a permanent body, and they elected and reelected me as its president until Hitler came.

Soon after the meeting, our adversaries began to act. The two critical gentlemen surprised us with a draft of regulations which could easily have strangled the schools and the young profession. They stipulated that students should have acquired both a nurse's and a kindergarten teacher's diploma before being admitted to a school of social work. Our school course was to be limited to eighteen months, and the subjects to be taught were mainly various aspects of health and hygiene. This would have extended the period of education over many years, at the same time lowering the academic standard.

Behind this expression of hostility was the distrust of learned and progressive women. They considered our endeavors as part of the struggle ever latent between men and women, now transferred to new spheres of life. They fought against a type of school which would prepare for a profession preeminently suited to women, conceived by women, and formed according to their scale of values. So far all professions—that of the nurse and the teacher included—had been shaped by men. Most educational institutions were directed by men, in conformity with men's notions of women's duties and capacities. The object of education for women had been to form men's "helpmates." Our opponents were right in guessing that we wanted more. We wanted to make women responsible for services in which human needs should be met with a woman's understanding. A man brought up in the tradition of German officialdom could not even grasp the nature of our aspirations, much less approve.

We fought their plan to the last minute, but the decree was signed and published two months before the revolution, when the war was practically lost. It was the eleventh hour for the empire and the reactionaries.

Under the new regime, the doors of the cabinet ministers were wide open. I asked the new minister of the interior, Wolfgang Heine, for a hearing. Although not a man of the people himself, he was for the people with all his heart, and he understood at once that these rules would wreck the profession, besides making it a monopoly of women with means. Within a short time, we had new regulations with which we could work.

Unfortunately, the revolution had affected only the most important positions; the bulk of the men in the administration remained and tried to pursue their policies by means of obstruction. My particular opponent in the Ministry of the Interior seized the opportunity for counteraction when the state examining commissioners were appointed and saw to it that he was assigned to my school. It turned out very differently from his expectations. I took matters into my own hands, and from the first I conducted the examinations; the two state commissioners, seated to the right and left of me, were simply in attendance.

The man from the Interior Ministry asserted his prestige by asking each candidate one question. I soon learned his two favorites. The first was: "What children's disease can be contracted more than once?" The answer he wanted was, "Diphtheria," to which he invariably added, "I know for certain, since I had it three times." The second question I found decidedly offensive: "What is illness and what is death?" The question upset the students. They were not prepared for it. It had never come up in their lectures or textbooks. With leading questions, he gradually extracted the answer: "Illness means that at least one organ does not function properly." He then added, as no student ever did: "Death is a state in which the heart has ceased to function." Certainly there were other possible answers. One might have replied, "Death is the beginning of a better life." Obscure questions create a bad atmosphere for an examination, so I did a wicked thing in later years and told the candidates beforehand. However, I do not think I shall be punished for it on Judgment Day!

We were especially lucky during these years of financial chaos, the inflation period, to have a Democrat, a liberal man of influence, as chairman of the Board of Trustees. He had been mayor of one of the city districts and, for a time, a cabinet minister. When the student fees lost all value and when it seemed impossible to balance the budget, he negotiated for grants with the authorities. Finally he arranged for a mixed administration—the teachers' salaries were paid by the municipality, and the school gained official status as an administrative unit.

Years before this development, I had been asked by a publishing house that specialized in schoolbooks to write textbooks on economics, civics, and social work. They were well received by vocational schools and went through many editions, so that I came to look upon the royalties as a sort of old-age insurance. This never materialized, however. When Hitler seized power in 1933, my volumes suddenly disappeared, as Germany set about eliminating the "non-Aryan" influence to which I had so copiously contributed.

While the profession of social workers was developing along with the schools of social work in Germany, a parallel development had occurred in other countries. When war restrictions had ended, I realized this at once. The British Joint University Council of Social Studies, a clearinghouse for the problems of schools for social work, had been organized in 1918; in the United States, the "American Association of Schools of Social Work" had come into existence in 1919; and Belgium, France, Switzerland, and other countries had followed suit. Everywhere the national and international emergency with the ensuing social problems had stimulated education in our field. A stage had been reached similar to that of the development of the nursing profession through the efforts of Florence Nightingale. Our profession had come of age.

My own social work activities had grown from insignificant Junior League services to the creation of a profession of national importance. At the same time, welfare work had lost its taint of charity, poor law, and philanthropy and had acquired the dignity of social justice, with the added merit of helping to level class differences.

I had put more than thirty years of my life into social work and over twenty-five years into educating social workers. After a serious illness, my friends urged me, in 1925, to withdraw officially as principal of the school and to lead a less strenuous life. I felt then that it might be time to let the younger generation take over. I had scarcely informed the trustees, when I received a letter from Dr. René Sand, of Brussels, the international expert on public health, asking for me to come to Paris for a meeting where an International Conference on Social Work was to be prepared. To my great surprise I was chosen there to arrange and preside over the section on education for social work.

When the conference took place in 1928, so many suggestions were made for permanent cooperation that an International Committee of Schools for Social Work emerged, heaping me with new work.

It is extremely difficult to find a common ground for international work of a specialized kind, but equally stimulating to observe people who have no such experience being initiated. There is no doubt that such meetings have [un]limited possibilities. Delegates can learn in what manner the work they do is being done in other countries, why it is done differently under different economic conditions and in countries with varied social, legal, and educational institutions—that social work and education for it depend, like industry, on location. We all have to learn not to be naively provincial in taking for granted that the systems of our own country can be made the yardstick for all continents.

We tried to come to an understanding on some very modest principles to be accepted by all schools, so that students who planned to continue their education for social work in foreign countries could receive credit, like university students who study abroad. No one guessed at that time how soon this problem would become acute; nevertheless, our agreements proved very useful in European countries.

Language difficulties and the tediousness of long translations are naturally the greatest hindrances at all international conventions. But fortunately we soon grew into something of a happy family. This committee, together with my many other activities, kept me constantly on the go—it was anything but a "retired life." Once the members of our International Committee realized the nature and cultural variety of our problems, the Paris conference afforded them a great deal of satisfaction. Porter Lee, then director of the New York School of Social Work, told me later, "I have never experienced anything like it. It was a great event in my life." All of us mourned his early death; it was a sad loss for all the schools.

Sometimes a small personal matter is associated in our minds with serious work. All conferences, certainly those in which large numbers of women take part, require preparations behind the scene of which the public is seldom aware. While I was getting ready for Paris in 1928, knowing that I should have to preside at one of the plenary meetings in the Salle Pleyel, I remembered that years ago, before I addressed a similar session in Washington, D.C., one of my sponsors had come to inspect the dress I meant to wear. I also knew that Parisians put emphasis on clothes and that German women had a bad reputation in this respect. Since I was quite affluent at that time, I decided to order a dress at Gerstel's, one of the best known custom shops. It was of pale gray crepe de chine, very simple, as I like my clothes to be, but lovely in cut and workmanship, with a hat and coat to match and accessories with a touch of blue. The bill was large, but I thought it worthwhile, and the outfit gave me much pleasure. Some time before the Paris conference, I had one of my recurrent attacks of appendicitis combined with heart trouble and was, as so often in life, confined to my bed and strictly forbidden to move. I cannot think of the Paris conference without remembering my anxiety over the receipted bill in my desk. I had always been a planner—not only for life but for death—and day and night during that illness I worried because, in case I should not recover, some member of my family would go through my papers to dispose of them. They did not address international meetings, and neither could they afford to buy that sort of thing. I knew, although I had often helped my family, that some of my relatives would resent this extravagance, and the first thing I did when I was able to move to the sitting room was to destroy that treacherous bill.

During the year of the Paris conference, circumstances compelled me to build up one more educational institute. One social worker after another came to me with the same complaint. They said, "Since social work has been taken over by public bodies, since I am employed in a state or a municipal department, I am subordinated to men who have a completely different outlook, the outlook of the 'administrator.' For them there is no difference between those employed in the department of taxes or of water supply and those who have to deal with human beings and their troubles. They reprove me if I do not handle a large number of records and files. How can I? Every record contains the struggles of a family. Sometimes it takes days to understand and disentangle the actual problems of one family alone."

This was a very sore spot. A German civil servant was educated to think in terms of functions, not in terms of life as a whole, of human beings as entities, or of dealing with human affairs. These highly educated and socially minded women with their desire to humanize the conditions of living had to work according to the standards of a bureaucratic machinery, to work like police investigators and renounce their own ideas of personal service. Similar complaints came from nurses who worked under administrators in municipal hospitals.

I could no longer doubt that all the reforms we had accomplished would be nullified if we could not get women appointed as directors in various branches of civil service. All the principals of the other schools endorsed my opinion, and together we prepared to organize, as a crowning central institution, a postgraduate college which would be concerned with the professions in which women were preeminent—not only social work, but nursing, household economics, and teaching in vocational schools. The "Deutsche Akademie für Soziale und Pädagogische Frauenarbeit" was to provide the academic armory and to stress those branches of scholarship which release the creative gifts of women. We decided to admit students who had, in addition to the state diploma for their respective professions, at least three years of professional experience.

This was once more an exciting experiment. It was new for Germany, where the universities remained limited to the traditional four faculties and had not added academic provisions for the newer professions. It was stimulating to teach mature women who pooled their experience in various fields of work, thus mutually enriching their minds. Teachers and students undertook research projects together. Among the publications I edited were thirteen volumes of an investigation on the status and decline of the modern family.[1] We had lectures from the great scholars of our time, from [Albert] Einstein, Carl Jung, Ludwig Klages, Eugen Fischer, Ernst Cassirer, Romano Guardini, and many others.[2]

These new undertakings would not have been possible had not the years from 1924 until 1929 been prosperous ones for everybody. The German industries worked at full speed, and I had friends who were glad at any time to offer help for one of my institutions. Economic conditions had improved, and in justice it must be said that the workers and the lower middle classes had more in the way of comforts than before the war. Perhaps this was not evident in the quality of the food they ate and the clothes they wore. Yet when I asked the owner of a small notions store in my neighborhood how so many small stores could exist—one almost in every block—he said, "Madam, don't you know that silk stockings have become articles of common use—even of general necessity?"

Many working-class people lived in better houses, and all had better medical care. They had amenities of which we did not dream during my childhood. Everyone smoked cigarettes, and all the girls bought cosmetics. Gramophones, movies, and radios furnished widespread entertainment, the circus of ancient times.

Many of my friends have asked themselves since, "Did we never realize that we lived at the foot of a volcano threatening momentary eruption?" No, I do not believe many people did, nor did I.

We are all guilty; we lived as though there were many ways in which to serve our country. This I think is still true. But ours was a dangerous period and we had not learned enough about the obligations of democracy. We have paid dearly for our collective guilt.

CHAPTER 15

# Fourteen Years of Democracy

## IV: Then Came the Collapse

All of us who believed in a German democracy and approved of the republic are guilty for our blindness. Men and women alike, we lived our narrow lives fulfilling the obligations of our particular field of work. We did not see the traitors in our midst. None of my friends and fellow workers, nobody among the ruling parties, thought the Nazis anything more than an unimportant party without influence, led by a group of gangsters who incited each other to murder—criminals the government should put behind bars. At best we thought of them as unruly people who, after the war, were incapable of returning to an orderly life with routine duties, a life without adventure and excitement. None of my friends would have believed that some day, not too far off, they would threaten the civilized world. The only ones who knew were the plotters themselves, who made the plans for overthrowing the regime, and they hid in the dark and did not show their true face.

The facts and events that brought about the collapse are so well known that only for completeness' sake I will briefly allude to them. In 1929 something happened in the United States. It was called a "depression," and it was a great calamity. Many rich people lost much of their wealth, a few lost all of it, and the people called the "underprivileged" became the "unemployed." The depression traveled across the Atlantic by the same route which thousands of wealthy Americans had taken on luxury liners for many summers in search of pleasure, the same route which middle-class Americans had taken on tourist liners to study or to educate themselves in European countries.

When it arrived in Germany on top of successive periods of privation and suffering from war, defeat, "peace treaties," and inflation, it was called by a stronger name, "the crisis." It became more than a calamity; it became a disaster.

What could be done about it? How could we, the individual citizens, help the standing army of unemployed, most of whom had been industrious people? There was the unemployment insurance, in which we had taken such pride, but it provided only for those who had been working before the crisis came and for a limited period; after that, they had to go on relief. It did not apply to the young generation, who graduated from school and had to proceed to idleness. For years they felt they were not needed, and they never learned that bread should be the fruit of toil—that its ingredients are not produced in relief agencies.

Other industrial countries weathered the storm; we attempted to do the same. Many small groups, private welfare agencies, public-spirited men and women, among them teachers and students of my school and academy, experimented with schemes for a voluntary labor service, and some municipalities made efforts to establish work relief. We were convinced that the unemployed needed more than money to buy food and to fill their bellies, that they needed something to fill their days, keep their hands busy and their minds alert. Most of all, they needed some belief in themselves and in the future to give meaning to their existence.

I wrote an article in 1932 for one of the liberal daily papers. It was returned. They considered it too radical for their readers. The *Berliner Tageblatt,* with Theodor Wolff as chief editor, accepted it.[1] I quote from it, for it suggests exactly what the Nazis did a few years later. It appeared with the title "There would be work if . . ." I said it was an economic fallacy to assume that unemployment was caused by overproduction or that modern technology had made labor superfluous. I gave figures on the families living in overcrowded rooms and on those who did not have a bed for each person. I spoke of the children who had only one shirt and were obliged to remain in bed while it was being washed, who had only one pair of shoes and could not let them dry after rain. As long as these were the living conditions of the masses, I maintained, no hand need be idle. There was not too much produce, but too little planning and rationality.

"There are more than five million who want work and are unemployed. They are insufficiently supported by the other twenty million, most of whom have barely enough themselves. People say it is impossible to build decent houses for more than small groups. But as long as the unhealthy and demoralizing slums are not pulled down and better housing made available for the masses, there will be people like myself, repeating that it is not impossible. We maintain that it is necessary and imperative to give the unemployed a chance to make bricks, to saw boards, to construct houses, to manufacture beds, sheets, and clothes.

"They say there is no money to pay for the houses, beds and sheets. But the unemployed still have to be supported, and most of them would be only too glad to work in return. As it is now, the state must put their maintenance on the debit side. It would be much more advantageous to exchange this debit for houses, furniture and health.

"They say that such a scheme would disturb the cycle of production. Is it not disturbed and shaken when those who want to work cannot find work, when the masses who long for health and decency have no dwelling space, no space to live, to satisfy their elementary needs?

"Whatever may be said about it, it is absurd to believe that we produce too much. Common sense does not accept this as a final statement. Common sense accuses the social order.

"There would be enough work if the standard of living which is desirable to the masses were the gauge and test of all economic actions."

Such appeals had no effect. The government had no dependable and stable majority, and organized labor did not back any such schemes for fear they would lower wages.

In 1931 the administration promised to support voluntary labor schemes and to cooperate with them. But what we needed was something much bigger—not only several hundred unemployed teachers teaching several thousand unemployed young people; not only shoemakers, tailors, and dressmakers out of a job teaching those who were in rags to do repairing; we needed a plan to provide all employables with a job. But it was too late.

Discontent had spread everywhere, even among those who were well employed, and the Nazi ideas had a devastating effect. Once, while discussing the Nazi principle of sending women back to the house as a means to make room for unemployed males, a most charming young colleague of mine unexpectedly launched into what I considered mutinous, treacherous remarks. She was highly educated, with university degrees, and held a position as headmistress of a vocational school. She declared the Nazi ideas on women were sound. To my comment that they would have made it impossible for her to acquire an education and to secure her interesting and influential position, she retorted that she would have been just as happy as a governess. Perhaps—but she had never tried, and now she rejected all the advantages for which generations of women had lived and struggled. However, she was honest at least and came out with her opinion. It soon became clear that she was not the only one, that women were joining the Nazis in larger numbers than men.[2]

The only influence on political events that I could exert as a citizen was through the vote, and for this there were plenty of opportunities. We were practically drilled in the technique of voting, as the Reichstag was continually dissolved and one general election followed the other. In 1932 we had four elections for the Reichstag within ten months. Yet none of them yielded a majority for any one party or a possible combination of parties, so that the government was constantly swinging about in search of reliable support.[3]

The Reichstag members were up to their necks in party politics; they could think in no other terms. This was true not only of the opposition—the communists and reactionaries—but just as much of the adherents of the parties in power. A woman of the intelligentsia, quite influential in the Liberal Party in the Reichstag, remarked to me deprecatingly that she feared a Stresemann cabinet could not be avoided—as though this were a calamity—whereas actually Stresemann protected Germany against the Junkers and Hindenburg and Hitler as long as he lived.

Old Hindenburg, who was then in his late eighties, was surrounded by competing conspirators claiming power for the nationalistic groups, for the army, or for the Junkers; and the best of the chancellors, like Schleicher and Brüning, who might have been able to steer the Republic through the rising waves of antagonism and intrigue, he chased out of office like mangy dogs.[4] Probably Hindenburg was too senile to understand the workings and laws of democracy. There was a story indicating the average man's opinion of his mental stability! He had been induced to appear on the balcony of his residence during a torchlight parade of Brownshirt and Blackshirt formations and, alluding to his World War victory at Tannenberg, he exclaimed, "Did we actually take so many Russian prisoners?"

Meanwhile, after unemployment had set in, the Nazis were becoming a formidable menace to the republic. The people who were compelled to live in idleness had found their way into Hitler's marching units and joined the revolutionary "Freikorps" and "Brigades," the forerunners of the Nazis. There they had again, as in 1914, flags, banners, badges, music, excitement. Hitler's bodyguard and the general staff of his party arranged meetings in the largest halls, and Hitler screamed to the unemployed, "Your country does not need you? *I* need you! I will build a new Germany if you follow me!" The audiences were delirious in their enthusiasm.

In 1930 the Nazis had their first electoral victory: they captured 18.6 percent of the Reichstag seats. No longer were they, as we had all believed, "a small, ineffective party." Two years later they reached their peak with 33 percent, but in justice to the German people it must be emphasized that they never attained a majority vote.[5]

In self-defense, the republican parties organized an "Iron Front" willing to fight the Nazis if necessary. The immediate result was that Hitler's men went into the streets, and pitched battles constantly took place between the two groups.

It was no longer safe in the Weimar Republic.

This was clearly demonstrated in the summer of 1932 when Papen,[6] the archconspirator though by name and affiliation a leader of the conservatives, attempted a coup d'état in Prussia, a rehearsal of what he and his Nazi friends intended for Germany. Without any authority whatsoever and accompanied by a handful of disloyal ruffians, he entered the Ministry of State and the Ministry of the Interior and ousted the legal officials, both ministers who had held office for long periods since 1920. Both of them yielded "to avoid bloodshed."

There are moments in the life of every soldier, sailor, pilot, in which he must be prepared to sacrifice his life, and the same attitude is essential for everyone in a responsible position. I should like to believe that the two socialist ministers were not lacking courage but were too surprised to know their duty. It is tragic that their sin of omission helped to bring about a situation in which two lives had become insignificant compared to the millions endangered.

From 1932 on the Nazis lost votes. They made common cause with anyone who would help to overthrow the Weimar Republic, with the so-called "conservatives"—Papen, Hugenberg,[7] Junker and big business groups today, or their archenemies, the communists, tomorrow. On January 30, 1933, Hindenburg signed, under pressure, the death sentence of the democratic republic, appointing Hitler as chancellor.

At once the traitors of democracy, who had never yet shown their colors, appeared on the surface. They crawled up like vermin from the fissures in a floor. They turned up in our midst, among women at least as much as men, among those near to me, among social workers, university women, even among those in evangelic mission work, and of course among middle-class women, who had voted for the new hero in full force and had helped him to power. There were even some former associates who came Heil-Hitlering into my home, but never beyond the foyer. My loyal and devoted housekeeper saw to that.

Hindenburg remained secluded on his East Prussian estate, guarded by the Junker camarilla and held incommunicado. He was, as people said, like a prisoner "in a one-man concentration camp." After a year and a half of Nazi terror, he died on August 2, 1934. As an orthodox Christian he would have been scandalized had he heard Hitler's pagan salute at his grave, "Farewell in Valhalla!"

Throughout its fourteen years, the democratic government had been on the defensive. No government could have achieved more under such circumstances without violating or sacrificing the parliamentary system. It never received the credit which was its due. It had given to labor more justice and influence than labor had ever known before; equal rights and liberty to women; better provision to the unemployed and the underprivileged; and educational facilities to the young so that they could develop their gifts and obtain a chance to overcome the divisions of class. The masses never consciously appreciated the benefits of the democratic regime. The liberty to speak, to write, to assemble, they took for granted. They did not know what the loss of these liberties involved. Probably they understand it now.

Democracy was defeated by men and women who bought from Hitler what they believed to be security or, as it was later expressed, butter and no guns. They had to pay with the loss of human rights and dignity, ultimately with the most cruel, bloody war in human history.

This was the inglorious end of the German republic.

CHAPTER 16

# The Golden Ring of Friendship

Once when I expressed my profound gratitude to a friend, he countered, "Don't you know the proverb, 'Friendship is a golden ring—you never know how much you give and how much you receive'?"

When my thoughts wander back to my life in Germany across the distance of time and space, I do not see it in pictures of committees, councils, institutions, and activities that filled my days. Rather, I visualize it as a stream of people, of individuals, broadening and swelling with the years, and many of these individuals as part of the golden ring. In earlier chapters I have dealt with friendships that grew out of my work; it now remains to give a testament of gratitude to those who—outside and apart from my causes or my career—lavishly contributed to the fullness of my life.

This book may sometimes seem as much a book about women, as though I had lived in a harem. Actually, I always had men and women, old and young, rich and poor, and sometimes whole families as my friends. The homes of those in the higher ranks of culture were centers for outstanding painters, musicians, writers. There was among others the Mendelssohn family, or rather the two families of the brothers Robert and Franz, who were grandsons of Moses Mendelssohn, the philosopher and friend of Gotthold Ephraim Lessing, and close relatives of Felix Mendelssohn-Bartholdy, whose "Midsummer Night's Dream" and symphonies and oratorios have been performed for more than a hundred years.[1]

There was a medley of languages and nationalities in Robert's house. His and Franz's mother had been a Frenchwoman of a Protestant family, and Robert had married an Italian musician, a Catholic and a highly gifted woman, who sang and played beautifully. They loved art and had a marvelous collection: Rembrandt's self-portrait and his portrait of Hendrike, his wife, a Rubens, a Goya, Manets, and exquisite Corot landscapes. But both Robert and Franz lived for music—although they were bankers, having inherited a banking house from their father which was well known for the issue of the Russian loans during the days of the czars. I owe it to these two families that I gained access to the enthralling realm of music, which at times lifted me out of the realities and problems of life and guided me into another fascinating world where emotions and sentiments and the innermost soul have a medium of expression far above and beyond words of any language.

Robert had been an intimate friend of Joseph Joachim, the violinist, and Eleonora Duse stayed at his home whenever she came to act in Berlin. His eldest daughter was her godchild and grew up to be an actress too. Strangely enough, she has something of the sound-color and timbre of Duse in her voice.

Robert died after a long illness in 1917, and his widow indulged in long absences from Germany, which seemed to affect her nerves. Meanwhile, the children were in the habit of inviting statesmen, noted painters, and musicians, and once, when they were out of their teens, I helped them out with a luncheon arranged so that Einstein could meet Gerhart Hauptmann,[2] both of whom had been honored by the Nobel Prize. I remember this party in particular, for Einstein hardly managed to get in a word and sat looking rather overwhelmed while the famous poet, the author of the naturalist drama *The Weavers,* talked about the flavors of different wines with nebulous loquaciousness.

Robert and Franz had bought acres of land and forest in the early days of the western suburb, the Grunewald. Their gardens adjoined, and there was much coming and going between the two families, since they always shared in performing or hearing music. The Franz von Mendelssohn family, equally gifted in the arts, were more normal in their habits, and a permanent family friendship developed between us. Naturally, their children, too, had to face the handicaps existing in European countries for those brought up in great wealth. They knew little about life outside the tall iron fence bordered by yew trees that surrounded their estate. One of their teachers, who had been associated with the parents for twenty years, told me how when the first of the girls was about to be married, the sisters had wanted to give her something different, something she had never owned before, and after pondering over this problem for some time they had hit on a change purse.

None of them had ever had one, probably because they had never needed to buy anything.

They were the most generous family I have ever known, and there were few young musicians who had not been helped or encouraged in this house. This was not done with a sense of the obligation of wealth; it was a natural trait, and it crops up in younger generations, even when there is a struggle to earn a living, as one of the granddaughters who is in this country demonstrates in keeping up the family tradition.

Music was sacred in the two families, and they asked for perfection. Once Franz von Mendelssohn had promised to play with a very famous scholar for charity in his own home. The scholar had a fine appreciation and intuition for music, but he did not practice and sometimes played carelessly. At the rehearsal, the day before the concert, his violin struck several false notes, and Franz lost his temper. He declared that unless the scholar practiced all day until he could perform well, he would refuse to play with him, and there would be no concert in his house. Scholar or no scholar, fame or no fame—music has its own rights and claims.

Robert replaced Hausman, the cellist of the Joachim Quartet, at public performances when Hausman was ill, and in both families some of the children also became expert musicians. All the great German musicians played in their homes: the Joachim and the Klingler Quartets, Arthur and Therese Schnabel, Bruno and Olga Eisner, later Micha Elman, and also Benjamino Gigli and Yvette Guilbert. There was always a crowd of young musicians with them. Adolf Busch and his wife belonged to their most intimate circle, and by and by they became close friends of mine as well.

Adolf was and is one of my favorite musicians. He had won fame as a violinist in all of Europe before he was thirty. He dedicated himself to the spirit of the composers whose works he rendered. He made no compromise, no concessions to impress the audience; rather, he seemed to carry the audience with him to a high office to which he was consecrated. And so he has remained—genuine, honest, and pure, as a musician and in character. He did not turn socialist as many others did during the revolution of 1918, nor did he—the prototype of a Nordic—adjust himself to the Nazis.

When I became acquainted with the Busch family, they were living in a suburb of Berlin, and one day in 1920, when we were still very short of food, they came back from a concert tour in Austria with a boy who looked much in need of being fed, with a shock of unruly dark hair and striking features. This was Rudolf—then Rudi—Serkin, just seventeen years old.[3] Somebody had told Adolf Busch about the exceptionally gifted son of Russian refugees who could not afford to let him have a musical education. Busch and his wife saw the boy and heard him play. Then and there, they invited him to come to Berlin with them and live under their roof as a big brother to their daughter, Irene, with time and opportunity to work out his talent undisturbed. I witnessed Rudi's dazzling ascent and also how in after years the brother-sister relationship gave way to marriage between the two. The little girl herself became a noted musician as well as his happy wife, while Serkin's art grew to wonderful perfection, perhaps under the influence of their love. For his friends, he remained what he had been before he became famous—kind, thoughtful and generous. Once when I admired the tropical fish in an aquarium, he said instantly in his sweet voice, "May I give you one?" And to this day he would say the same kind of thing.

All this belongs to the story of a culture that is past. The enormous wealth is gone, partly through financial losses and partly through taxes. The large homes have been handed over to public bodies. The younger generation live like the rest of mankind: they have to earn their living, and many do it as musicians. What is left us is the memory of a culture in which people were honored not for their wealth but for what they did with it, and the memory of superb art that lives permanently as a luminous gift for all who shared in it.

With my social consciousness I should approve of the changes that have taken place, if the wealth and art and beauty were not now in the hands of individuals who own material things without the appreciation of tradition and values. Margaret MacDonald, the wife of Ramsay, who died years before he became prime minister, used to say, "I regard the luxurious life of my wealthy friends exactly as I do the torn clothes and black tea of my poor friends. I am sorry for both and as anxious to change one as the other." This is an evolution which must be achieved everywhere, and it is in the first and last sense what I have lived for: to even differences of class and opportunity. Otherwise, there can be no peace and no brotherhood.

Many of my personal friends were artists or lovers of art. In 1905 I met a woman of my own age, a painter, who had a similar background, living as I did with a mother. I met Martha [?] at a farmhouse in the Engadin, where I arrived with the mail coach one morning to visit friends. Toward evening, we two were sitting in the tiny garden plot, on the brim of the old-fashioned well, after long and intimate talks during the day, when she suddenly said quite seriously, "I still remember exactly when you arrived." It was as if we had known each other for ages. I often teased her about her observation, but it marked the beginning of our friendship. She was a beautiful woman, gentle, with long delicate hands. She had studied for years with Max Liebermann,[4] one of the pioneers of the impressionist school of painting, and among a number of people who were anxious to paint me, she was the only one to produce a good portrait. I have to admit, however, that when she had finished it, she withdrew to a convalescent home to recuperate. She insisted that she had never seen anyone whose expression changed as quickly and constantly as mine. Martha could do everything; she was Martha and Mary of the New Testament combined. For twenty years we interchanged social and artistic interests, until she died prematurely, leaving everyone who had known her bereaved.

There were other artists among my friends, some of them very poor. In Berlin a joking expression was, "He is a painter, and she has no money either." There were many whose difficulties I shared over long years, but in the end it was more than returned in lasting loyalty.

I had given up working for family welfare organizations when I started the school, since I no longer had time for it. I had my hands full with "cases" or human problems among students and sometimes among teachers, and in expanding institutions, the number of employees grows, and some of them step into the line of friends.

There was, for example, a woman who had been cook in my mother's home. I will call her Rosa. She was competent, honest, and clean, but when she married, her husband turned out to be altogether inferior, physically and morally. My friend insisted that I built the house for the school just to give Rosa a job as caretaker and to provide a home for her child. Her husband worked as an electrician, but during the war he deserted from the army, was caught and sentenced to a long term of penal servitude. After the revolution in 1918, when the prisons had been thrown open, he reappeared. He began to drink and became violently destructive, a danger to the house and the neighborhood. This could not go on, so I spent the best part of a Sunday coaxing and threatening to make him join a league of abstainers, which he called "the pious hypocrites." I would not exactly include him in a family friendship. But the child grew into a sturdy, intelligent girl and was much attached to me. Rosa took as much interest in my affairs as I did in hers. We were very fond of each other and this persisted until Hitler had seized power and I could not go to the schoolhouse any more. But a teacher once came to see me with a bunch of violets from the little front garden I had planted and told me how fiercely Rosa guarded the flowers, allowing no one to touch them until she was convinced that they were intended for me. For her I remained the rightful owner of the schoolhouse. We had been associated for more than thirty years; the place seemed deserted to her, and she felt it was time for her to retire.

Some of my most delightful friendships, those with men, came into my life late, like the rare blue flower of romance, and I cherished them as unexpected gifts. Though I had always been more interested in girls than in boys, I like men better than women. There had been little to show off at a time when most young women have their beaux. When I grew older, with an interesting life behind me, I was probably more interesting myself, and these friendships were based on intellectual affinity and now and then on a warmer shade of feeling. There was, of course, a problem, for these men had usually been married long since, and their wives did not share in our intellectual intimacy. So at times life was not easy for me and very likely not for these men either. But friendship and love must like gold be purified in fire, and at their best they become unselfish. In all humility, I think I have been striving to achieve this.

Through all my joys and many sorrows, I had grown old when the shadows of coming disaster spread over Germany. If I had done what was expected of me as a young woman, I should have had children and grandchildren long before. I have mentioned that instead of children of my own, I had a crop of nephews and nieces—and now there are eight children in the third generation. For these I have coined a word, quite untranslatable, but since I have used it dedicating to the six girls when they were still little a book on "Heroic Women"—biographies of great reformers—as a challenge to their future, I might as well put it down here. It is *Enkelnichten,* which means both grandchildren and daughters of my nieces and nephews.

I know that none of the mothers of these children would forgive me if I admitted that I have a dearest of the dear in the youngest generation. My niece, Lotte, who has twelve-year-old twins, watches carefully to see that I do not pay less attention to her little boy than to the little girl. Therefore, to prove my impartiality, I will tell a story about my grandfather. Whenever our family gathered for a dinner party, he would say, "The prettiest of the children has stained the tablecloth!" However often he said this, to his great amusement, each one of them would invariably look down at his or her own place. Like him, I leave it for them to decide.

There are some elaborate plays and operas which end with a massing of the complete cast on the stage, not for a bow but as a magnificent finale, an apotheosis.

Before the curtain went down and finished my life in Germany, my friends held a festival, encompassing all those who were bound to me in friendship: relatives and friends, social workers, university women, councilwomen and my employees, musicians and painters. It was a birthday party for me, less than a year before Hitler came to power. A woman is not supposed to give away her age, but as I have already remarked that I counted my years from the day I began to work, I may as well say that according to this yardstick I was exactly thirty-nine. A good age for a woman—an age when many stop counting!

The hundreds of letters I received moved me most, all of them beginning with "You will not remember me, but . . ." Some of them said, "I notice your influence not only in all I do, but already in the attitude of my children." Edith Geheeb, who had come to me for guidance at fourteen and who later married a famous educational reformer, wrote, "It may have cost you much not to marry, but it is good as it is. Otherwise you would never have been able to do for us what you did." Else Jaffé-Richthofen, who had remained close to me from our early student days when she indirectly got me into the university, said, "Nothing in you has withered. If every complete human being has some male as well as female elements, the male element in you has had full opportunity for expression. But the mother in you has had it still more completely. And the playful child, who is the parent of the grown-up man and woman, was always alive in your moments of freedom and relaxation."

The government of the Weimar Republic and other official bodies sent representatives to the party to prove that they appreciated what women were doing for the nation. The Prussian cabinet, through the minister of welfare, sent me a beautifully chased silver medal bearing my name and the words "For Special Services to the State." The dean of the medical faculty of the Friederich-Wilhelm University in Berlin presented the document awarding me the dignity of honorary doctor of medicine. A former minister of the interior and president of the

Board of Trustees of the School of Social Work announced that they had decided to change the name of the school to the "Alice Salomon School for Social Work."

A year later, the name disappeared quickly, and the dark days of terror and the reign of hate began. It is hard for me to deal with them, but like everything in my life, this is an obligation laid on me by my destiny.

CHAPTER 17

# The Stream of Lava

I had a painful awakening from the dream of "German idealism," which was nothing more than hiding, ostrich-like, from reality.

It was one of the last days of March 1933, and I was on a train between Bolzano and Merano, in the beautiful, fertile Tyrol, that had been given by the Big Four in Paris to the Italians in payment for breaking the three-power pact with Germany and Austria. Like many people from Berlin, I meant to spend my Easter vacation there and meet the spring before it came north. The newspaper another passenger in my compartment was reading intrigued me because of the red banner headlines, unusual at that time. He left it behind when he got off the train, and I looked at it. It was Hitler's *Völkischer Beobachter,* with an announcement of the first pogrom, to be staged on April 1, in Berlin.[1]

Could this really happen in the twentieth century in the heart of Europe? That all doctors of Jewish origin see no patients and have their houses smeared with swastikas ... that Brownshirt armies dominate the streets, forcing the Jews to close their stores and hide like owls in their homes!

A few weeks earlier, the politicians had declared, "Hitler has no majority; he cannot do a thing without the backing of another party." They still thought in terms of constitutional government—not of terror, atrocities, arson, and hate propaganda. But on February 27, the Nazis had set fire to the Reichstag, arrested all its Communist members, and cancelled the seats of all Socialists.

So much has happened since that this first pogrom seems like a game of children, cruel as children sometimes are. In 1938, when the second pogrom was organized—on a much larger scale, far more sadistic and lunatic—I was no longer in Germany. Mercifully, we forget at moments. Otherwise, we could scarcely live with the knowledge of the suffering and distress which the Nazis and the other fascists have inflicted on the people of this globe; on the refugees fleeing along the highways of Europe and Asia; those under the heel of the conquerors and those tortured in concentration camps; the thousands who committed suicide, and those deported, "destination unknown," of whom we never hear again.

Although Hitler's most passionate hatred and his first assault was directed against people "of Jewish blood," it must be remembered that there were many others on the blacklist—the Socialists, Catholics, pacifists, and those who defended Christianity against Hitler's paganism. Altogether, there were millions of threatened people, and abroad no one except a few political groups and some Jewish organizations lifted a hand to save them.

Most of these groups were nonexistent in 1933. The Jewish congregations had no centralized office, and the endangered people no representative bodies that could speak for them. They had to be organized, and this took time.

In Merano at Easter 1933, there were a few men and women who like myself had international contacts. We came together and discussed ways of using these channels to arouse the interest of the democracies. While still outside of Germany and immune to Nazi censorship, we wrote to friends abroad, urging them to influence their governments to let the threatened people in. I suggested further that they convey to religious and political leaders a plan to start an international emergency committee with Jewish, Catholic, and Protestant representatives in each country. All of us got the same reply: "You ask the one thing I cannot do, because of the depression." The ancient challenge was forgotten and denied—"Who is my neighbor?" Soon a political slogan grew out of the democratic soil which we heard from our best friends and closest associates when we were individually threatened: "We cannot interfere with Hitler's internal policy." They have since learned that internal policy does not remain as such when hundreds of thousands of human beings are chased across the borders.

There is no frontier, be it ever so strictly guarded, that cannot be crossed secretly, via rivers or mountain passes. Such escape may bring terrible misery to those who succeed and have to live on without passports, but it happened all the time. The first to leave were the radical politicians, communists, and socialists, some Catholic leaders, liberals, pacifists, and practically everyone who opposed the Nazis politically. In the summer of 1933 there were more than twenty thousand of these refugees in France and large numbers in Holland, Switzerland, Czechoslovakia, and Austria, most of whom fell prey to the Nazis after the invasions later on.

Concentration camps had been established and filled overnight.[2] The Nazis seized everyone against whom they had a grudge, if for no other reason than his holding a coveted office or possessions. Those who were not seized in the first onslaught fled for their lives, if necessary without (or with faked) passports. Some hid temporarily in the homes of friends; others were warned and helped by foreign journalists or embassy secretaries, who had sources of information which they often used for the benefit of their imperiled friends.

Naturally, my friends abroad wished to hear more than I could tell them in letters, and my Scottish friends sent a countryman to me who was in Germany on business. He told me that he had talked to lots of people—businessmen, train conductors, waiters—and that Germany was flourishing. Many people like him who wanted to "see things for themselves" went to Germany up to the fall of 1939, and many returned enthusiastic about the Nazi regime—its cleanliness and order, which actually were in no sense a Nazi contribution but an inheritance from imperial and republican days. The filth and the disorder were invisible to visitors. They had been implanted in the minds of the people.

My Scottish visitor could not see it. He said this was "just a Jewish problem" and that the Jews should solve it themselves. When I mentioned the non-Aryan Christians, he asserted there was no intermarriage between Christians and Jews in Great Britain, and that settled the matter for him.

It was certainly a peculiar characteristic of pre-Nazi Germany that while people of Jewish religion were barred from professions, social life knew no such barriers. The emperor favored marriage between officers and daughters of wealthy Jews—"gilding the old crests." The nobility was interfused with Jews. Intermarriage was very common and in no way considered a problem.

Now it became a very intricate one, with hair-splitting distinctions. In 1933 the Nazis ruled that one Jewish grandparent made one a Jew, even if both parents had been brought up as Christians. I had two friends in this category. The single Jewish grandparent of one had been baptized as an infant, carried in his mother's arms; he was adjudged an

Aryan. The grandfather of the other had been baptized when a few years old, standing during the ceremony on his own small feet. His descendant was pronounced a Jew. This is not a story: it was the outcome of a rule distinguishing between "a lying and a standing baptism." Another friend of mine satisfied the conditions, but his grandmother had borne the name of a world-famous family of Jewish origin whose members had been Christians for generations. When the official in charge of the case read the grandmother's name, he turned down the application. In another case with an equally famous name, the ruling was handed down with the comment, "A Kru-nigger remains a Kru-nigger"—whatever that may mean. Such proceedings would have been merely silly but that they meant doom for a family.

From time to time, the interpretations changed. In 1935, when the racial laws "for the protection of German blood and honor" were imposed,[3] a more complex problem resulted: Who may marry whom? This became almost an occult science, requiring more than ordinary arithmetic. A girl among my friends, one-quarter Jewish, after submitting to endless medical tests and supplying about fifty-six documents establishing her and her fiancé's ancestry, was forbidden to marry him because he was the son of a mixed marriage—"fifty-fifty," we called them. She was not permitted to marry anyone with a higher percentage of Jewish blood than herself, nor even a man of the same composition. It was her "duty" through marriage to become more "Nordic." She would have been allowed to marry a pure Aryan, but should he marry her, this possible husband would lose any official position he held in the state, the municipality, or the party; if he were an army officer, he would lose his rank; and as head of a firm doing business with public bodies, he would forfeit government orders. In this particular case, the "fifty-fifty" young man was lucky. He had an aunt in the United States who provided the affidavit, and the two young people left Germany and married on arrival in this free country.

Another clause of the "blood and honor" law had the most demoralizing effects. It provided that a mixed marriage contracted before the Nazis invented their race theory could be annulled on the assertion that the "Aryan" had not been aware of contamination and losing caste. Many close couples were confronted with the choice between divorce and loss of job and income. The matter was simplified later, when the dissolution of these marriages was made compulsory.

The most shocking case that came to my attention was that of a man who was prominent in the air force, whose name was known to everyone in Germany. He was born and brought up as the son of a Gentile mother and a Jewish father. According to all Nazi rules, this semi-Aryan would have lost his position. But he forced his mother to swear under oath that he was not the true son of his father but the result of an intimate relationship carried on by his mother with a Gentile during her married life. Later, this method of acquiring a birth certificate as a Gentile became quite common. If words have a meaning, the law would much more correctly be termed "for the promotion of dishonor."

The defamation of having the wrong kind of blood weighs heaviest on children. I knew two families with this problem, but since they had means, a solution was possible in each case. One was the very intellectual family of a professor of law whose wife had been a fellow student of mine. The children, three sons and a little girl, had been brought up as Christians. Two sons, whose brilliant careers had been cut short by the Nazis, went to Spain and Italy, respectively. The third son went to Paris, where he competed successfully in state examinations. The little girl, Ada, who had been born late, wanted to stay at home with her parents, and they were reluctant to let her go, too. At that period, such children still went to school with the "Aryans," and she insisted that she was not suffering from prejudice or intolerance. "The teacher is nice and the children are nice," was always her story. But one day she came home humiliated: "It was not so nice today." What had happened? The teacher had sent the Aryan children to one side of the classroom, the non-Aryans to the other. Then the teacher had told the Aryans to study the appearance of the others and to point out the marks of their Jewish race. They stood separated as if by a gulf, children who had played together as friends the day before. The Gentiles scrutinized their former playmates. Poor things—what else could they do? Finally, a child said about little Ada, "She has curly hair." Needless to say, in the United States curly hair is anything but a sign of inferiority! But in Nazi Germany this child was marked, isolated from that day on, and her parents had to send her abroad.

In another family with a Jewish father and a Gentile mother, the children were divided in their sentiments. The older girl was anxious to adjust herself and to be accepted. She went to a labor camp after these admitted "fifty-fifty" children, if they were strong and good-looking, and thus acquired the privilege of living in Germany. The second, a fair-haired, lovely girl, was too sensitive. She could not endure to be singled out at school, and her parents sent her to England when she was still a child. The war cut her off completely from her parents, and then she had to earn her living. I have recently heard that she is doing well and has grown into a courageous personality.

To the limit of my ability, I tried to help individuals by asking friends and colleagues abroad for aid to emigrants on their arrival. Some of the people of the international committee of schools of social work were wonderfully helpful. With some friends, I started an aid committee on a modest scale, and when the Jewish refugee service was established, we kept it on for Christians.

Remembering some of the problems we handled, I can still feel a giddiness come over me.

The most discouraging cases were those of young people who had never been told of the Jewish ancestry of one of their parents. Suddenly they had to know. One of them was a beautiful, sensitive adolescent girl, an only child, in one of those small northern towns where people must conform in order to exist. She was athletic and fond of sports, consequently eager to join the "Hitler Girls." When she heard that this could not be and why, she did not want to live. Her parents found her after she had killed herself.

One young woman had been born of an "Aryan" mother who had been a prostitute. The father was unknown, and since the home was unfit for a child, she was brought up in a Christian orphanage and trained, in time, to be a nurse. She was ambitious and saved every penny toward an education as a social worker, finally getting a job with the Health Insurance Service. Then the law barring "non-Aryans" from the professions came into force. In filling out the customary questionnaire she stated that her mother was Aryan and her father unknown. The case was turned over to the Race Department for investigation, and they discovered that her mother had received a large sum of money from a Jew during the year the girl was born. On this "evidence," the report concluded that "Aryan" descent could not be proven, and the girl was dismissed from her position. She had no memory of her mother and had never even heard anything about her father. Naturally, she was embittered and wanted a job, any job, as far away from Germany as possible. She found one as a midwife in a South American hospital.

There was also a young artist, the son of an "Aryan" and a woman of Jewish ancestry who were eventually divorced. He was successful at painting and learned to restore damaged pictures to supplement his income. When the Hitler regime began, he was forbidden to paint, to exhibit, or to restore, and he applied for work as a housepainter. But since he had not been apprenticed in the trade, he could only work secretly, without knowledge of the Labor Front. Realizing that this could not go on, the young man decided to emigrate to South Africa, where the building trade was prospering. The South African government gave visas only to people who could deposit considerable sums, and hardly any money could be taken out of Germany. I finally persuaded the English Society of Friends to give or guarantee half the sum if I raised the other half. I got it literally in five pound notes while spending a few weeks in England, and when everything at last seemed settled, the South African government issued new regulations: the steamship companies would not sell a ticket unless the return fare was deposited. This had to be raised too, but we got him there safe and sound just before emigration to South Africa came to an end.

The people who were doomed talked of nothing but the possibility of emigration. When I was in England, I visited a friend from Germany whose husband had succeeded in bringing out his own family and that of his brother-in-law through business connections. My friend's mother had joined them only a few days before. She said to me, "Miss Salomon, for years we have discussed only whether we would emigrate, when we would emigrate, how we would emigrate, and to what country we were going to immigrate. Now that we are all here together, I wonder what we are going to talk about."

Even those who emigrated early during the Nazi regime cannot imagine how difficult it soon became to get out of Germany and find a haven.[4] Before we started our committee, I had to secure official sanction from the Ministry of the Interior and protection for the man we engaged as our secretary. The official knew me very well. He said over the phone, "Do I understand correctly that you advise non-Aryans who have no property how to start life in other countries?" I replied that this was so. His answer was, "That complies perfectly with the intentions of our ministry." At that time, the Nazis had not yet chosen the tactic of blunt, outright robbery. Later on, it took months and months before one could get a passport, in order to get a visa, and when the passport was granted, it was for another few months only. People had no choice but to go to any country, no matter where, that would let them in quickly.

When the secret police compelled me to leave at three weeks' notice, I got letters of advice: "Do not decide rashly where you will go. Look around first. Come here on a visit. You can certainly get a visitor's visa." What did they know about it? Who would give a visitor's visa to an emigrant with a six months' passport no good in his own country, with no money and no prospects? We had to "thank heaven, fasting" if anyone took us in. I did not even see my passport until I arrived at the German frontier, where I had to report to the secret police. It was valid exactly long enough for a short visit to London, where I had the luck to obtain a visa that brought me to the United States three days before it lapsed.

CHAPTER 18

# The Mystery of Individual Adjustments

Much has been written about the tragedies of those victim of the Nazis who were starved, deported, tortured, and killed, and I cannot relieve the suffering of those who may still be alive by telling their stories. I can only add to the picture of Nazi Germany by describing the attitudes of individuals and groups within my range of contact.

One evening in April 1933, two young women, one of them closely connected with my work, the other the assistant of an outstanding "Aryan" active in public life, invited friends and colleagues who were endangered by the racial doctrines or by their former party affiliations for a discussion of their various plights and to make decisions.

The "Aryan" and I, who were much the oldest, were asked to give our opinions. I said bluntly that all who were under forty years of age had better decide at once on emigration, that there was no future for them in Germany. My advice was not dictated by personal resentment—I believed that they should not be encouraged to hope for a change they could not help bring about. How modest it seems today! But my "Aryan" colleague was shocked. She could not understand that anyone loyal to her country could even think of such a solution. "This phase will pass," she said, and in a tone that betrayed her scorn for the susceptibility of the "non-Aryan" woman.

In spite of the misery and ruin that has come to the Jews and those of mixed ancestry, I have always considered them lucky in one thing. They did not have to make the wretched choice of accepting the Nazi creed or not. The Gentile *had* to make that choice. It was, "My position, my income, my family and their security, with my oath to Adolf Hitler—or for me and for them daily risk and danger." It was far from easy.

The attitudes of my most intimate group of fellow workers, the staff of the School of Social Work and the Academy, most of whom were Protestant in predominantly Protestant Berlin, were typical of educated women. There were instances of human strength and human weakness. Some came out of the battle finer and stronger personalities; others lost whatever moral poise they had ever possessed. There were some women on our staff who would have been considered irreproachable by Nazi standards but for having worked closely with me. They tried to atone for this with redoubled fervor, saying "Heil Hitler" twice where others said it once. Long before Aryans were forbidden to talk to the "wrong" people, it was painful for me to see them because with every word they felt a nervous urge to declare their new faith.

On the other hand, we had a devout Catholic teacher, also a "hundred percent Aryan." After the ferocious sterilization laws were enacted, it fell to her lot to instruct the students in this subject. She stated that she would explain the laws and even abstain from expressing her personal views about them but that she could not possibly speak in their favor, since this would violate the laws of her Church. She resigned of her own accord. If she had not resigned, she would have been denounced by some student sooner or later and dismissed.[1]

One of the Protestant teachers would have been perfectly acceptable to the Nazis but for her Jewish fiancé, a tenor who had been forced to leave the opera. They had known each other for years and had discussed marriage but never set a date. The woman now came into the open, discarding the position based on her university education, acquired at great sacrifice. She declared that she belonged to him and married him. Together they went to Palestine, where two children were born to them while they struggled desperately for a living.

We had no full-time teacher on the school staff who was Jewish, but there was a widowed Jewish physician employed at the Pestalozzi-Froebel Haus, with which we were affiliated. She taught hygiene and looked after the health of our students. It developed that her six-year-old little boy, seeing that all the other children had swastika buttons on their coats, put one on too—and was brought home to his mother on one of the first days of the "new glorious period of German history," beaten up beyond description. That same evening she left Germany with her two children and sought refuge with a sister living abroad. Some of the "Aryan" colleagues condemned her sharply for not having asked for a leave of absence. We also had a teacher who was born a

Lutheran but of Jewish descent. She had lived exclusively among Christians, and it was only when she was nearly grown up that she heard of her so-called Jewish "race and blood." A Nazi administrator imposed on the college dismissed her at once. She felt that she had lost not only her profession and her income but her church and her country as well.

Since I was no longer officially associated with the school, these cases were outside my sphere of influence. But a case arose in the academy of which I was president, and there I was compelled to take quick action. One day an official of the Ministry of Education came to urge me to dismiss the director of the academy, who was a Jewess.[2] She said, "The new minister of education is being bombarded with letters complaining that the Women's Academy is a hotbed of communism." This was, of course, absurd; if anything, the staff and students tended to be conservative. The scholarship for the year 1933 had even gone to a conservative woman who turned out to be a Nazi. The official, who was a personal friend of mine, knew this perfectly well but said that she could no longer hide the letters from the minister. Her own position was none too secure—every official was battling for time. She made her demand very urgent, but I refused. I explained that Dr. [Hilde] Lion, whom we had appointed because she was the best person for the job and one of the most gifted women of her generation, had a life contract. I told her I would rather destroy the academy, as dear to me as the youngest child, than betray a fellow worker and that I would never dismiss anyone on the grounds of race or religion. "Today you come for her," I said, "tomorrow you will come for me."

I remembered seeing a desolate ruin during the war, formerly a fortress which had served as headquarters for the Russian army. The Russians had burned it to the ground rather than deliver it to the approaching enemy. I resolved to do what they had done. My visitor agreed and said, "But hurry, Miss Salomon. Don't wait till next week. Don't even wait till tomorrow. If you do not act soon, the storm troopers will be in the house, and once they're in, they will confiscate the whole institution."

I summoned the board of trustees by telegram for the following day. I told them what had happened and added that an institution of higher education preparing women for executive positions would have no scope under the Nazi regime, which was eliminating and suppressing the influence of women in public life. The crisis had developed so rapidly within twenty-four hours that I was only anxious, by this time, to have my suggestion to dissolve the academy accepted. When the Nazis finally did appear, they came too late. We had destroyed the list of students and members and all our archives; nothing was left for requisitioning.

Students, too, had the courage of their convictions. One morning I went to answer my bell and found a girl I had never seen before. It was no time to be asking strangers in. I inquired what she wanted at the door. She said, "Miss Salomon, I am a student of the Alice Salomon School." I remarked, "There is no such thing any more." "When I applied for admission," she said, "there was, and I entered the school to learn from you." I asked her in, and she told me that a group of students like herself had arranged a course of private lectures from people who had officially ceased to exist. She had come to ask me for a lecture. But what good could come of it?

A student of mine who had been working in a factory with the aim of appointment as factory inspector was horrified by the sudden volte-face of the workers who discarded their leftist "red buttons" for "swastika buttons" and changed their affiliations overnight. If they did not change their opinions, they at least changed their badges. We called these people "rare hamburgers—brown outside, red inside." That there are some who have stayed "red inside" cannot be doubted, particularly among the older generation with socialist traditions. One of them told me of an incident during the funeral of an old trade union leader, which he had attended. Thousands had come—too many for the police to arrest—and when the casket was lowered into the grave, they all raised their fists and, as if with one voice and once accord, they shouted three times, "Freiheit!" which means liberty.

In the higher ranks of the professions, among teachers and artists, physicians and lawyers, the adjustment was made with few exceptions.[3] They became interpreters of the Nazi doctrine of blood and soil, changing their ideas, their theories, and their vocabularies. Many, not only in Germany but in neighboring countries, were eager to replace their colleagues, often former friends, when these were ousted from their jobs or forbidden to practice, to perform, to publish, or to exhibit. There were a few shining exceptions. Adolf Busch, of whom I have spoken before, replied from his home in Switzerland after being asked to replace Hubermann: "Sorry. Am not R.S."—Richard Strauss, who had swiftly appeared in place of Bruno Walter at a Berlin performance.⁴ Another conductor, in Holland, when urged to send an "Aryan" to replace Schey in the role of Jesus in *St. Matthew's Passion,* wired, "Impossible. Have no Aryan Jesus."

In the places which had been the shrines of truth, of the humanities, and of intellectual integrity—the universities—adjustment was the most complete.

In my own alma mater in Berlin, after the Easter recess of 1933, a notice appeared on the students' blackboard with the statement, "Jews, whether teachers or students, are no longer tolerated in the universities. Jews who speak German are liars. Their language is Hebrew." There it was—people read it and went their way. One "Nordic" professor only, a teacher of philosophy and education, took offense. He went to the president and asked to have the sign removed. Until this was done, he said, he would not resume his courses. The president reported after a time that the statement was written on the blackboard of the Nazi students' league, which gave him no authority in the matter. The professor then approached the minister of education, who, like the president, had served under the democratic republic and was still in office. The minister also promised to act and also sent word that he had not succeeded. The professor kept his word—he asked for an indefinite leave of absence. He looked for a job in neighboring countries, but scholars abroad had not yet been aroused, and they failed him. After a year, the German authorities threatened to deprive him of his salary and his claim for a pension unless he returned. Then he submitted. He came to see me to explain why he had come back to his job. "A teacher must have contact with students," he said. "One cannot even write or do research without the stimulation of their reactions and response. I cannot go on editing my magazine without this stimulus, even if I should be permitted to, after resigning as professor. I used to grade large numbers of theses for Ph.D. degrees all year round. Suddenly this stopped. At first I received letters of sympathy and appreciation—visits from colleagues. After a few weeks, that stopped, too. The mail brought nothing but advertisements for soap flakes. I felt mentally stifled. I could not endure such a life." He was far from young, in delicate health, and he had a wife. He added, "I had expected solidarity from the others, but not a single one backed me up. My sacrifice would have been in vain."⁵

Even if the highly educated Germans could not have stopped the flood, a declaration of faith would have redeemed their own conscience and their standing before the world. The First World War had produced the very ill-advised declaration of ninety-nine leading scholars in which they asserted that Germany was without guilt for the outbreak of the war. Now, when it was a matter of testifying to something they were truly qualified to judge, where did they stand and what did they do?

They got what they deserved. Academic self-administration was abolished during the first year of Nazi rule. The president of Berlin University was dropped, and they got a new one appointed by Hitler—a young man in his early twenties whose education consisted solely of training as a veterinary. The light of culture was extinguished.

The few who could not live and breathe in an atmosphere of intellectual regimentation and moral corruption, where scholarship went hand in hand with Nazi propaganda, left and expressed their opposition in comparative safety from abroad. Of course, all the Jewish teachers emigrated sooner or later. Hitler's promise that those Jews who had fought during the war would be allowed to continue in their professions was, like so many others, repealed in 1935. The Nazis had realized meanwhile that with a total of five hundred thousand German Jews, one hundred thousand had served in the army; out of eighty thousand in the front lines, ten thousand had been volunteers, and more than twelve thousand had died for their country. Under these circumstances, the Nazis preferred to brush the inconvenient claims aside. One of their answers was, "No one can doubt that thousands of Negroes fought in the French army, but this would not lead anyone to consider them French citizens."

How insular the Nazis were! They knew so little about the habits and opinions of other nations. A short time before the secret police told me to get out, front-page headlines reported, "Adolf Hitler has talked to a French journalist." Even at that, it was one in sympathy with the Nazi movement. Where else in the modern world would it be conceived as news that the head of the state talked to a foreigner! Naturally, being so provincial, they did not foresee that their intolerance might arouse general indignation. But in a situation that called for a hurricane of censure, it came rather as a mild breeze. The aid committees were sadly incommensurate with an emergency calling for the concerted protests and efforts of the governments of all civilized nations. Whenever the wind increased at some fresh explosion of Nazi barbarism and cruelty, a new official committee—League of Nations or intergovernmental—was set up to survey the world for open spaces that could absorb Hitler's victims. After listening to negative declarations from all the great powers, its members put on their blinkers to keep from seeing the unpopulated areas that exist on all continents and passed feeble resolutions, with no serious attempt at action. No country could be persuaded to abrogate its immigration laws—even for a boatload of children, although many nations had a declining birthrate and the threat of a diminishing population.

There would have been, at the start, only one way of destroying the Nazi specter. If the great powers had ruled that persecution of political opponents and racial minorities is *not* an internal affair, that maintenance of racial decrees and further persecution would be considered as hostile acts in the sphere of international politics—thus leading to a severance of diplomatic relations with the Nazi government of murder and arson—civilized Germans would have joined them in opposition to Hitler. The overthrow of the Nazi regime would have been highly probable.

But their policy was too hesitant. They did not understand, or they would not take the risk for civilization. Later, they had to risk everything. It became too late, not only for Hitler's German victims but for all the nations that were hurled into the war.

CHAPTER 19

# A Spy Stands behind You

In a country dominated by a tyrant, virtually everyone is spied upon from morning till night and from night till morning. What is worse—almost everyone is liable to become a spy.

People quickly learned to take all possible precautions. One high officer in command of army maneuvers in East Prussia was billeted with his staff in the best hotel of the provincial capital. The first thing he did there was to send for army engineers, who searched, according to his order, and found a number of microphones put in by the secret police to spy on the general—on whom, after all, the safety of the whole nation might depend.

One day I was told that a professor whom I knew as a harmless person, averse to politics and quite beyond suspicion, had been taken to prison. Finally, the mystery was cleared up. The secret police had searched the house of a certain young man and found a copy of the "open letter" which Thomas Mann wrote after his university degree was cancelled.[1] It was very outspoken and of course forbidden in Germany, but pamphlets like this were sometimes smuggled in. Taken by surprise, the young man in whose possession it was found admitted how he had got it. They jailed him and arrested the man whose name he had given. He too was caught off guard and gave the name of a third, who was jailed in turn. . . . And so it went on, ironically like a parlor game, until the professor I knew was taken as the seventh in the chain. For months they all remained in prison, without trial, without knowing if they would ever be released.

In Switzerland and in other neighboring countries, until these were overrun by the German armies, people commented on the "German gesture." They meant that even after passing the frontier, no German ever said a word without looking over his shoulder—not in the street, not in a restaurant, not even at home. No German ever talked freely in a room with a telephone. They had too much experience with microphones.

In July 1937, when Germany belonged to my past, some friends asked a bishop of the Church of England to receive me for a discussion of the churches in Germany. He had befriended Hitler's victims as no one else had done and thoroughly understood the struggle of the churches. I met him exactly a week after Niemöller's arrest.[2] The bishop told me that the German church problem was to be considered in August at the conference of the World Federation of Churches in Oxford. I thought something should be done for those Germans who worked, through their churches, on a committee to aid the victims of Hitler and who were themselves in immediate danger. Many congregations bereft of their ministers, too, were deeply affected, not to mention the wives and children of the imprisoned clergymen. I urged that someone be sent to them with the information that the churches abroad offered them moral support. The bishop, a compassionate man willing to listen and to understand, acted at once on the suggestion.

Several months later, I met him again. He said, "Miss Salomon, I did what you considered necessary. I asked my dean to go to Germany. He went unofficially, not to attract attention. He saw only two clergymen, in their homes, in different cities. The evening after the dean left Germany, both ministers were taken to prison for having spoken to him. Every word that was said had been taken down on 'gramophone records.'"

People say this is impossible. I cannot explain how it was done—I am no engineer or technician—but that is what happened.

The German atmosphere was nicely summarized in a cabaret skit whose producer was a witty man and, for Nazi Germany, a courageous one. The curtain rose on a room furnished sparsely with a table and two chairs; a canary cage and a goldfish bowl were on the windowsill. Doors opened at opposite ends of the room, and two men came in. Without a word they shook hands. They looked around. One seized the telephone and took it out of the room, while the other bore away the cage with the canary. They returned, looked around once more, and removed the goldfish bowl. Then they sat down, and the curtain fell.

Yet, in spite of pogroms, danger, spying, many of my friends remained in Germany. We were convinced that our duty was there, that we had to take a stand and defend a tradition, that we must not give in. One of the leaders of the Jewish community expressed this with the words, "If the history of German Jewry must be liquidated, it should be done with dignity." Had we all left at the first stroke, the world would have been justified in reproaching us for yielding without resistance.

The younger people who could no longer follow their professions or work at their trades could not stay; their lives were not yet lived. The older ones who had lost their income also had to go. But I believed that emigration should be organized and directed. For people like myself, it seemed obligatory not to compete abroad with others for the few jobs that could be had, and in Berlin I would still be useful in a modest way. Like the captain of a small vessel, I wanted to help my young friends into the lifeboat.

CHAPTER 20

# Exit Modern Woman

A drastic method was employed to erase the status and the rights of women, won during a hard and persistent struggle of fifty years or more. Probably at the request of his female followers, Hitler appointed a young woman outside of public life as leader-organizer for all affairs of women, with the duty of coordinating women with the party.[1]

In May 1933, she summoned the president of the National Council of Women, the central body to which all organizations of progressive women were affiliated. Fortunately, the Council then had for president a woman of exceptional wisdom and dignity, Agnes von Zahn-Harnack. The Nazi leader enumerated her orders and gave an ultimatum: (1) The Executive Committee of the National Council as well as the hundreds of affiliated associations were to accept the "Aryan clause." (2) All important positions within the Council were to be given to members of the Nazi Party. (3) All elections and all democratic forms were to be abolished and the leader principle accepted. (4) The Council was to pledge itself to carry out the work which Hitler and the woman leader would assign to it.

Agnes von Zahn[-Harnack] inquired what the work would be. The answer was philanthropic and charitable work exclusively, since the Third Reich had no place for women in public life. Hitler saw in the conception of equality of the sexes, as in everything else he disliked, "a product of decadent Jewish intellectualism." The acceptance of these orders was to be signed within forty-eight hours or the Council would be dissolved.

Our president explained that she had no authority to make a decision, that the Council was organized on democratic principles, and that the members had to be consulted. She called them together by telegram for the next day and invited me, as international vice president, by courtesy. Naturally, the ultimatum could not be accepted. The Council had been organized on the principle of the International Council of Women: to bring together and to further understanding between women of all classes, creeds, and races. Moreover, the Council was a body formed to promote the development of women to the full measure of their capacities and to let them share public responsibilities with men. It would have given up its very substance if it had submitted.

My friends well knew the consequences if we merely refused to obey. The Nazis would search the office, confiscate archives and assets, and imprison the leading women. Our international affiliations alone would have been considered treason. With great solemnity, it was decided to dissolve the Council at once.

The same fate overtook all the other women's organizations; only some church societies and the women's branch of the German Red Cross survived, the latter completely coordinated.

All of us who had held official positions, whether in public office or in the institutions built up by women, disappeared into an abyss of obscurity. We did not even have opportunities, except in isolated instances, to meet any of the Nazi women.

The rank and file, our younger colleagues whom we had prepared for professions or offices, were much harder hit. It was part of the Nazi doctrine to "lead women out of the factories, workshops, and professions and back to the home." After years of depression, men hoped to eliminate women as competitors. The Nazis, on coming to power, met their demand with fanaticism by ousting women from all paid work, even secretaries and waitresses. The new women leaders behaved as if wage-earning women had left their homes out of sheer perversity.

It must have been early in 1933, before I left the house I had built for my school, that one of the teachers appeared excitedly with the first issue of a Nazi women's magazine. She read to us, "Women must be educated to have sound bodies and to withstand the stress of war, but far more important is the need for a mental outlook which includes war as a necessity and a law of life." There it was: the new goal was war. Women, good for nothing else, were to be used in the preparation of war. A few months after the publication of this article, Hitler addressed a meeting of Nazi women, and I heard him shouting on the radio, "You ask me what I have done for German women! In my new army I have provided you with the finest fathers of children in the whole world. That is what I have done for German women. You must produce more and more children who will be as fine soldiers as their fathers are." Women as potential mothers, the child as potential soldier, the country with the greatest number of soldiers ultimately on top and able to dominate the world—this was the new order.

A handful of younger women protested against the role allotted to them. They sent an open letter to Hitler in which they proclaimed their loyalty to the Nazi ideology in general but demanded some elementary rights for women. However, the majority cheered him, and only those attained distinction and influence who submitted and accepted the humiliation of their sex.

In a country with a female surplus of two million, women had been lured into the party by the promise of "a husband for each and a happy family life." But the Nazis never intended a legal husband for every woman, only a man to be the father of her children. They were soon outspokenly in favor of sex relations between unmarried people, particularly the very young. The results were often tragic. One of our former students, a Lutheran minister's daughter who had been brought up strictly in a small town, returned from a labor camp pregnant. She could not conceal her plight much longer, and her only concern was to keep it from her parents. She approached one of her former teachers for help. She wanted to leave the country, never to come back, in order to be out of reach of her parents. The alternative was to absent herself under false pretenses for the necessary time and give the child away. The teacher's offer to intervene and explain to her parents was stubbornly refused. The girl felt that according to the standards of the group into which she was born, her life was spoiled, that her family would be deeply afflicted and torn asunder.

Illegitimacy has been a problem at all times. In nations of Western culture it was mostly considered as an individual misfortune. Under the Nazi regime it occurred under the auspices of the party-state, in state institutions, encouraged and sanctioned by the government. Mr. Rosenberg,[2] the cultural leader of Nazi Germany, had said, "A childless woman, whether married or unmarried, is not of full value to the community." Others went a little farther and said that "the childless woman should be dishonored." The most filthy ideas were expressed by a German professor, author of some mystical books, who wrote, "Fortunately, one boy of good race can associate with twenty girls, and these girls would gladly fulfill the demand for children, were it not for the nonsensical so-called civilized idea of permanent monogamous marriage, an idea in complete contradiction to all natural facts."

But thousands of years ago, the prophet Isaiah had said, "Break forth into singing, thou that didst not bear, for more are the children of the desolate than the children of the married wife."

There were more than enough girls who lived up to the Nazi ideas. I knew one, just fourteen years old, with a baby. When her father reproached her for her conduct and her lack of restraint, she retorted, "I cannot tolerate the manner in which you talk to a German mother."

When the Nazis marched into Poland and started the recent war, Himmler, chief of the secret police, published a decree: "It is now the duty of German women and girls of good blood to become mothers, even without marriage, of children of our soldiers going off to war, of whom fate alone knows whether they will return or die for their country." He promised that a personal representative of his would act as guardian to these illegitimate offspring to relieve the soldier-fathers of worry concerning their future. The message was read to the elite guards, who had to testify by signature of their knowledge of the order. However, the decree seemed to arouse some opposition, for a little later it was made known that the task of having children outside the marriage bond did not apply to wives but only to unmarried, widowed, or divorced women.

At a time when the boys' and girls' labor camps were close together, a welfare worker showed me a postcard, a printed form which one of her clients had received from a labor camp for girls. It ran: "Fetch you daughter . . . home; she is pregnant in the . . . month." Only the name and a figure had been filled in. It simplified the matter, at least, for the camp administration. But what of the girl? And the girl's parents? In this particular case they had old-fashioned ideas about morality in addition to having to meet the unexpected financial responsibility.

In all countries, modern women have tried to raise the "age of consent" for the protection of young girls. Among the Nazis, every girl of sixteen, every boy of eighteen, could acquire a certificate of matrimonial fitness if a child was on the way. Nobody asked how they were going to bring up this child! Perhaps it did not matter, for a German child belonged to the state. For the Nazis, education was a political function, it was in the hands of the "party," and well-established families struggled in vain to keep some influence over the minds and souls—and even the bodies—of their own sons and daughters.

One of my friends, a prominent university woman, had a small boy of about ten who remarked, "I can't stand it any longer. At school I hear all the time what a wonderful man Adolf Hitler is, and at home I never hear a good word about him!" The mother, a wise woman, said, "All right, if you can't bear it, we won't talk about Hitler any more in your presence. But then you won't really be one of the family." A few years later, no parent would have dared to utter these words before a child. The Fifth Commandment—like most of the others—had become invalid. Children were admonished in the Hitler Youth to respect and obey not their father and mother but their squad leader, a sixteen- or seventeen-year-old youth. They were told to spy and report on their parents, and in many cases children actually did. Another acquaintance of mine surprised his son in the act of searching his bookshelves and writing desk. The boy explained brashly, "I am only obeying the order of my squad leader. I am looking to see whom you correspond with and if you have forbidden books." The outraged father boxed his ears, whereupon his son threatened that he would report him to the authorities.

Mothers were kept in constant anxiety for more reasons than one. One friend, whose only child had a weak heart, was at a loss what to do with her and how to provide for her future. The girl was not fit for the strenuous physical drill of the Hitler Youth or labor camps, and without this training she would not be permitted to become a teacher—or even be apprenticed to a dressmaker. What was to become of her?

On a bus that stopped in the public square—renamed like thousands of others in Germany "Adolf-Hitlerplatz"—I heard a little girl suddenly say in the high-pitched voice of the very young: "Mummy, why is the square named after that wicked man?" The mother, horribly frightened, took the child under her arm and jumped off just as the bus started. Another child's voice, equally shrill, cried, "Mother, there's a dumb little thing. She hasn't got enough sense to know that we mustn't talk about him in public!" It was truly a difficult proposition to bring up children in the Nazi atmosphere.

During the years before complete coordination, at least on the surface, parents constantly conflicted with the school authorities. Before leaving school or a higher institution of learning, children and young people had to learn about the Nazi race theories, about eugenics, about Nordic supremacy, and the history of the Nazi movement—with dates of putsches, imprisonments, and murders. In a very refined high school for girls in a western suburb of Berlin, the headmistress, an ambitious woman, was anxious to excel in the final state examinations, to be held in the presence of state deputies, especially in the new subjects prescribed by the Nazis. She conducted a sort of "dress rehearsal," where she asked, among other questions, "Which diseases make it necessary for a man to be sterilized so that he cannot become a father?" One of the girls, quick and witty as many Berlin children are, said, "For instance, if he has a clubfoot." The children giggled. Everyone knew that Dr. Goebbels[3] had a clubfoot. The headmistress was also quick. She replied, "You are quite right! This is one of the traits that may be inherited, but need not be. As you know, Dr. Goebbels' little girl is quite normal. But I would advise you not to mention this particular deformity if the question should turn up during state examinations."

Even adults had to learn Nazi "history" and its concocted anecdotes before taking an examination. A law student I knew, compelled to belong to some Nazi group, took part in this drill. The method of the so-called teacher, who had got his job for services to the party, was to repeat a series of silly questions until he extracted the orthodox answer and then let his "class" of young university men repeat the answer in chorus. Question: "Who was Adolf Hitler's best friend when he was young and poor in Vienna, without hope for the future?" Answer: "Hunger was his best friend." Again: "When did Hitler cry for the first time in his life?" Answer: "When he had recovered from his war blindness and could see the distress of the German nation with his own eyes." This is so stupid, so infantile, that no one could even have invented such a story.

There was scarcely one family of whom I knew without internal tensions and conflicts. One cultured, sensitive boy of nineteen or twenty, while doing military service, had been among the officers commandeered to carry out the mass purge of June 1934.[4] He had been forced to shoot one man after another, not as in war but eye to eye, while the victims waited their turn. He came home appalled and sick, hating his own life, in revolt against the "Leader" and his system. On top of this, the boy's sister joined the Nazis and became frantically enthusiastic. I have often wondered about their family relationship. And there were many others.

To be sure, not all Germany ladles Hitler's brew. Whenever the Nazis organized an atrocity campaign, they insisted that it was a spontaneous act of the "seething soul" of the people. A friend of mine witnessed a very different outburst of anger. This was in the streets of Berlin during the pogrom of November 1938.[5] A Hitler Youth group—boys who participated in a demonstration according to orders—were helping to demolish Jewish stores and to destroy a temple, amid much excitement and hooliganism. Suddenly, a woman broke through the crowd—she had recognized her own son among the Hitler boys. She rushed at him and slapped him violently in the face.

In a provincial town, a very popular minister from the ranks of those opposing Hitler's paganism was arrested shortly before Easter. He had prepared a large number of children for the confirmation service. In his place, a more obliging man was appointed. However, on Palm Sunday, when the new "pastor" entered the church, he found it empty. After a quick and quiet conference, within forty-eight hours, all the parents had taken their children on the train to a nearby town, where they were confirmed by a loyal minister in place of his imprisoned colleague.

The former leaders of women and their causes, who were cut off from the world in which they had lived, met from time to time in one another's homes to keep the torch glimmering, at least, for another generation to rekindle. This was during the early days of the Nazi revolution, before we were required by special decree to inform the police when we expected more than eight guests. I remember in particular one evening when a rather insignificant colleague, still head of the central employment service, talked about her work. She reported that the attempt to bar women from all work was bound to fail. Even then, employers in certain factories were declaring that they could not operate without women and calling them back. This at a time when people were aghast at the pogroms, at the persecution of political opponents, and the savage cruelty revealed in carrying them out.

I was sitting next to a friend whose racial background was not "pure." She was engaged in a passionate struggle involving her lifework and her future. I whispered to her, "Are they speaking a foreign language? Or are we on another planet? After all suppression of law and justice, of charity and mercy, what does it matter whether a few hundred women are allowed to work in this or that factory and move this or that wheel? Other matters are at stake." A gulf had opened between those who were out of the running and those who hoped to carry on. The woman who spoke about the employment situation soon "adjusted" herself and kept her job.

With few exceptions, my friends remained loyal. Those who were financially independent retired. All of us wrote—reminiscences, novels, biographies. The others looked for work in which they were not obliged to "bear false witness," in private teaching, domestic or parochial service, or keeping small shops.

I, too, settled down to writing. Years before, I had published a book on outstanding men in social reform,[6] and it struck me that their motives were fundamentally different from those of women reformers. The men came by their work more or less accidentally, sidetracked from their professions as clergymen, politicians, and writers, while most of the women were drawn by a conscious or unconscious inspiration from childhood on. I had always meant to give the women a book of their own, and I worked on this the first year or two of the Nazi regime. *Heroic Women,*[7] which I have already mentioned, was published in Switzerland with a motto borrowed from William of Orange: "We need no hope for action and no success for perseverance," although some of my friends thought this alone would be enough to bring down the wrath of the Nazis. Then I spent six months in Geneva, working in the library of the International Labor Office on an international survey of schools of social work. The survey was written in English, printed in Germany, published in Switzerland, supported by Americans (the Russell Sage Foundation), and paid for by an international organization.[8] This was characteristic of the vicissitudes of those excluded from work in their homeland but at the same time appropriate for one who had always wanted the whole world to be her country.

Presently, when unemployed men had been absorbed by the army, the storm troops, and labor camps and when the armament industries began to work at full speed, women were brought back into the factories as instruments—handmaidens of the god of war. The state, which had thrown women out for its own ends, drove them back for its own ends. The principle had not changed, only the practice. Those women who had held prestigious jobs or highly paid positions that were coveted by men stayed out. Women could vote, but they could not be elected, however low that privilege had fallen in a land where public bodies assembled only to hear a message and to cheer it. They were discouraged from entering the universities; they had few facilities for training. The proportion of women in the teaching profession had changed to women's disadvantage. The health insurance bodies, which handled 80 percent of all medical services, had to give preference on their staff to married men and to exclude married women. In the civil service, women were employed only if unmarried and over thirty-five and, as marriage among the lower and middle classes in Germany was to a large extent a selection of the best, the administration cannot have had a very good crop. In case they married after being appointed, they were dismissed if the husband had an income.

The only time I ever met one of the influential Nazi women was in connection with my international work. There was a Miss Unger attached to the Ministry of Propaganda, whose department it was to provide women in other countries with Nazi ideas and take charge of foreign women visiting Germany. I had been obliged to go to the Ministry of Propaganda for a permit to publish a pamphlet on women who had won the Nobel Peace Prize abroad, and when my business was finished, I was told that Miss Unger wanted to see me. A meeting of the International Council of Women was about to be held in Paris, and I knew that Miss Unger had written to the president about the possibility of Nazi affiliation.

As first vice president, elected not as representative of any nation but as an individual, I knew that the Council expected me to participate. I also knew that if I went I would be arrested on my return to Germany. All of us who were officers of international bodies made it a rule never to resign unless so directed officially. We compelled the Ministry of Propaganda to give us written answers to the communications in which we expressed our intention of taking part—knowing that they would order us to stay away. This helped to relieve our feelings and justify our absence before our colleagues of other nations, who would not believe that we lived under such terror, some of whom even insisted that in our place *they* would not have yielded.

Miss Unger told me that the letter forbidding me to go was already on the way and broached her hope that Nazi women could obtain representation in the International Council. She even asked me to use my influence with Lady Aberdeen—apparently well informed about this—on their behalf! I referred to the basic principle of the Council, "to bring together women of all classes, races, creeds, and nations," and I said, "You must bear in mind that you would meet Jewish women from France and Great Britain and the United States." She retorted, "The constitution of the International Council excludes interference with the internal policy of any country. We only refuse to let Jews take part in our own cultural life; we do not mind meeting Jewish women of other nations." The question remained open as to whether those women, respected members of their national councils, would object to meeting the Nazis, advocates of a creed inciting hatred against the Jews—especially in an organization founded to overcome such antagonism. This happened in 1934. Later on, the Nazi policy was clarified, and all affiliations with international bodies were forbidden. The Nazis were preparing for world domination. They had no use for friendly relations with people whom they intended to conquer.

In spite of enormous numbers organized in compulsory Nazi groups, women had ceased to exert any influence or to impress the woman's point of view on the country that was "totally" dominated by men. Yet the humanizing mission remains that of women in our modern world. It is for them to kindle the light of truth, charity, and mercy in a barbarous age of power politics and superstition, to further the invincible faith in the ultimate victory of love.

If, as I firmly believe, modern women liberated forces that God and nature had given to us for this purpose, then some day they will break forth again.

CHAPTER 21

# The Strong and the Weak

Everything I had done during my life had one object: to help bring about a social order with more justice, more equality of opportunity, and a deeper sense of solidarity and brotherhood. Hitler, whose henchmen have rewritten the Sermon on the Mount, has not only renounced this goal but has put another in its place. "So-called humanitarianism is merely a compound of stupidity, cowardice, and arrogance. . . . In constant war mankind has become great. In eternal peace it must perish. . . . The world is not for weak peoples." If he had been almighty, he would have had the strong inherit the earth.

Hitler's first speech in the Reichstag as chancellor, on May 17, 1933, in which he declared that Germany would work for peace on the basis of equal rights, was nothing but camouflage directed at other governments and at the German masses. He alone was entitled to speak for peace. Several others who did, in sincerity, were imprisoned. Pacifism, never popular, became a crime subject to the highest penalty.

This became clear to me during an episode following a suggestion of my Norwegian friend, Betsy Kjelsberg, who knew that I had been cut off from work in Germany and was anxious that my influence should not be completely lost. She said if I would write the stories of the two women who had been awarded the Nobel Peace Prize—Bertha von Suttner and Jane Addams—they would be published in Norway.

Since she would not agree to anonymous publication, I decided to ask permission of the Cultural Department of the Foreign Office in order to avoid unnecessary difficulties with the Nazis. I knew that Suttner's books had been burned, although she had never said a word that did not conform with Hitler's peace speech, its pledges and professions. The head of the Department of Culture in the Foreign Office, who had frequently been my dinner partner at social gatherings, grew rigid at my request: It was for the propaganda ministry to deal with such affairs. I protested, "This is not propaganda. This is literature, it is history." But he could not even be persuaded to hand the manuscript over to Dr. Goebbels' staff—or to keep it in his office overnight!

The Norwegian section of the Propaganda Ministry was in charge of a Herr Zuechner, quite affable. His qualification for office was his knowledge of Norwegian, acquired in Oslo, where his brother had a store but was primarily active as a Nazi agent. He took advantage of our meetings mainly to thrash out our divergent opinions on anti-Semitism. As to my request, he claimed that they were never narrow minded and that he himself had read *Lay Down Your Arms* years before. Would I leave my manuscript? I would hear from him. I did not feel obliged to enlighten him about the auto-da-fé of the Suttner book: it could not harm him to read my story without bias. After weeks of waiting, I called him up. He declared, "We cannot allow you to publish anything about this woman. We have burned her books. Her name is on the index. What you have asked is altogether impossible."

A lively dialogue followed. "But the Leader is also in favor of peace. I quoted his speech in my preface, to prove that I have the support of his opinion."

He retorted, "Yes, he's in favor of peace, but what sort of peace? Not the peace of Versailles!"

"But Baroness von Suttner died before the war broke out—she had nothing to do with the Versailles Treaty."

"Never mind, Miss Salomon. *You* cannot understand how we feel about that so-called treaty."

"What do you mean to imply? Why should I feel differently from you? My family has lived here for seven generations. Look up my records in the Foreign Office. I attacked this treaty in other countries at a time when very few Germans could do it."

After further discussion, I said, "All right. If you cannot allow me to publish it, I give up. I want to live in peace. But you must let me have your answer in writing. My friends abroad will not believe that I'm not allowed to publish anything if I cannot prove it." I worked myself up into a temper and added, "If this should be taken up by the foreign press, I should much rather have them attack your ministry than reproach me with cowardice."

To my surprise, he asked me to give him a few more days and he would try to find a way out. The Nazis were, in spite of their defiance, very touchy about foreign public opinion at that time.

After two days, the man called me up to say that if I would change one paragraph, they would give me permission. "If a difficulty arises over the matter, we must be able to explain that we induced you to accept our conditions." I changed the wording (without weakening the content) and received the permit in writing. The pamphlet was not worth half the fuss, but my experience was.

In the field of organized labor, the Nazis soon proved what they thought of solidarity and mutual aid. In April 1933 Hitler proclaimed May 1 an official national holiday. Labor rejoiced, but the joy did not last long. The same fate that had overtaken the women's organizations was in store for the trade unions and even for the nonpolitical labor organizations. They had been a powerful school of democracy and administration for the masses. They had taught individuals and minorities to accept the vote of the majority. They had made the first experiments with unemployment insurance and had founded the workmen's bank. Like the medieval cathedrals and city halls, built with contributions in kind and by the labor of guilds and corporations, beautiful buildings for the administration of the trade unions had been constructed—by the carpenters with exquisite woodwork, the metalworkers with priceless wrought ironwork. The trade unions had established schools for adult education, they had made theaters and concerts available to the masses. All this was a result of their solidarity.

Immediately upon seizing power, the Nazis "coordinated" the trade unions. When the nonacceptable board members had been replaced, there seemed to be no pretext for further interference. On May 1, 1933, for the first time in industrial history, employers and workers marched together, by order of Hitler. They had worked together under the republic, deliberated collectively on wages, and sat together in factory councils. But back of this were years of antagonism, of class war with strikes and lockouts. Now they demonstrated together by an order that must have been distasteful to both factions alike. Nobody quite understood for what or why they demonstrated. Hitler made a speech on the dignity of work and the workers. Promptly, the next day, the storm troopers seized the trade union buildings; they imprisoned the officials by order of Dr. Robert Ley, the leader of the newly formed Labor Front, "for the protection of national labor." Two days later, all unions were dissolved and their property confiscated. The labor movement, which had been a supreme attempt at mutuality for the welfare of the masses, belonged to the past. The reforms fought for through generations were canceled—the eight-hour day, unemployment insurance, collective bargaining, and even those labor laws for the protection of children and young people.

In its stead, the Nazi Labor Front was only a section of the party, with compulsory membership for employers and employees, conforming to the leader principle by appointment of Hitler. Its activities were virtually restricted to philanthropy and propaganda and had no influence on working conditions. Foreigners were often impressed when they heard of the enormous income of the Labor Front, but the workers complained that they were severely taxed for it, apart from state taxes and contributions to insurance funds. They also had to buy *Mein Kampf*[1] in an edition costing seven marks. The wife of a workingman resented this bitterly as an utter waste, since they would not read it anyway. She never guessed what nuisance value it acquired in Germany and far beyond her frontiers while making of the former housepainter a wealthy man.

Employers, whether businessmen or manufacturers, were equally subjected to the authorities and had to put up with heavier burdens. If they were suspect[ed] of hostility toward the Nazi regime, they were arbitrarily assessed by some party official as an easy method of driving them into bankruptcy.

A complete reversal of motives and objectives was imposed on my own field—that of social and welfare work, the final flowering of centuries of religious and moral culture. Love and care for the weaker members had developed humanizing and civilizing attitudes first within the family, later within the community. Now we were confronted with the principle of the survival of the fittest.[2]

At best the Nazis merely continued the services which they took out of our hands. But the new guiding principle was to increase the population and strengthen the race through welfare work and to subject the work not to humanitarian but to military aims. A new emphasis was placed on two branches of social work—the welfare of mothers and infants and on collective leisure activities. Neither was new or original, but they were now conducted on a scale beyond imagination and, like all welfare work, even in the women's auxiliary of the party, under masculine leadership. Hundreds of schools for mothers or prospective mothers were set up, well attended, more or less under compulsion, for the elite guards could marry only girls who had taken these courses. The beneficiaries, as in all welfare work, were exclusively women from eugenically sound families—it was part of the high-pressure campaign for a higher birthrate.

The second, more interesting branch was the organization for leisure activities, "Strength through Joy" (*Kraft durch Freude*), which had been preceded by the "Worker's Welfare League" of Germany's democratic period, and also in fascist Italy.[3]

Years ago I had gone hiking with two friends in Switzerland in the region of the Jungfrau. The air was thin and exhilarating, the glaciers were shining silver, and avalanches like translucent veils. I felt something like a pang of conscience. We were wonderfully privileged to live through these unforgettable days on this magnificent scene. I thought of the millions who never have such an opportunity. My companions shared my feeling, as would anyone who had caught the social virus. How little did we know that only a few years later, hundreds of thousands would be journeying without expense or effort to mountain and seaside resorts, on summer cruises, and that this would be made possible by an antidemocratic regime!

"Strength through Joy" had its own steamships; built its own summer resorts; rented theaters and concert halls; arranged community evenings, sports festivals, and lectures. When a new excursion was under way, I used to see them assembling on the square in my neighborhood. All over the city and throughout the country, one might have seen identical groups standing around a Nazi flag and placard, waiting for the command to board the bus or lorry or march to the railway station in the famous Nazi "marching column." Sometimes I had the impression that half the working population was going for a holiday.

How was it done? Here, too, we encounter the financial mystery of the whole regime, the efficiency in raising money by whatever means. Officially, there were two sources of funds for the welfare work. One was the so-called "winter-help," for which they had an excellent device. It was the monthly stew Sunday, when no household was allowed anything but stew for the main meal, while the difference in price from the usual Sunday dinner was given to the collectors going from door to door.

The second source was the income of the Labor Front. Employers were also taxed for the excursions in proportion to the number of their people who participated. A nominal fee was charged to the excursionists. No dependable figures have been published, for the money went in and out of the party treasury, and no accounts were given. A Berlin wit said of the first blackouts that they had been ordered for a certain night because the funds in the winter-help treasury were to be counted.

A few people refrained from taking part in the trips because they objected to being herded together like a pack of animals. What had come to my mind in Switzerland was the joy of the individual, not only in appreciation of the scenery but as the reward of individual toil. These people, however, were not permitted to feel as individuals; they were parts of a collectivity of the ubiquitous state. The Nazis' welfare work was degraded by political exploitation and, like all their activities, had only the most superficial relation to its avowed purpose. Consequently, the excursionists were given no rest, even on these holidays, from glorification of the Leader and the state, which was dinned into their ears from morning to night. "They must," as one of the leaders said, "have no private life. They must never be left alone; otherwise they might be inclined, in spite of all training and discipline, to think independently." Anyone questioning the regime, even if only in his mind, was doomed. He could no longer endure it.

While the "Strength through Joy" movement remained, within these obvious limitations, an asset of the Nazis, the weakest point in their welfare work was the reversal of humanitarian thought and moral codes.

From the beginning the social workers, thousands of women I had trained to help the weak and physically afflicted, received orders to foster only the sound members of the community. They were informed in Hitler's words that "to care for defectives is a reversal of true humanitarianism. . . . The money spent on defectives is not merely wasted. It is taken away from the healthy members of the community." The Nazis furthered this concept with motion pictures of institutions for imbeciles and the text, "Shall we pay taxes to provide for these people in expensive institutions?" Many social workers were in despair. They said to me, "There is no sense to it. Only people who have never lived among the poor or attended to their needs can give such orders. The people who need us are weak and unfortunate as the cause and effect of their poverty. How can we obey!"

But here was indeed a problem, one which we had discussed at conferences of social work for many years: the discrepancy between the money a workingman, or even a white-collar man, can afford to spend on the upbringing of a family and the enormous cost of institutional care for mentally defectives, incurables, and criminals. It was a problem to be handled with great care and a strong moral code for guidance.

The Nazis soon realized that merely to leave the weak without support would not solve the problem and decided on a rigorous policy of sterilization. In any society this is a grave step, involving the most serious measures on both the scientific and ethical planes. But the Nazis had no inhibitions. They published a decree on sterilization "for the prevention of inherently defective offspring" on July 14, 1933, intending to apply it within one year to 350,000 cases, and actually performing 84,000 operations (1.3 per thousand of the population). It was done without regard for restrictions imposed by any code or by the limits of our scientific knowledge.[4]

We still know little about the laws of heredity, the transmission of diseases. We only know that a taint may crop out unexpectedly after generations, perhaps lying dormant in other members of the family. And how little do we know of the psychic effects of the operation on women! Women I met who had been subjected to it felt humiliated and degraded. Others lost their inhibitions, knowing that they could no more become pregnant and were considered free game, particularly in small cities, where the summons for the operation were published at the courthouse.

In democratic countries, experiments with sterilization have been made for years—the first one in the United States as far back as 1907—yet the approach is still reluctant and deals mostly with feebleminded inmates of institutions who are incapable of responsible parenthood.[5] More and more, as the data on genetics increase, sterilization is based less on purely eugenic than on social considerations.

To foster only the sound in body is not merely incompatible with welfare work but also with the religious belief in the value of the individual soul, in which democracy is rooted as well. It rates only the physical being and overlooks entirely the fact that the laws of civilization differ from those of nature, that moral and social ideals cannot be founded on biology. Some of the greatest benefactors of mankind have been physically handicapped but mighty in intellect and willpower. Beethoven was already deaf when he composed some of his immortal music, and [John] Milton blind when he wrote some of the world's greatest epic poetry. [Louis] Pasteur continued his invaluable research after he was paralyzed at the age of forty-six.

The recent war has proved what men perverted by inhuman doctrines are capable of doing. The Nazis have gone from sterilization to murder and from murder to wholesale extermination, not only of the weak but of all who were in their way.

The only profitable, creative strife is not for material goods among individuals, not for domination among tribes or nations; it is the struggle against the physical universe—against microbes and insects, floods and droughts, hurricanes and earthquakes. In this struggle, success comes only with cooperation, with mutual aid. It comes with the forces of charity, solidarity, brotherhood, entrenched against social injustice and inequality, against rapacity and callousness.

No civilization known to history has achieved a moral order without religious sanctions for the rights of individuals, without protection of the weak against the strong, even of the individual against the state. The Nazis, who refused to acknowledge the rights and the worth of the individual, were warring not only against their own minorities, not only against other nations, but against the Hebrew and Christian religions which for thousands of years have taught mankind to believe in the universal fatherhood of God and the brotherhood of man. If there is anything to be learned from the suffering inflicted by the Nazis, it is that our deepest need is for a renewal of the springs of religious life—a return to the ancient wisdom "to do justly, to love mercy, and to walk humbly with God."

CHAPTER 22

# God and Caesar

Bismarck, who united the German states into an empire after three victorious wars of aggression, suffered one irreparable defeat—his battle with the Catholic Church. Intending to suppress its educational influence, he had banned from German soil the Jesuit order, founded to counteract the spreading Reformation. But in the worldwide organization of the Church backed by the Holy See, he had chosen too powerful an opponent. The laws that were to give the Prussian state far-reaching authority over the affairs of the Catholic Church gradually had to be canceled.

Hitler, by birth a Catholic but alienated from the Church, apparently thought that he would prove stronger than Bismarck. The Nazis tried to bring Church members into the party fold with insincere and demagogic proclamations, promising both Churches new influence and a secure and respected position. In a Reichstag speech in March 1933, Hitler said, "The two Christian Churches are important elements in the preservation of German national individuality, and their rights shall not be touched." He sought friendly relations with the Holy See, and in a concordat with the Catholic Church he offered guarantees including the preservation of parochial schools and free circulation of pastoral letters. However, a clash with the Protestant and Catholic Churches was unavoidable, considering the avowed Nazi principle that might is right, that the strong must dominate the weak, that men are not of one blood and are not equal before God. The ensuing conflict, and the peculiar situation of the German Evangelical Church, was of the greatest importance to hundreds of thousands in Germany.

Since Luther's reformation, the Protestant Church had been a constituent part of Prussia, Saxony, and other individual states. It was a state church, protected and supported by the state, whose prince, in each case, was her supreme bishop. The altar was tied to the throne, and it is not surprising under these circumstances that most of the pastors were conservative and many even nationalistic. Church taxes were paid together with other taxes to the state, which was responsible for the salaries of the clergy. The Weimar Republic severed relations between church and state, intending gradually to give the Protestant churches complete self-administration. Their new freedom might have provided new religious impetus if the socialists, who had always insisted that religion led to bigotry, had not favored withdrawal from church membership. Large groups of the working class had been estranged. For many intellectuals, Jews and Gentiles alike, religion was nothing more than a luxury, appropriate for festivals only. Even active church members took Christianity very much for granted.

Therefore, Hitler's promise to the churches raised their hopes, until, only a few weeks later, it was officially announced that the totalitarian slogan was to be "One Nation, One State, One Leader" and that this might include "One Church." People asked each other, "What does he mean? He can't possibly try to turn Catholics into Protestants or cancel the Reformation."

There was, at first, no question of a direct threat to the churches. The only demands were acquiescence to a change in the Creed—only a small change, said the Nazis—and a change in the administration of the Church. Why should the clergy not do what the universities had done? Everything else was coordinated. Why should not the churches, too, become totalitarian? Although the party program stated that the Jews would be driven out of Germany, not even the Jews themselves believed until April 1933 that it could and would be carried out. And yet it was a challenge for the Christian churches. The clergy would betray their mission if they witnessed without protest a persecution in direct contrast to basic Christian principles—the attack on a race in which the New Testament had its origin.

Many incidents merged in initiating the clergy's opposition to Hitler's church policy: the order to amalgamate the Protestant Churches, Lutheran, Reformed (Calvinist), and "United," into a "German Christian Church" which was to be an instrument of Nazi propaganda; Hitler's order for the elections of a national Church synod, which were held true to Nazi methods, with the looming threat of the concentration camp for those who would not vote "German Christian"; or Hitler's move in introducing, against all Protestant traditions, the post of a primate (*Reichsbischof*).

Yielding for the sake of peace, the Churches elected the beloved and trusted Pastor Friedrich von Bodelschwingh. Hitler cancelled this choice and appointed one of his personal friends, a former army chaplain named [Ludwig] Mueller, to the highest office in the Church. A queer sort of bishop, Mueller was antagonistic not only to the Semitic but to the pacifist elements in Church theology. During the [First] World War he had preached an evangel of hatred: "In the name of Jesus Christ, you must kill your enemies. Blessed is he who throws bombs. In the name of God, plunge your bayonet into the heart of the enemy. Thus you will fulfill the will of God. Amen."

No one could doubt that the future of the Church was at stake, and people were thronging into the churches in greater numbers than ever looking for guidance. Some of my younger friends, among them "non-Aryan Christians," were in doubt as to whether the sacraments of the Church were valid or not. I advised them to ask the ministers who had baptized, confirmed, and married them, in some cases their children as well. The answer came from many sides: "Will you just be patient for a little while? As guardians of the Church, we are preparing for concerted action."

The clergy had quietly begun to organize opposition against the religion of "race, blood, and soil." They were not by nature fighting pastors and did not go into battle lightheartedly. But within a few months, they had formed the "Pastors' Emergency League of Defenders of the True Protestant Faith," which was instantly joined by two thousand and at one time included as many as eight thousand out of a total of sixteen thousand Protestant pastors—an achievement that can only be truly recognized by people who have been threatened themselves. The ministers who submitted and joined the "German Christians" were an insignificant minority. The third group vacillated and called itself "neutral." Lay elements combined in what has become known as the Confessional Church (the Church acknowledging the unalterable Creed, the "Confession of Faith"), which I joined with most of my Protestant friends.[1]

Hitler did not attain his object of uniting the Churches; he split them instead.

One of the most urgent problems for the Confessional Church

(*Bekennende Kirche*) arose from the discovery that there were between three and four hundred Protestant pastors partly or wholly of Jewish descent. No one had been aware of their existence, and they caused a considerable stir. The Confessional Church supported them, keeping them in their parishes as long as possible and then finding new openings for them.

In November 1933 the so-called "German Christians" staged a demonstration at the Berlin Sports Palace. It was a call to battle. The speaker was a high school teacher, one of the radicals of the Nazi Party. He declared himself in favor of a neopagan movement, since the teachings of Christ were in his opinion apt to pervert and weaken the Nordic character. He ridiculed the Church, condemned the Old Testament in drastic terms, and demanded that it be dropped from use in church and school. Backed by the new authorities, the "German Christians" now claimed the introduction of an "Aryan" paragraph into the Church to free it from "Semitic materialism," thereby annulling the sacrament of baptism.

The news of the meeting spread like fire. The masses were roused—even those ordinarily indifferent to religious matters. They realized that this was an avowed intent to destroy religion, the displacement of God by Caesar.

Meanwhile, all important offices in the Protestant Church had been filled with men who professed the anti-Christian, pagan attitude. Alfred Rosenberg, author of *The Myth of the Twentieth Century,* was made leader and adviser of the party in all affairs of education. He had written, "By blood is the divine nature of man manifested," and, "Nordic blood represents the mystery which takes the place of the sacrament of old." Primate Mueller rewrote and improved the Lord's Prayer and the Sermon on the Mount according to his ideas of heroism. "Blessed are the peacemakers, for they shall be called the children of God" was replaced by "Happy are they who keep peace with their fellow nationals; they do God's will." In a sermon, the primate said, "A Church is a foreign body among the Aryan German people. . . . My aim is to promote a general racial religiosity. The faith of the German people must be turned toward the things of this world and not toward the world to come." And the minister of church affairs, Kerll,[2] remarked, "Germans in the early days of Christianity were naive enough to accept a foreign-clothed answer to their ideological questions."

The appointment of these people, and their fantastic proclamations, stirred up constant commotion. It also became known that pagan exercises were held by the storm troopers and elite guards and that instructions for new "tribal rites" had been circulated. There was a pagan "creed." Hitler was worshiped as the messenger of God, as his revealer and the savior of Germany.

Although in general the Germans appreciate economic security more than personal independence, social order more than individual rights, there are many who can be roused when their religious freedom is threatened. These were determined to defy the new Caesar who claimed whole and undivided allegiance. They were willing to follow the clergy in the battle for the realm and the Word of God.

CHAPTER 23

# The Pastors . . . Martin Niemöller

President Hindenburg had at least attempted to check the "Pagan Church," but soon after his death, Primate Mueller ordered that every pastor was to commit himself under oath to the spiritual as well as the political leadership of Hitler. The Confessional clergy then did what Martin Luther had done in his time. At the end of the service, in August 1934, they read a manifesto rejecting any pledge that interfered with their office as "servants of the Word" and protesting against an Aryan paragraph within the Church as a violation of the Christian religion. They did what no other professional group had dared to do. Living witnesses to the belief that the spirit does not die with the body, they knew they might have to die for their faith. They are the real heroes of Germany.

While the churches were under attack as intruders in the life of the state, people of all classes rallied to their defense. The churches were crowded. Mass meetings were held in the Sports Palace and all over the country to inform the public of the war against the Church and to organize for defense. Latent religious feeling came passionately to the fore. At times, when reciting the Creed, the people joined hands and formed a chain of thousands, spontaneously expressing the strength that is in unity of faith. One of Luther's hymns developed in the same way into the fighting song of the movement: "Keep us, O Lord, to Thy Word: check Thine enemies in their murdering."

The Nazis could not let this revival go on. They forbade any Church meetings and barred them from public halls. They made it unlawful, by decree, for the Church to publish anything about the struggle against the heretic movements. All Church magazines were suppressed; the display of the Bible in bookshops was stopped and its sale allowed only when specially ordered. Religious broadcasts were discontinued. The correspondence of the clergy was watched and often confiscated; their telephone calls were intercepted; their homes were raided. Ministers were summoned by the secret police and questioned for hours, standing until the old and weak among them collapsed. Many thousands were arrested repeatedly, and we heard our pastors talk about imprisonment as of an everyday occurrence. In trying to break their spirit, the police kept many imprisoned without a trial, expelled them from their parishes, or sent them to concentration camps. From the beginning of 1935, the churches existed very much like the early Christians in the catacombs, and the struggle of the clergy became the struggle of every member of the congregation.

All Christian institutions were suspect. It was told all over Berlin that the Nazis had raided and searched the headquarters of the YWCA. Absurd as it seemed, it proved to be true. Two lorries full of Nazi police had arrived to search the house for contraband literature. All they had found were some Nazi propaganda leaflets that one of the young women had undoubtedly received from a Nazi boyfriend.

The Catholic Church was attacked somewhat later and in a different manner but with the same ruthlessness. The concordat was violated; Catholic schools were closed and Catholic children deprived of religious education. It was made difficult for hospital patients to receive the Sacrament, and prison inmates were left without religious consolation. The circulation of papal messages and those of bishops was forbidden; the Holy See was insulted in the paper of the elite guards. Printing and publishing firms were expropriated merely because they printed a papal encyclical. Exaggerated stories charging priests and nuns with misconduct ranging from gross immorality to infringements of the currency exchange laws were widely circulated in an effort to incite the population. In spite of all this, the churches kept moral standards high and the tradition of mercy alive. Several weeks before the death of Field Marshal General Ludendorff, who had thrown the weight of his reputation behind the pagan movement, I heard that he had entered the Roman Catholic Josefinum Hospital and was under the care of Catholic sisters. About that time I met a Catholic friend in New York. "Do you remember," she asked me, "how Ludendorff boasted that he, like the ancient Germans, despised those who died 'on straw' and said that any death except in battle was ignoble? What an example of Christian charity for a Catholic hospital to take him in, after all he has done to try and destroy Christianity!"

The name of Martin Niemöller, the Dahlem pastor, is well known as the driving force of the Confessional Church. Since his incarceration in a concentration camp, he has become a symbol of the persecuted churches and of all the unknown priests, ministers, and deacons who exposed themselves as he did. Among them was Asmussen of Hamburg,[1] the first to be deprived of his church and the first to address a public meeting on the subject of the impending battle. I heard him preach in Berlin, while he was traveling in the service of the Confessional synod. He was probably the sternest in his faith, much like a character in the literature on early Calvinism. He was handicapped by asthma or emphysema and constantly gasped for breath, but his solemn words, wrung out of him, cut deeply into our minds and hearts.

Another early rebel was [Otto] Dibelius, whom I had met and found to be a learned and worldly man of many interests, although by nature formal and rather inaccessible. He had been driven out of high office as superintendent of a Church province and, to support his many children, had preached in a small German congregation in a French or Italian holiday resort. On the Sunday after Niemöller's arrest, he took over his pulpit. He had always been a powerful orator; now his eloquence rose to the pathos of the ancient prophets.

I came to the Dahlem church through one of its young ministers, Franz Hildebrandt. He had been ordained at the age of twenty-three and was highly esteemed by Niemöller. When the halls were barred for religious purposes, my friends and I followed him to Dahlem, where services were held in two churches, a very old baroque village church and a large, airy, modern one with only a huge wooden cross behind the altar and the words of the Creed in gold on the wall for decoration. I attended them regularly for years and learned to know Niemöller so well that I could sense the meaning of each of his expressions and gestures.

Niemöller has written the story of his younger days, of his navy training and his brilliant record as a submarine commander; how, intensely patriotic, he resigned his commission after the armistice, unwilling to take two submarines to Scapa Flow, where they were to be surrendered. Planning to become a farmer, he served his apprenticeship as a farmhand, but at the age of twenty-seven he felt the urge to enter the ministry. He claims that it was not an interest in theology that prompted him but a desire, simply and modestly, to preach the Word of God as his father did. He had come to believe that this was the best service he could render to restore order and self-confidence in a nation debased by war, hunger, and defeat. He was already married, and two children were born before he finished his studies. He had periods of terrible hardship and stark poverty. During the inflation, while he was preparing for his examinations, he worked at laying cross ties on the railway to earn a living for his family. He tells how he sold the gold braid his wife ripped off his old uniforms to a jeweler for just enough money to live on for a few days.

Nothing in Niemöller's early career as a pastor pointed to his future leadership. He seemed fitted for a parish where childlike faith and trust were uppermost, for spiritual ministration rather than sophisticated scholarship. When he came to the Dahlem parish, in a fairly wealthy suburb of Berlin, his future was apparently assured. He had a beautiful home, and his family life was gradually enriched by seven children. As a man of nationalistic tendencies, he had hoped the Nazi movement would free Germany from the fetters of Versailles and had joined the party in its early days. He left it when the Nazis seized power, at the very moment when he could have profited by the connection, because now he began to see clearly what it stood for.

Niemöller's congregation knew that he never recovered from his disappointment over Hitler's betrayal of the Church. At first he believed that irresponsible party members were to blame for the attack and that Hitler's intervention must be sought. We heard from one of the Dahlem pastors that Hitler's staff and bodyguards tried to prevent an audience with Niemöller's delegation, but when they finally got through, Hitler seemed to unbend. One of his aides—Goering, I believe—asked to be allowed to contribute something before a decision was reached. He turned on a gramophone record of Niemöller's remarks during a private telephone conversation the day before. It contained outspoken criticism of the primate and was perhaps too confident of a successful outcome of the impending interview with Hitler. That finished it. Hitler was in a rage, and from that day Niemöller and the Church were doomed.

While resisting the domination of the Church by the state, Niemöller changed gradually in appearance; the energy expressed in his face gave way to asceticism as the weight of his responsibility bowed him down. But his sermons, although carefully written out as a precaution against vicious charges, became increasingly powerful and penetrating. An assurance and a certainty of the reality of God and his laws that radiated from him took hold of us, filling our need in a world that defied all moral standards. Our faith became simpler and stronger. It was this absolute surrender to God, his passionate earnestness and his courage, that attracted people from all parts of the city to Niemöller's church in such numbers that the ticket collectors in the Dahlem subway station had to be reinforced. People arrived an hour before the service began; some brought folding chairs, others stood through the long service, and the rest stayed outside to hear as much as they could. Toward the end, Niemöller spoke or preached every single day, well aware that his liberty and perhaps his life would soon be over.

During the last year of his freedom, we had the feeling that he was consciously walking toward his Golgotha. Again and again he stressed the claim of God for His Realm: "There shall be no stranger set over thee; thou art mine," and "Thou art mine, follow me." We felt the direct application to our own time and our own minister when he introduced a sermon with the words, "This was written by Paul when he was in prison, accused of being a traitor to his country and his Caesar." After the sermon, he read the names of the pastors and elders who were in prison, forbidden to preach, or expelled from their parishes—as did all the pastors of the *Bekennende Kirche,* while the congregation was standing, sometimes for twenty minutes.

At the beginning of the struggle, Niemöller had asked people to his home for evening discussions of their individual religious problems. As the number increased, he moved these meetings to the parish hall, where he also informed us of every phase of the Church struggle after the publication of Church news had been forbidden. Only those holding membership cards of the Confessional Church were admitted. We applied for the cards to our pastors, and in return we gave a pledge of loyalty and, if necessary, of sacrifice for the Church. Yet the secret police prided themselves on being in possession of at least forty membership cards. Niemöller told them frankly what he thought of the work of spies and said he hoped it would do them good to hear something of the ethics of the Gospel. At these meetings, he was not so much the priest of apostle but more simply a combatant, talking more freely, fighting more and more grimly as the persecution increased in brutality.

One Sunday in March 1935 is unforgettable. Alfred Rosenberg had publicly declared that "Eternal Germany shall replace the Kingdom of God." The Prussian Confessional clergy drew up an answer, warning against such teachings. The minister of the interior was informed of this by his spies, and the publication and circulation of the document was forbidden. Nevertheless, the clergy decided to read it from the pulpit. Niemöller read it at the end of the liturgy, before the altar, as an act performed in the service of God. The secret police had often arrested pastors at the altar—many in the congregation felt as if the beat of their hearts were suspended. On the same day, Niemöller, together with seven hundred other pastors, was placed under arrest, although only briefly that time.

Early in 1937, Hans Kerll, the cabinet minister for church affairs, summoned the leaders of the Protestant and Catholic Churches and gave the following order: "The authority of the state over the Church must be accepted. The primary assumptions of the state, as it stands today, expressed in terms of race, blood, and soil, must be inviolable also for the Church. The National Socialist Party represents positive Christianity. The question of the divinity of Christ is ridiculous and irrelevant. We have a new authority on the real meaning of Christ and Christianity: Adolf Hitler."

The Confessional clergy, in a bold proclamation, refused to accept this authority in Church affairs.

For a long time, the secret police had not dared to touch Niemöller. Attempts of the authorities to pension him off or forbid him to preach had been useless; he went on preaching. In 1935, when his seventh child was born, the parish people said that this child was proof of his faith in the future of the Church. Yet, on July 1, 1937, he was imprisoned because he preached the Word of God and not the word of Adolf Hitler. The Nazis called it "treason."

After many months, his case was brought before a people's tribunal, where even the Nazi-appointed judges, holding the trial behind closed doors, were so impressed with Niemöller that they acquitted him. While his friends waited triumphantly to take him home, he was rearrested by the secret police—at the order of Hitler, it was said—and taken through a back door of the courthouse to a concentration camp. Essentially a social being, Niemöller was in solitary confinement for nearly eight years, as if buried alive.

He remained a living influence on many people for whom the Dahlem church was the redeeming feature of existence in Germany. We have had the unique experience of living in a congregation where the Gospel was renewed and became contemporary with the Holy Scriptures. Through persecution and in bondage, we had this refuge. No tyrant and dictator could take it from us.

CHAPTER 24

# New Lease on Life

The secret police summoned me in May 1937 to appear the following morning for a "report on my trips abroad." After four hours of questioning, I was ordered to leave Germany within three weeks.

It might seem strange that I should not have expected this from the beginning of Nazi rule. However, so far, people who were in danger had either left of their own accord or disappeared suddenly into a concentration camp. This was before the bestial pogrom in the fall of 1938 and before the mass deportations. To be expelled and expatriated was still a mark of particular distinction, although it was meant as a humiliation.

"For what crime? What have you done? Were you a citizen?" my friends abroad wanted to know. My German friends knew that there need not be any such excuses for Nazi actions; they asked merely what charges were made and whether the secret police had any material evidence on which to base their order—the recording of a telephone conversation, the photostat of a letter, the finding of an "open letter" by Thomas Mann or Einstein,[1] or any such contraband.

They had nothing except the reproach of my frequent and lengthy sojourns abroad. Of course, though I had never been in party politics, I represented everything the Nazis detested. I was of Jewish "race"; I belonged to the fighting Protestant Church; I was a progressive woman, internationally minded and therefore of pacifist tendencies. Undoubtedly, they believed I would do less harm outside the country than within. They were mistaken.

The son of one of my friends warned me of the danger of writing many letters on behalf of people who wanted to emigrate. I said, "If it's no longer possible to do even that, I would rather not live." But I did not expect trouble. The Nazis wanted non-Aryans to get out—my activities should have been welcome. They had never searched or raided my home. When the summons came, I never even considered the possibility of being in danger.

Individual mishaps have become rather irrelevant since the recent holocaust. I was, after all, not deported like my youngest sister, my brother's youngest son, and so many of my friends. It would not be worthwhile to mention my inquisition by the secret police but for the futility of matters into which they pried, the stupidity of their accusations and judgment, that may contribute to the unsavory picture of totalitarianism.

The iron gate of the huge red brick police building in central Berlin was locked behind me as I passed through, and I was asked to produce the summons. In a bare, characterless office room, a young official questioned me and noted down my answers, while an older one who pretended to be at work on some files acted as watchdog and interrupted curtly several times. I remembered novels about czarist Russia that I had read in my young days, portrayals of distrust and suspicion in an atmosphere where even spies were spied upon. Incredibly, I now found in real life, in my own country, the same system with a secret police whose members were no less distrusted, watched and controlled by their own superiors from the highest down.

I was questioned extensively about my various trips, their dates and routes, and the friends and places I visited. "How did you make that acquaintance?" was a favorite question. How does friendship begin? Sometimes with a glance, sometimes with an accord in the course of a conversation, sometimes through interest or cooperation in a common cause.... I explained each case.

Apparently the names of my titled friends disturbed them, for these they took down when I produced letters of invitation. I had been collecting these "alibis" for years. Everyone did, during the Nazi regime, to protect themselves against possible charges of having spent money abroad. We were allowed to accept hospitality and railroad tickets from foreign friends, but no money even for the smallest expenses. The usual joke, when we commented on this ruling, was to say, "All right, but what about tips?"

They pounced on the name of an American hostess, a Mrs. Johnson, after I had given the address of Mrs. Emilia Johnston, a Scottish friend.

"You just told me that Johnston was in Scotland," the officer said, warily.

"Johnson," I replied, "is a common name in Anglo-Saxon countries."

The fact that I had spent every summer in Engelsberg was also suspicious in their eyes. Why go to the same place for so many consecutive summers, if not for some intrigue or underground work—even if it is only a quiet mountain valley?

"With whom did you talk there?" I answered that I had gone for a rest and lived very quietly.

"Do you mean to suggest that you never talked with anyone?"

"No, I do not. In a hotel you eventually talk to people."

"Then give us the names."

I mentioned the family of the proprietor, whom I had known all my life, the Cattanis. The absence of any Jewish name was rather disappointing. Quite obviously they were out to discover my connection with some Jewish plot or underground activity.

A trip I had made the winter before to the United States was my greatest offense. This had occurred about the time when Mayor La Guardia and Bishop Mundelein had commented on Hitler in terms that were far from complimentary.[2] Evidently the secret police traced these remarks to my influence, which, however flattering, sadly overestimated my importance. The watchdog interfered curtly: "Do not keep asking her *where* she went, but *why* she traveled."

The significance attached to my innocent movements seemed so ridiculous that I burst out, "Why do you ask me all these things? So far as I know, it is not forbidden to travel. To whom should I apply for permission next time I plan to go abroad?"

I was already contemplating another trip without dreaming what sort of final journey lay before me. It was only later I realized that these subalterns had received orders to throw me out of Germany and that it was left to them to find some warrant for the action. Toward the end of four hours of cross-examination I had arrived at a stage of exhaustion where I would have admitted anything. I began to understand how under pressure people will sometimes admit things they have never done.

For a long interval, I was sent out into a corridor closed by iron bars. They called me in again and inquired about the organizations to which I belonged. This time my inquisitor attempted to imitate Hitler's famous "hypnotic glance." I had to admit that my organizations were all very mild, harmless groups concerned with women's activities and social work. His attention focused on the International Council of Women. Probably he assumed it was a communist or Jewish organization in conspiracy against the Nazi government. He noted the names and addresses of all board members of the Council and also of the International Committee of Schools of Social Work, of which I was chairman. Then he demanded, again with the hypnotic glare, "Fräulein Doktor, did you meet any emigrants?"

Although the whole of Nazi policy had been framed to force all nonconformists, pacifists, republican politicians, Jews, and many Christians to emigrate, yet the Nazis behaved as if all emigrants were criminals. Mere contact with one of them made a German a leper.

I admitted having met quite a few, among others Dr. [Bernhard] Weiss, former vice president of the Berlin police, at the home of the Hon. Mrs. Franklin, who had offered him refuge. The Franklins were old friends of mine, and I had visited them for many years. The watchdog was most anxious to know what Dr. Weiss was doing in London. I informed him that he was the representative of a stationery firm. I might have added that a certain former cabinet minister represented a company making electric bulbs, and another, a Catholic, sold oil and incense to churches, and that all three had accidentally met in a motion picture studio where each was trying to place an order. I also named some very distinguished professors, several of them world famous. He expressed surprise when I explained that some of them had called on me in the United States. Apparently he considered such visits improbable unless we were agents of an underground organization. What had we talked about?

I answered, "Mostly about America. The United States is a very interesting country, and people who have recently arrived there are in the habit of discussing its institutions and customs."

"So you had scientific discussions?"

"Yes."

"But people must have asked you about Germany as well."

"Certainly; some wanted to hear about mutual friends."

Then he asked, somewhat comprehensively, what the American people talked about and whether the general feeling was favorable to Germany. My answers were correspondingly vague.

Meanwhile, I had repeated my request to make a telephone call to my housekeeper, who would be waiting for me with a friend I had asked to lunch. But my inquisitors seemed to fear that I would call for help. Although I explained exactly why I wished to telephone, it was not permitted.

After a long time—it was then after three o'clock—I was called into another room where a rather vulgar man asked me, "Miss Salomon, what had you in mind when you traveled abroad?"

"In mind? I traveled, as I have done frequently all my life."

"Do you intend to remain in Germany?"

"Certainly."

"That is impossible. You must leave this country within three weeks."

After a moment of shock, I said, "It seems pretty short notice!"

"Why so? What have you got to do here?"

"For example, to dissolve a home."

I did not add, "To say 'good-bye' to lifelong friends whom I shall never see again," nor "To find a refuge"; nor "To go over the papers accumulated by a scholar and author and teacher during forty years, to decide what would best serve me in my profession in new and alien surroundings"; nor "To liquidate funds that have been entrusted to me."

He was quite uninterested in my personal reactions and demanded, "By which frontier station will you leave Germany, and where will you live?"

"I cannot possibly decide at a moment's notice. I may go to Switzerland, via Basel. But I can't tell."

Ironically, that very morning I had received word from my local police station that my routine application for a new passport (the old one having expired) had been granted, "as nothing unfavorable was known against me."

He continued, "Your passport has expired. When you get the new one, come back to this room and tell me what day you will leave Germany and by which frontier station."

That was all.

I drove home. My friend and the housekeeper were upset over the long delay, and both broke down when I told them the verdict. "I accept it," I said, "and you must do the same for my sake."

Overnight I decided to ask my British friends, the Franklins, if they would take me in for a time. I wrote to American friends for an affidavit so I could get an immigration visa for the United States, where an exile is allowed to work for a living. Two days later, I told the

New Lease on Life 225

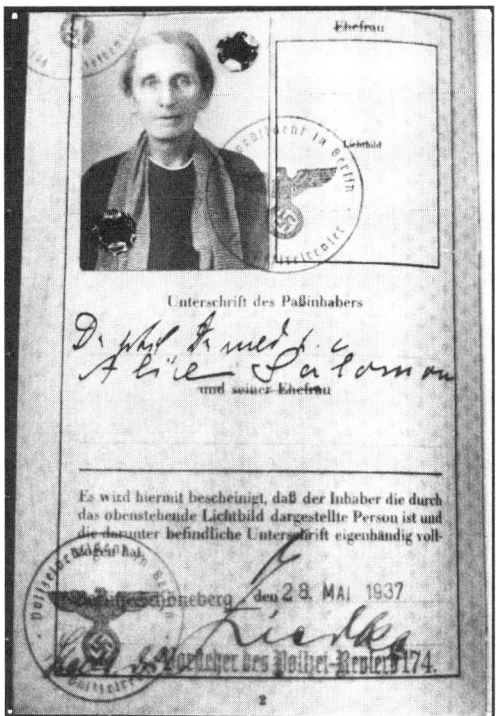

Picture page from the passport used by Alice Salomon to emigrate from Germany in 1937. (Photograph courtesy of the Leo Baeck Institute New York City.)

secret police that I would leave by Bentheim, Holland, and was informed that I should have to travel without a passport until I claimed it at the frontier. I then asked to have the order of expulsion in writing. This infuriated the official. He jumped to his feet: "That can't be done under any circumstances! We never give anything in writing."

I said, "This is an enforced emigration."

"It is an order to emigrate," he corrected, "so as to avoid the concentration camp."

That was my sentence. They might have saved themselves and me the trouble of endless questioning. The order for expatriation had gone through, and it was a stupid order. So long as I lived in Germany, I was powerless. In sending me away, the Nazis loosened my tongue. Inadvertently, they gave me, after empty dreary years, a new lease on life, the need to work again, and the freedom to do it. I have always considered this one of life's greatest gifts.

To have been marked by the Gestapo provides an insight into human nature beyond anything the psychologists can teach. It is a supreme test of friendship, loyalty, and courage, for any communication with a marked individual may endanger the others.

Immediately after the inquisition at Gestapo headquarters, I telephoned a friend who was a lawyer. Curt was a bachelor in his early forties and had frequently been my guest—a pleasant asset to small dinner parties and a good conversationalist. I told him that I had to see him. He came at once. I explained what had happened and asked him to advise me how to liquidate my German life. It was not easy: I needed an exit permit, for which in turn I needed proof that all my taxes, beside the emigration tax, had been paid, and none of these papers were granted without a certificate of "good behavior." I also had to give up the lease on my home, dispose of my books and furniture, and get a permit for the things I wished to take with me. My pension from the Berlin municipality, as former director of my college, and a life annuity on capital I had donated for the purchase of a dormitory would stop, but a fraction of my remaining funds could perhaps be transferred before my bank accounts were blocked. All this in three weeks.

Curt was dumbfounded. There was no regulation whatever that justified the expulsion of a citizen, in this case an aged women with a record of public usefulness. People still thought in terms of the law. He considered my request for a moment. Then he said, "Alice, I am going to do it for you and am not going to take any money from you. On the one condition that you follow my advice and that you don't let others meddle who may think you could get a more favorable arrangement in some roundabout way. And I beg you not to talk about it. Keep the whole affair as secret as you can. Who knows what else these gangsters will do to you if it is discussed?" He faithfully took care of everything.

One of the astonishing things about Nazi Germany was the speed with which news traveled in spite of fear, spying, and intimidation. Curt was so upset that he did himself what he had warned me not to do. He told a few people, and soon everybody knew. Since I have been blessed with the kind of innocence that never anticipates disloyalty or disappointment in human relations, I did not realize then how great was the service I had asked of him and that it might prove very inconvenient for his law office. Before my summons, I had promised to dine at the home of very dear friends. Now I went to say good-bye. My heart was pounding, my hands were jittery, and when I told them, I spilled their best Bordeaux over my best dress. Only later it dawned on me that I might have been traced to their house.

Soon there were incidents that made me understand the situation. I noticed that the telephone never rang unless someone was calling from a public booth. A very intimate friend of mine, a prominent citizen of eighty years, rang up and said, "How are you, my dear friend?" "I am all right." He said, "People are telling so many stories nowadays. There are rumors about everyone." I told him, "Everything you may have heard is true. I shall come and explain." It turned out that someone had mentioned my case at a party the night before. He would not believe it but did not dare to reassure himself by telephone. Early in the morning he had come to my apartment. The elevator was out of order, so he had climbed four flights of stairs. He rang, but I did not hear the bell, and my housekeeper had gone to early mass. This alarmed him still more. About noon he had gone to a public telephone booth to call.

Some people dared to come, but mostly after dark. A friend and former student of mine who was known for her courage came every day in her car, parking it ostentatiously in front of my house. Meaning to take my thoughts off my problem and to let me have a last glimpse to remember, she urged me to drive out to the lake district and see the beauty of spring. I told her, "The banks of the Hudson are beautiful, too."

Paul [?], the great banker, came with his brother, Frederick. They wanted to try to have the order canceled, but I explained that life in Germany would be impossible for me after this. I mentioned that the money I had earned during the lecture tour in the United States had been turned over to the Nazi government in exchange for worthless German marks. Max Warburg, in whose lovely home in Hamburg I had spent a day on my return from the States, had promptly had his bank exchange it for me.[3] Paul volunteered to talk to Dr. Schacht or one of his aides, pointing out that it would be unspeakable to withhold money earned on a trip for which they turned me out of Germany. He actually succeeded in getting the few hundred dollars transferred at a better rate. These and a good many others were and remained my steadfast friends. There were some with whom I had worked for forty years and from whom I have never heard again.

I could not possibly say good-bye to the great number of people who meant much to me, so I decided to send them a letter of farewell, explaining that I would have left Germany, never to come back, by the time they received it.

Several people warned me not to send it through the mail, for it would endanger every addressee. I was advised to employ the method of the Confessional Church—to have them delivered by car, with a second person along to drop them into the mailboxes, ready to drive on before the letters were discovered. A friend promised to do it for me, and I asked my secretary to sort the letters in the order of their delivery and to accompany him. The next morning she declared, "I put the letters in order, but I will not drive in the car. According to the map I saw, it will have to take so many turns it can't fail to draw attention." But the young man did it anyway.

I had told Curt that I wanted to get out as soon as possible, and it was settled that I would leave on June 12, two and a half weeks after the order. My friends were distressed that I had to go alone, without money and without a passport. Ursula [?], who had been secretary for the non-Aryan Christian Refugee Committee, welcomed the opportunity to visit an aunt in England, and it was arranged that she would go on the same train. Of course, she had to buy her ticket somewhere else, travel in another car, and board the train at another station. When we had passed the frontier, where the secret police gave me my passport, I asked her into my compartment. We looked out on Dutch houses covered with crimson ramblers, on gardens in bloom and cherry trees bending under the weight of their fruit. I said, "Look at this. Isn't God's world beautiful everywhere?" In amazement she told me, "We were all convinced you would collapse the minute we passed the frontier."

I waited in England for my visa, encouraged by the kindness of my English and Scottish friends. In September 1937 I arrived in New York for my new lease on life.

It has not all been bliss. It is hard work to lecture for a living, and I have always been physically frail. Also, it has been said so often that I hesitate to repeat it, the refugee loses caste. I lost many former friends, and sometimes when I see them at a public function I think of Henry George, who said, "These people once gave a banquet for me."[4] A few of my old friends have been guardian angels and, as I have always been lucky, I have found new ones, and a church where people tell me that they have missed me when for weeks I have not been well enough to attend services.

It took me four years to start a home, and I am now rather proud of having learned in my seventieth year how to cook from a cookbook. A home requires an aura that the most luxurious hotel suite can never have. It is made up of the people who go in and out. So I could be happy if the thought of this most cruel of wars, the suffering it inflicted, and its aftermath, would not intrude.

The germs of aggressive nationalism have long been latent in the German organism, as they have been and are at times in other nations. The only hope for a cure of Germany's delirium lies in the potential growth of her moral forces and a rediscovery of the basic law of human relations: the law of interdependence. Or as it was expressed two thousand years ago: the law of human brotherhood.

# Appendix A: The Significance of the Women's Movement for Social Life

A few years ago, a German scholar summarized his views with regard to the significance of the women's movement for the life of the community as follows: "When I survey the great achievements of modern culture, I have to conclude that all of them are men's works." A member of the women's movement has, however, expressed a quite different view. She says, "Other images tend to enforce upon those of us who are women contrasting conclusions. When we see soldiers marching by us on the street or when the gates of a factory open and a horde of workers streams forth, the thought spontaneously occurs to us: each of these, the son of a mother! Each born with pain and brought up with care and toil; purchased at such a great price and yet, in our social life, so little valued. Does woman really have no functions in our communal life, no significance for our culture?"

In these two statements lies the social core of the women's question. We live in an age of shining economic development, of rising wealth, and of marvelous technological advances, in which, however, all of men's planning and effort is directed toward production, achievement, and the mastery of nature. Human life as such—its emergence and its passing, its inner development—is held in low esteem.

In all countries, it is a concomitant of the new structure of the economy, of the development of industry and of the growth of the big cities, that the health and life of human beings is neglected and recklessly abandoned to accident or to economic forces, that one attends to the dead machine more carefully than to the "human machine." We invent ever more means of facilitating transportation and communication, improvements that make the railroads run more quickly and introduce the telephone to places that lie farther and farther away. But despite all of these new means of social intercourse, the relationships between people, far from being eased and improved, have been loosened and made worse. We know less than our ancestors did about our fellow countrymen, about their needs and their longings. In the place of patriarchal relationships there has emerged the conflict among opposed interests, a wild struggle for economic advantage.

This view of the social life of our time can be made concrete by means of several examples.

Every year in Germany, three hundred thousand children who have barely seen the light of day die before they reach their first birthdays because their mothers had to drag themselves, despite their exhaustion, to work up until shortly before giving birth; because, in order to earn money for food, they could not take care of their children during the weeks immediately after they were born; or because no one had ever taught them how a child should be reared.

So much in the way of lost vitality sinks with these children into the earth! So much in the way of wasted energy that has been expended by women disappears with them!

Thousands of additional children languish slowly away, becoming unproductive, morally weak, or dissolute creatures, because their parents cannot care for them; because they are malnourished and they spend their childhoods cooped up in unhealthy apartments; and because they are abandoned to the influences and temptations of the street.

So much vital and youthful energy is weakened and made useless for the struggle of life!

Then there are the additional hordes of boys and girls who are forced at a too early age to enter into employment: children fourteen years old, whom the law regards and treats as "young people" and "youthful workers." There are youths who have sacrificed limbs because they have been put to work at machines that demand ceaseless watchfulness, from morning until evening, from Monday to Saturday, all year long—constant concentration, of which even adults are incapable and which one can scarcely expect from youngsters. There are girls who give up their youth and the sacred right to become mothers because they work too long or work in unhealthy ways in shops or at machines in factories. In addition, others are exposed to moral dangers, because they work alone, without protection, for men who take no interest in their personal fate.

So much in the way of promising life, which is physically and spiritually endangered!

We observe, moreover, thousands of people who are incapable of working, people who require assistance, people who are homeless, who are blown around by the economy like grains of sand, who are like foreigners when need overcomes them; ne'er-do-wells, who have been shipwrecked and stranded. Perhaps they are worthless beings from the standpoint of the economy. They are, nonetheless, creatures like us, with desires and hopes like ours, and with living souls which yearn for consolation and uplift.

Finally, we see around us a world that is full of class splits and conflicts, which are nowhere sharper anywhere in the world than in Germany. Rich and poor, businessmen and workers, oppose one another like members of two parties that are armed to the teeth, without mutual understanding, often also without any sympathy for members of the opposing group. It is as if our people consisted of two groups that can be described in the words of [Benjamin] Disraeli: "Two nations [the rich and the poor], between whom there is no intercourse and sympathy, who are as ignorant of each other's habits, thoughts and feelings, as if they were dwellers in different zones, or inhabitants of different planets."[1]

Wherever we look in the social realm, there we see—despite numerous efforts to ameliorate and eliminate social abuses—a lack of social services, of helpfulness, of educational measures; everywhere, a neglect of what is human and personal as opposed to what is technical; of the soul as opposed to what is material.

Under these circumstances, do women really have no communal responsibilities? Can they be of no value or significance for cultural development?

When the women's movement demands new opportunities and new possibilities for the unfolding of women's energies, it does so with the clear intention that through these opportunities, women will be led toward a higher level of social effectiveness. The basic idea of our movement—that women have tasks to perform beyond the realm of the household—does not mean that we simply intend to acquire "new rights." It means instead that we believe in women's ability to add something to cultural development, increasing the wealth and fullness of human striving and creativity in the social sphere. The insistence on new chances for development rests therefore on the deeply rooted conviction that there are social problems that women can, because of their nature, deal with better than can men; that women can introduce a new and valuable admixture into cultural life if they are able to make use of their special gifts and their special peculiarity in the public realm.

Much has been said in the women's movement and also during the past few days at this congress about the particular nature of women, and people have sought in a variety of ways to describe and characterize it. The definition that seems to me to be the most suitable and to which I would like to adhere is the one by Oda Olberg,[2] who once wrote, "It is the essence of women's peculiar nature to prize human life highly." Just as it is the natural task of the woman to produce life, so too, it seems to me, is it her cultural mission to preserve life by striving against its dissipation and destruction. It is her responsibility to uphold in society what is personal and individual, that which economic forces tend to schematize and extinguish, thereby working to bridge class differences and diminish class conflicts.

If one asks oneself how the women's movement can realize its social ideals in the social sphere and how it can seek to solve the social problem (in the first instance for women themselves), and if one wishes to summarize the strivings of the women's movement in this area, one can say the following: the movement seeks to bring about a better balance between the life of the woman who is confined to her household and wishes to add new and deeper content to that life and the life of the woman who is forced by material need to leave her house and her family behind her. The movement seeks to bring these two worlds closer together.

Numerous demands voiced by the women's movement are linked to this goal. There is the call for more intensive education and particularly the call for greater emphasis on socially oriented education for young women; then, too, the demand for admission to public office and the granting of civil rights, for better vocational training, the creation of women's organizations, protection for female workers, and motherhood insurance. All of this points on the one hand toward one group of women taking on new responsibilities and another group, whose members are oppressed, having its burdens lightened. One sort of woman should leave her household so as, at least to a modest extent, to enable another sort to return to hers.

Inasmuch as the educational and care-oriented functions that women formerly fulfilled within the family have now migrated into the areas of state and local government, women must similarly make the leap from the family into the area of public life. They must emerge from the familial and private sphere, performing their activities in public institutions if their influence is not to be lost for the purpose of cultural development. For this reason, the women's movement must demand the vote. This demand emerges organically from all other strivings by women, because without full recognition as a citizen in the state and in the municipality, a woman is hindered in her efforts to become socially effective. Only when spheres of influence are opened up for women in the area of public life will it become possible for them to become and to achieve that which, according to their essential nature, they are capable of becoming and achieving and that which, according to this essence, they are destined to become and to achieve for the life of society.

As a consequence of these demands by members of the women's movement—admission of women to public office and protection of working women (and not just unpropertied women but also middle-class women)—there emerges an abundance of concrete goals. For us, it is a matter not only of assisting, through poor relief and care for orphans, the impoverished and the afflicted in a narrow sense but also of taking positive steps to combat all destructive influences of a general sort that threaten life and militate against culture. We must not wait to provide help until the beggar asks us for alms, until we encounter children as wards of the youth court after they have broken the law, or until women who have become desperate in the struggle to survive have sacrificed their honor and dignity as women by selling their sexuality. We must instead seek in the first place to prevent all of these people from stumbling into such situations.

Just as it has long been the natural and self-evident duty of women to feed the hungry and care for the sick, so too is it now our duty to advocate that our collective life be organized according to the principle of greater fairness and perfection. This entails a wide range of particular objectives. We must see to it that young people are well prepared for vocations. We must take part in all efforts to improve public health in order to combat widespread diseases. We must work against the devastating consequences of alcoholism and seek to provide answers for the housing question by providing support for housing inspection as a means of bringing about better and healthier residential conditions. In addition, it is important to participate in endeavors in the area of popular education, to insist on the right to share in the work of educational administration, and in this way to strive toward a situation in which members of the unpropertied classes as well as others can taste more of the fruits of intellectual culture. It is, moreover, essential to strengthen the working classes for the struggle for better living standards by supporting demands for more extensive factory legislation and for advances in the area of social policy more generally. Women should do so by promoting employment offices, occupational organizations, factory inspection by females, and advances in the area of social insurance toward the establishment of motherhood insurance. It is necessary to combat the tendency for work to become increasingly boring, the general mechanization of life, and alienation from nature, from which wide sectors of the population suffer, by fostering positive influences in the areas of leisure and recreation. It is our further task to try to place fair limitations on the struggles among opposed interest groups and to work toward a situation in which economic life coincides more closely with our moral demands for fairness and justice. As housewives, as employers, and as consumers, women enjoy a multitude of opportunities for expressing feelings of social responsibility that point in this direction.

All of this should help to foster, everywhere in our nation, conditions under which the growth of technical and material culture—which will continue to be more strongly influenced by male than by female productivity—will be accompanied by the growth of moral culture. It should also help to resolve class tensions.

Only because the women's movement has acknowledged these duties, displayed this social character, and oriented its demands toward social ideals; only because it has demanded not only new rights that benefit certain classes of women but also new safeguards and additional justice for other classes of women; only on this basis could the women's movement forge to a certain extent among its own members what it seeks for society more generally: new personal and human relationships, the diminution of social prejudices and conflicts. Only because the women's movement has formulated both its demands vis-à-vis others and its definition of its own responsibilities in ways that encompassed women of all classes, striving to help all women adjust to modern life, have women of all classes been prepared to participate in it, finding there common ground and a common home. Even though the women who belong to one political party [the Social Democratic Party] keep their distance from us, because their dogma rejects cooperation with others, this cannot prevent us from uniting women of all classes, of all occupations, and all religious confessions— and, in our International Council of Women,[3] women from all countries—in collaborative endeavors.

It is a fact that all of us—whether we take a particular interest in cooking schools, in the right to vote, or in any one of the other areas that lie between these two poles—wish to enhance women's influence in collective life. Belief in this goal points beyond our personal interests and our individual lives. This all-encompassing awareness of a great collective responsibility creates a sense of gender-based solidarity among women, leading us toward a unity that transcends all philosophical and ideological differences. Consciousness of this fact—that women are adjusting to the new circumstances of society in order not only to gain something for themselves and for other women but also to help all of humanity—confers on the women's movement its majestic significance, enabling it to enjoy an impressive and irresistible influence in modern life.

I thus come to the end of my remarks, which I would like to summarize as follows: We believe in women's social mission. We believe that the abundant culture that has arisen around us can flourish still more abundantly, brilliantly, and beautifully if women gain a sphere of influence in social life. We believe that certain social ills can be eliminated only if women are enabled to become and accomplish that which, according to their essential nature, they are destined to be and do.

We also know, however, that although we must raise these demands in assemblies and at congresses, we cannot bring them there to fruition.

We can do the latter only through social action.

We must all strive through our conduct to give proof of the convictions we share.

Outside these meeting rooms, thousands await our help and our influence: children, whom we can rescue from death; women, whom we can rescue from moral ruin; youths, who need our assistance to find the right paths for themselves in life. They stand on our streets and in front of the doors to our houses.

Are we ready to hear their call and to meet them in their need?

May a sacred fire be ignited in our hearts. This will not be a destructive fire but instead one that projects new light and warmth into the area of social life, kindling additional fires as well.

# Appendix B: The Revolution of the Mother

It may be just a story, but I heard it from the teachers of one of the finest German universities. They told it when these universities were still cradles of culture, citadels of light, when a student, on receiving his diploma as a doctor of philosophy, had to pledge under his oath to search for truth and to proclaim it. It was many years before "the age of Hitler," before scholars who held unpopular beliefs had to flee for their lives, before the Nazis openly vented their contempt for learning and intellectual pursuits by erasing from a university building in Heidelberg the inscription "To the Living Mind." Thus I assume that the story is founded on facts.

This story, which seems very appropriate for present days, was that some of the Indian tribes in South America, when overwhelmed by Spanish invaders with mechanized arms and subjugated into slavery, decided to abstain from procreation. Life for them had lost its value when freedom went. They would not bear children doomed to the cruel fate that had struck them down.

We shall never know authentically whether it was the men or the women of these Indian tribes who led the way. But we do know that never in modern times has the womanhood of any nation revolted against a ruler who wantonly led their husbands and sons into a war of aggression and conquest. Women have fanatically supported bloody upheavals, against this or that form of government, for the overturn of one ruling class or another, for the suppression of a religion or the conquest of other nations. But with the exception of small and ineffective groups, they have accepted the leadership of men in these matters. They have adopted men's political slogans, men's aims and methods, men's passions and hatreds. Often they have been more cruel and bloodthirsty, more extremist, nullifying what potential motherhood meant them to be.

All over the ages, women have continued to bear children so that men might kill them.

During the classical period of Greek history, in the midst of the great war between the Athenians and the Spartans which lasted for twenty-seven years, an immortal poet dealt with this problem. The stage was then an institution with moral objectives, and poets were also philosophers. In this atmosphere Aristophanes wrote his *Lysistrata,* a play in which the heroine voiced her will to restore peace, urging women to exert the power which they possess to bring the war to an end. Women should refuse to bear children and to raise them that they may be killed or that they may kill the sons of other mothers, who bore them with travail and pains and raised them with solicitude and care exactly as they had done: lives dearly paid for and yet so lightly valued. She urged an organized strike of mothers to make future wars impossible. This was the role the poet had conceived for an enlightened womanhood!

Here now is the reality: three dictators, three European nations backing these leaders, hailing them when they wantonly assail and invade peaceful countries, slaughtering men, women, and children, wrecking the civilization, built up through many centuries, with the most ingenious means of destruction, laying a continent in ruins.[1] And the women of these countries? They do not follow the course taken by the Indian tribes. They do not convert the hopes of the Greek poet into reality. They increase the birthrate at an astounding pace—the result of a propaganda "to fill the cradles" such as the world has never known, and they hand their children over to the state, which alone controls the lives of the young, physically, mentally, spiritually. They cannot doubt that these children are to be brought up as warriors. They have been exhorted constantly "that they and their children must be trained not only to have sound bodies to withstand the stress of war but also to have a mental outlook which accepts war as a necessity and a law of life."

They have learned their lesson well. This is a German mother's voice: Her only son has been killed in action. She only grieves, so the papers report, that she has not six sons to give to her country, to her Leader. Another, who has lost within one week her only son as well as her son-in-law, the husband of her only daughter, leaves her home, shuts herself up during three days in a hotel, returns to her war work, and refuses to have her losses mentioned or to accept expressions of sympathy. She is determined, so her friends tell me, to behave as if all this had never been. This is not true heroism. It is a contortion and suffocation of maternal instincts.

Edith Cavell, the British nurse, helped hundreds of allied soldiers, prisoners in occupied Belgium, to escape and to rejoin their armies, while at the same time she attended with meticulous care the wounded German soldiers in a Brussels hospital.[2] Her memory is exalted, monuments have been erected to her, not for her patriotism but for her dignity and ultimate wisdom when she had been sentenced by a German court-martial to be shot and faced execution and eternity. "Patriotism is not enough," she said to the British chaplain who administered the last sacrament to her, expressing a much abused but eternal wisdom.

Indeed, patriotism is a great, a natural and indispensable virtue, but if it fills the human mind to the exclusion of all other considerations, if it diverts the heart from a higher loyalty, that to humanity, patriotism is not enough for the well-being and the happiness of mankind.

Two impulses are deeply implanted in human nature: the instinct to fight and the impulse to save and protect life. It has been attempted to attribute the first to men and the other to women. But this generalization leaves out the fact that there have been at all times some saintly men and also, sometimes, very devilish women. However, we cannot doubt that it is characteristic for women, potential mothers, to help the afflicted in body and mind, to comfort them that grieve, to heal the brokenhearted. It is not merely by chance that all those women who broke through tradition to win influence in public life were motivated by the same urge, to enter a neglected field of human suffering in order to abolish injustices, to right wrongs.

Even the demand for women's rights arose in connection with the abolitionist and the temperance movement. When, exactly a hundred years ago, American women delegates were refused admission to an antislavery convention in England, they recognized that there were not only slaves to be emancipated but women, and that is more than half of mankind.[3] They realized about the same time that in the backwoods, in rough and primitive ways of life, women needed protection against the brutality of drunken husbands, children against ruthless fathers who alone had the rights of guardianship, the right practically over life and death. Thus, the abolitionist and the temperance movements, both originating in the churches, produced the modern woman, who asserts that individual freedom is the birthright of both sexes.

More than one generation of women has been deeply stirred by the heroic and touching figure of Susan B. Anthony. Pathetic in her perseverance, she moved from place to place for sixty years of her life, always with the same thought in her mind, the same claims on her lips: converting women to the cause of suffrage. From the very beginning she was aware that women must unite—not the women of one nation only. She sent out a call for a "Women's International" (the International Council of Women, she named it). Women of the world, unite! Women of all classes, creeds, and nations, combine and assume the responsibility which has too long been withheld from you.[4]

It meant actually the revolution of women, of the mothers of the race, with the object of having a voice in the affairs of their nations and for the welfare of humanity. Suffrage as a means, a world of peace as the goal. Susan Anthony died without having attained her end. Others followed. We are the heirs.

The [First] World War was the first test for the Women's International. It proved its worth. Women of the belligerent nations appealed to each other by means of the neutrals when they were convinced that some avoidable suffering could be removed. The French women asked the Germans to intervene with their military authorities against the recruiting, under pressure, of respectable girls from the occupied territories into German brothels. The German woman appealed to the French against the destructive policy of the invasion of the Ruhr industrial area [in 1923]. Many other instances can be given. In every case, the request was followed up, with more or less success. An International League for Peace and Freedom was formed by the most progressive women soon after the outbreak of the war, with Jane Addams as leader, and they sent a delegation to the leading statesmen of all belligerent countries to negotiate for peace. There was, of course, much sadness and grief and sometimes misunderstanding among these organized women, but no personal bitterness, no hatred. They knew each other.

It seems paradoxical that women of many countries secured the rights for which they had long striven as a fruit of the war. Certainly, militaristic countries had never before allotted women a respected and dignified position. Officially, women were enfranchised in recognition of the war services they had rendered. But more or less consciously men may have realized what an important factor women are, that they are capable of promoting or preventing wars of aggression.

The problem of our time is what enfranchised women are going to do about it.

I have frequently been asked by intelligent and public-spirited men, even here in this land of freedom and democracy, "Does this suffrage mean anything to you? Has it changed your life?" My answer is, "If it had changed nothing else, it has given me and all women the sense of new responsibilities. We could not be blamed for wars waged in the past by governments which confined us to the home and family duties. Now we are challenged."

American women know. They understood. Within the short period of twenty years, since they became citizens, they have gained enormous influence. Though the pioneer women are dead, yet their spirit lives. New leaders took over the torch. Carrie Chapman Catt led American women into a passionate policy of peace. They have a right to ask the women of the totalitarian countries, "What have *you* done about it?"

When Hitler came into power, German women had the right to vote. They had more women in parliament than the women of other countries. These women had exerted a humanizing influence. German women knew from their program what the Nazis had in store for them: that humanitarian influences were not desired and that Hitler meant to send women back to their homes and to confine them there. Yet Hitler was supported by women. Large numbers thronged into the party that was going to subdue them. They cheered Hitler to the echo at a meeting when he told them, "I will provide you with the best husbands in the world—my soldiers. You must go and have more and more children who will be just as good soldiers as their fathers." The women obeyed with fervor. German women have always been enthusiastic about the army, about men in a uniform of many colors.

What happened to them was that Hitler ordered all women to be dismissed from gainful employment, and, with German thoroughness, they were not only ousted from important positions but even from secretarial jobs and as waitresses. Later, when unemployed men had been absorbed by the regular army and by the Nazi formations, when armament factories began to work at full speed, women were called back and actually conscripted to make shells, without any regard to the physical effects of such work, not even on their reproductive capacity. They are nothing but instruments of war. The state threw them out for its own ends, and it drove them back for its ends. They are in every respect enslaved as they have never been before.

They could not expect anything else from Hitler. They knew that in his book [*Mein Kampf*], he had written, "In constant war mankind has become great; in eternal peace it would perish. The world is not for cowardly people."

Women of the totalitarian countries, you cannot believe that there is sense in this. It is for you to break the vicious circle, the race between an increase of population and wars. You are responsible to the world of today, to your own offspring, and to posterity to stop future aggression. You receive honor crosses from Hitler, in bronze after you have four children, in silver for more than six, in gold when you have more than eight. The inscription on it runs, "The child ennobles the mother." You should not be proud about this nobility, which you share with the animal world. The child ennobles the parent only if it is conceived and cared for with dedication to the task of educating the child for noble aims—to further civilization, not to destroy it. It is from such an attitude only that the evolution of the spiritual motherhood can result.

It is true, there are many women in Germany who loathe Hitler and his policy, who feel that their womanhood is being insulted. But like all dissenters from the Nazi creed, they were silenced and disappeared overnight as if the earth had cracked and swallowed them. All their organizations were given two days to submit or to be broken up, to forswear their beliefs, to betray their ideals, to give formal allegiance to a movement that negates all [to which] they have aspired and [all they have] achieved. The German branches of all international bodies of women were swept away, clubwomen and councilwomen, university women and business- and professional women: all their organizations went overboard. The Women's International was damaged; a strong link was broken.

Wherever Hitler invades it is the same. Women have to serve his policy. Already his latest victim, France, warns her women to seek no other profession than that of wife, mother, and housekeeper, to turn toward the task of repopulation. If Hitler is to rule for any length of time over Europe and maybe beyond the limits of one continent, women's influence will be wiped out, women's rights will be buried. This must by necessity have repercussions even for the women of the United States.

We have been learning lately a cruel lesson. Like patriotism, so pacifism is not enough, not as long as dictators threaten the world. We here, and the women of the invaded and defeated countries, also the women of the British Empire in its heroic battle of defense, we must appeal to the women of the aggressor countries. Only if they join, then our pacifism will be vindicated. Only if they stop marching and return to the mission of true womanhood, only then will the revolution of the mother be complete. It may take them many years, even decades. It may cost them a terrible price in anguish, martyrdom, sacrifice, even of life itself. No one knows this better than one who has lived among them, one of them, one who was a German, subject to the totalitarian terror, who still bears the scars of persecution.

There is an ancient Roman story about an abyss which had split open the earth and which could be closed only if a citizen, offering his life in sacrifice, would jump into it. Such an abyss is here, in our days. It has torn humankind asunder. Thousands on both sides are killed, bombed, torpedoed day by day in their attempt to cross it. Perhaps its needs the "last full measure of devotion" of women in the totalitarian countries to close it. They would save future generations and at the same time prevent the downfall of Western civilization.

# Appendix C: Preface to an Early Version of Salomon's Autobiography

This is an autobiography, but it may help to throw light on the warp of the German mind that has been responsible for plunging mankind into a titanic struggle for survival.

The life of a nation is made up of the lives of individuals, and the fate of the individual, passing his early years in the shelter of the family, gradually spreads out into its nation. It is therefore natural that my story begins as a strictly personal narrative and that, as it progresses, national events and the world situation become more distinct while my personal adventures recede and appear like a light pattern on a background of many constantly changing colors.

My life experience parallels a long period of German history. It covers the reign of the three emperors, fourteen years of democracy, and ultimately, Hitler's savage tyranny (years that count double), until in 1937 I was expelled by his secret police.

Many books have been written about the terrible infectious mental and moral disease that has befallen Germany since 1933.

My story is primarily concerned with the germs that were embedded in the soil and only in the later chapters with the disease itself. These germs are the militaristic, aggressive, self-asserting, and domineering spirit that has been inculcated into the minds of the Germans through education and tradition and that are active in women as well as men.

After years in my new country, I have gained new perspectives and can see many incidents in my former life not as individual and isolated happenings so much as products of the social fabric to which I belonged by birth. Having spent my life among educated and leading progressive women, I have written my story in the hope of contributing a new aspect to the German problem with which the United Nations will have to deal.

It seems to me that my life has been exceptionally happy and complete, not only because of the achievements but also because of the setbacks which constantly stirred me to exertions and endeavors. Today, I realize that all the troubled periods of my life—apart from family griefs and personal loss—were caused by the arrogance and blindness of the reactionaries and by the militaristic spirit of the Germans, both male and female.

It is their attitude that helped the Nazis to conquer the German people before they overran Europe.

# Notes

INTRODUCTION

1. Much of what appears here is based on a chapter on Salomon in my *Cities, Sin, and Social Reform in Imperial Germany* (Ann Arbor: University of Michigan Press, 2002), 287–317. For the most up to date and the fullest treatment of Salomon's life through 1933, see Anja Schüler, *Frauenbewegung und soziale Reform im transatlantischen Dialog: Jane Addams und Alice Salomon, 1889–1933* (Stuttgart: Steiner, 2003), chapters 8–13. For the fullest selection from among Salomon's numerous writings, see Alice Salomon, *Frauenemanzipation und soziale Verantwortung: Ausgewählte Schriften,* ed. Adriane Feustel, 3 vols. (Neuwied: Luchterhand, 1997–2003). These volumes also contain thorough essays by Feustel on Salomon's life and thought and extensive lists of Salomon's writings. See also Iris Schröder, *Arbeiten für eine bessere Welt: Frauenbewegung und Sozialreform 1890–1914* (Frankfurt a.M.: Campus, 2001), in which Salomon figures prominently. For the importance of the Jewish factor, see Marion A. Kaplan, *The Making of the Jewish Middle Class: Women, Family, and Identity in Imperial Germany* (New York: Oxford University Press, 1991; on Salomon, 214–17); and Harriet Pass Freidenreich, *Female, Jewish, Educated: The Lives of Central European University Women* (Bloomington: Indiana University Press, 2002). For Salomon's views of her life as a whole toward the end of it, see appendix C.

2. See Kathryn Kish Sklar, Anja Schüler, and Susan Strasser, eds., *Social Justice Feminists in the United States and Germany: A Dialogue in Documents, 1885–1933* (Ithaca: Cornell University Press, 1998), which contains both a lengthy and informative introduction and translations of several essays by Salomon.

3. On this tradition, see Ann Taylor Allen, *Feminism and Motherhood in Germany, 1800–1914* (New Brunswick: Rutgers University Press, 1991; on Salomon, 208–15). For a particularly strong instance of it, see appendix A. For the larger context, see Seth Koven and Sonya Michel, eds., *Mothers of a New World: Maternalist Politics and the Origins of Welfare States* (New York: Routledge, 1993).

4. Alice Salomon, "Ausbildung zur Sozialarbeit," in Salomon, *Was wir uns und anderen schuldig sind: Ansprachen und Aufsätze für jungen Menschen* (Leipzig: Teubner, 1912), 37.

5. On the Federation of German Women's Organizations (the Bund

deutscher Frauenvereine, to which Salomon usually refers as the German Council and sometimes as the National Council), see Richard J. Evans, *The Feminist Movement in Germany, 1894–1933* (London: Sage, 1976). On the International Council of Women, see Leila J. Rupp, *Worlds of Women: The Making of an International Women's Movement* (Princeton: Princeton University Press, 1997), esp. 15–21.

6. See Lynne M. Healy, *International Social Work: Professional Action in an Interdependent World* (New York: Oxford University Press, 2001).

7. On Salomon's later years, see Joachim Wieler, *Er-Innerung eines zerstörten Lebensabends: Alice Salomon während der NS-Zeit (1933–1937) und im Exil (1937–1948)* (Darmstadt: Lingbach, 1987), 57–416.

8. One of the few works about her to appear before the 1980s was Hans Muthesius, ed., *Alice Salomon: Die Begründerin des sozialen Frauenberufs in Deutschland* (Cologne: Heymann, 1958). This work contains a biographical sketch (pp. 9–121) written by Salomon's former secretary, Dora Peyser, that was based largely on Salomon's then unpublished memoirs. Peyser's essay long remained the standard source for information about Salomon and has only recently been superseded by Salomon, *Frauenemanzipation,* and Schüler, *Frauenbewegung.*

9. Alice Salomon, *Education for Social Work: A Sociological Interpretation Based on an International Survey* (Zurich: Verlag für Recht und Gesellschaft, 1937).

10. The most noteworthy exposition of this viewpoint in recent decades appears in Carol Gilligan, *In a Different Voice: Psychological Theory and Women's Development* (Cambridge: Harvard University Press, 1982).

CHAPTER 1

1. The three wars occurred in 1864, 1866, and 1870–71 and culminated in the establishment of the German Empire on January 18, 1871.

2. The son of Kaiser Wilhelm I, Kaiser Friedrich II was mortally ill as a result of throat cancer when he ascended the throne in 1888.

3. As the wife of Kronprinz Friedrich, she was generally known as Kronprinzessin Viktoria. When he became emperor, she became known as Kaiserin Friedrich, a designation on which she continued to insist after his death.

CHAPTER 2

1. This organization was the Girls' and Women's Groups for Social Assistance, known as "the Groups." On its origins, see Lees, *Cities,* 298–301.

2. In 1893, before he became Germany's most famous sociologist, Max Weber (1864–1920) lectured on "Basic Features of Modern Social Development." Other lecturers treated "Welfare Arrangements for the Working Classes," "Social Assistance (Particularly by Women) in England and America," "Organization of Public and Private Care for the Poor," "Basic Features of Hygiene," and "Health Care for Children."

3. Jane Addams (1860–1935) took the lead in establishing Hull House in 1889,

and Lillian Wald (1867–1940) founded her settlement house in 1895. They cooperated in 1914 in opposing militarism. On links between Addams and Salomon, see Sklar, Schüler, and Strasser, eds., *Social Justice Feminists.* On examples set in England, see Standish Meacham, *Toynbee Hall and Social Reform* (New Haven: Yale University Press, 1987). Salomon first traveled to England in 1896, and it is likely that she first became aware of the settlement-house movement at that time.

4. The Social Democrats had actually received almost one-quarter of the votes in the 1893 Reichstag elections.

5. Between 1881 and 1889, at Bismarck's behest, the Reichstag passed legislation that provided for insurance—mainly for industrial workers—against sickness, accidents, and old age. See Lees, *Cities,* 363–71.

6. The founders included teachers, clergymen, physicians, lawyers, economists, officials, reformers, and other representatives of Berlin's educated middle class. From the outset, several women, among them the mayor's wife, played important parts in the organization's leadership.

7. Women remained legally excluded from this domain until around the turn of the century, when the larger cities began to admit them to it.

8. Public authorities did not give poor relief to anyone who possessed more than what was considered to be the bare minimum required for existence.

9. The organizers of the club used midday meals, sewing courses, social evenings, and information about job openings to attract girls to a setting in which they would experience the benefits of "higher culture." Salomon summarized her overall objective at the time as being "to get them to appreciate not only material goods but also ideal values" (Alice Salomon, "Ein Arbeiterinnen-Klub in Berlin," *Soziale Praxis* 12 [1903]: 994–96).

10. Lily Braun (1865–1916), albeit the daughter of an aristocratic general, joined the Social Democratic Party in 1894. She was a prolific writer, best known for her works on women's issues.

11. Jeanette Schwerin (1852–1899), a cofounder of the German Society for Ethical Culture, helped to found the Groups and served as their director between 1897 and 1899. Lady Ishbel Maria Aberdeen (1857–1939) was a leader of the English women's movement who chaired the International Council of Women for all but five years between 1893 and 1935.

12. This was the Bund Deutscher Frauenvereine, a name that Salomon usually translates as the German Council of Women. The BDF was an umbrella group of moderate and politically nonpartisan women's organizations. For more on this group, see Evans, *Feminist Movement.*

13. The great Russian novelist Leo Tolstoy (1852–1910) eloquently preached the need for loving one's fellow human beings.

14. After writing several novels, Benjamin Disraeli (1804–81) became a leader of Great Britain's Tory Party, serving as prime minister in 1868 and between 1874 and 1880. John Ruskin (1819–1900) was a British essayist, critic, and reformer. Johann Wolfgang von Goethe (1749–1832) is generally regarded as the greatest German writer. Disraeli, Ruskin, and the British authors mentioned in the next two paragraphs wrote influentially about social questions during the mid- and late nineteenth century.

15. Mary Augusta Arnold Ward (1851–1920); Walter Besant (1836–1901). The People's Palace was a cultural center where efforts were made to provide uplifting entertainment for ordinary Londoners.

16. Charles Kingsley (1819—75) and Charles Dickens (1812–70). Both wrote socially critical fiction.

17. Edna Ferber (1887–1968) was a socially engaged writer best known for novels for women written during the 1920s.

CHAPTER 3

1. Salomon was elected during the summer of 1899, her predecessor Jeanette Schwerin having died earlier in the year.

2. By 1905, about seven hundred women were working in the Groups. The subdivisions that attracted the most participation centered on child care and on assistance for the poor.

3. The Deutsche Verein für Armenpflege und Wohltätigkeit (German Association for Poor Relief and Charity) had been founded in 1880 under the leadership of Berlin's poor-law officials as a means of bringing expert opinion to bear on poverty and related themes.

4. Friedrich Wilhelm Foerster (1869–1966) was the son of one of the founders of the Groups. Foerster spent a good deal of time in Switzerland before the First World War and received right-wing attacks because of his wartime pacifism, and he withdrew from his teaching position at the University of Munich. The Nazis burned his books, and, like Salomon, he later emigrated to the United States.

5. August Bebel (1840–1913) was one of the founders of the German Social Democratic Party and remained its chairman until his death.

6. August Bebel, *Die Frau und der Sozialismus* (1883; trans. in 1904 as *Woman under Socialism*).

7. Prussian universities had admitted women who obtained ministerial permission as auditors in 1896, but they were allowed to matriculate only in 1908; see James C. Albisetti, *Schooling German Girls and Women: Secondary and Higher Education in the Nineteenth Century* (Princeton: Princeton University Press, 1988).

8. Alice Salomon, *Soziale Frauenpflichten: Vorträge gehalten in deutschen Frauenvereinen* [Women's Social Duties: Lectures Held in German Women's Associations] (Berlin: Liebmann, 1902); Salomon, "Die Frau in der sozialen Hilfsthätigkeit [Women in the Area of Social Assistance]," in *Handbuch der Frauenbewegung* [Handbook of the Women's Movement], ed. Helene Lange and Gertrud Bäumer, 2 vols. (Berlin: Moeser, 1901–2); and Salomon, *Was wir uns und anderen schuldig sind* (see "Introduction," n. 4), which appeared several years later than Salomon indicates here.

9. Salomon began to study at Berlin's Friedrich Wilhelm University in the autumn of 1902. She received her doctorate with a specialization in economics and a secondary field in history.

10. Max Sering (1857–1939), a professor of political science, had helped to found the Groups.

11. Gustav Schmoller (1838–1917) and Adolf Wagner (1835–1917) were influen-

tial economists who advocated an active state role in the solution of social problems, along the lines supported by Bismarck. Their viewpoint was often referred to as *Kathedersozialismus* (socialism of the lectern).

12. Alfred Weber (1868–1958), a younger brother of Max Weber, was an economist and a sociologist.

13. Salomon's dissertation treated unequal pay for men and women, which she traced to what she regarded as "the dilettantish, provisional, and haphazard character of women's work."

14. The minister could force the faculty to consider Salomon's application, but unanimous agreement by the faculty was required for the application to be accepted, and two professors remained opposed.

CHAPTER 4

1. On the International Council, see Rupp, *Worlds,* 15–21.

2. Susan B. Anthony (1820–1906) chaired the National Woman Suffrage Association and its successor, the National American Women Suffrage Association, in the United States.

3. May Wright Sewall (1844–1920) was an American teacher and an activist in the women's suffrage movement. She headed the International Council between 1899 and 1904.

4. Charlotte Perkins Gilman (1860–1935) was an American writer who took advanced positions in support of equality for men and women. The book to which Salomon refers was Gilman's *Women and Economics: A Study of the Economic Relation between Men and Women* (Boston: Small, Maynard, 1898).

5. Anna Shaw (1847–1919) received a divinity degree from Boston University but decided not to pursue a clerical career and instead became a leader in the movement for women's suffrage.

6. The Rothschilds were an international family of wealthy bankers. Josephine Butler (1828–1906) established in 1875 the International Abolitionist Federation, which aimed at eliminating instead of regulating prostitution.

7. Beatrice Webb (1858–1943), together with her husband, Sidney, played a leading part among Great Britain's moderate socialists (known as Fabians). For autobiography, see Beatrice Webb, *My Apprenticeship* (London: Longmans, 1926).

8. The central character in Mary Augusta Arnold Ward's novel *Marcella* (1890).

9. Hedwig Heyl (1850–1934) was deeply involved in various projects that concerned not only families in households headed by the workers at her factory but also women and children elsewhere in and around Berlin.

10. The congress took place in June 1904. Sessions concentrated on "women's education," "women's work and professions," "social institutions and efforts," and "women's legal position." There were hundreds of presentations.

11. Bertha von Suttner (1843–1914), an Austrian writer, was a leader among European pacifists. She received the Nobel Peace Prize in 1905. Her novel *Die Waffen nieder* (1889) was translated as *Lay Down Your Arms* (1892).

12. Charles Darwin (1809–82), Herbert Spencer (1820–1903), Carus Sterne (pseudonym for Ernst Ludwig Krause [1839–1903]), and Henry Thomas Buckle

(1821–62) were widely read during the nineteenth century. Darwin was a famous biologist. Krause sought to popularize natural science. Spencer and Buckle sought to apply it to the study of society.

CHAPTER 5

1. John Campbell Gordon (1847–1934), a Liberal statesman who held important positions in Ireland and Canada.
2. George Edmund Street (1824–81) was one of the foremost champions of the Gothic revival in architecture.
3. William Gladstone (1809–98) and Sir Henry Campbell-Bannerman (1836–1908) were Liberal statesmen and prime ministers.

CHAPTER 6

1. The Gesellschaft für Soziale Reform was founded in 1901 as the German section of the International Association for the Legal Protection of Workers. It counted among its members trade unions, employers' groups, and agencies that helped to administer social insurance.
2. Bernhard von Bülow (1849–1929) worked in the foreign service and served as imperial chancellor between 1900 and 1909. He is not generally regarded as a progressive, and his refusal to enter into an alliance with Great Britain exacerbated Germany's growing isolation before 1914.
3. Helene Simon (1862–1947) was a supporter of social reform who belonged to the Fabian Society in England, and she emigrated there in 1938.
4. The Pestalozzi-Froebel Haus was founded in 1874 to promote kindergartens, and it later served as a center for training teachers of young children and women who needed help in household management. See Allen, *Feminism and Motherhood,* 114–21.
5. Thomas Carlyle (1795–1887), an English essayist, historian, and philosopher, was greatly influenced by German romanticism, and it seems fitting that he in turn influenced Salomon.
6. Salomon seems to be referring here to her book on economics, *Einführung in die Volkswirtschaftslehre: Lehrbuch für Frauenschulen* [An Introduction to Economics: A Textbook for Schools for Women] (Berlin: Teubner, 1909; eight later editions), and to a book on social work that she coauthored with Siddy Wronsky, *Leitfaden der Wohlfahrtspflege* [A Guide to Welfare Work] (Berlin: Teubner, 1921; three later editions).
7. Flower Days were introduced into Germany from Scandinavia and England in 1904. Profits from sales were supposed to provide benefits for charities, but actual profits were negligible.

CHAPTER 8

1. The growing literature on social reform in the German Empire includes Kevin Repp, *Reformers, Critics, and the Paths of German Modernity: Anti-Politics and the Search for Alternatives, 1890–1914* (Cambridge: Harvard University Press,

2000); and Lees, *Cities* (see 355–89 for discussion of governmental measures). Readers of German should also consult Rüdiger vom Bruch, *"Weder Kapitalismus noch Kommunismus": Bürgerliche Sozialreform in Deutschland vom Vormärz bis zur Ära Adenauer* (Munich: Beck, 1985).

2. Friedrich Naumann (1860–1919) was an influential proponent of social changes that he hoped would encourage workers to support a reformed but still monarchical state. He served as a member of the Reichstag between 1907 and 1918 (except for a short period in 1912–13) and briefly was a leading member of the Democratic Party formed after the end of the First World War.

3. The Deutsche Verein für Armenpflege und Wohltätigkeit was renamed the Deutsche Verein für Öffentliche und Private Fürsorge.

4. Marie Baum had already spoken at a 1905 meeting of this association.

5. The city was a major center of a highly conservative women's movement known as the Deutsch-Evangelisch Frauenbund (German Protestant Women's League) and headed by Paula Müller. On this organization and the context within which it operated, see Nancy R. Reagin, *A German Women's Movement: Class and Gender in Hanover, 1880–1933* (Chapel Hill: University of North Carolina Press, 1995).

6. Alice Salomon, *Mutterschutz und Mutterschaftsversicherung* (Leipzig: Duncker und Humblot, 1908).

7. Carrick-on-Shannon is a town in Ireland. Nacross was presumably some sort of fine textile.

8. Eleonora Duse (1859–1924) was an actress who enjoyed a great reputation both in her native Italy and abroad.

CHAPTER 9

Salomon's chapter title echoes biblical passages in 2 Corinthians 4:18 and Romans 8:24.

1. Salomon was one of a substantial number of Germans who drifted away from Judaism during the nineteenth century as they sought to assimilate more fully into German society. On her efforts and those of others like her to find in a community of social reform a substitute for a community of coreligionists, see Kaplan, *Making*, 208–19.

2. Adolf von Harnack (1851–1930), an Evangelical theologian, served both as a professor of church history and of the history of religion at the University of Berlin and as a chairman of the Evangelisch-Sozialer Kongreß (Evangelical-Social Congress), an organization of liberal Protestants. On this group, see Harry Liebersohn, *Religion and Industrial Society: The Protestant Social Congress in Wilhelmine Germany* (Philadelphia: American Philosophical Society, 1986).

CHAPTER 10

1. An 1870 defeat of France during the Franco-Prussian War.

2. Because of German opposition to more far-reaching agreements, the

results of the 1899 conference were quite limited. German opposition in 1907 prevented any agreements.

3. This reference is to Gertrud Bäumer (1873–1954), whom Salomon mentions only once by name in her autobiography, no doubt in part because of lingering resentment over Bäumer's role in blocking an anticipated career move by Salomon in 1920 (see chap. 13). Like Salomon, Bäumer received a doctorate from the University of Berlin (in 1905). She headed the German Council of Women between 1910 and 1920. Between 1919 and 1932, she served as a Democratic member of the Reichstag, and between 1920 and 1933 she also held a national administrative position in the area of youth work. She continued to edit *Die Frau,* a journal devoted to women's issues, after 1933. See Repp, *Reformers,* 104–47.

4. *The British "White Paper" Giving the Diplomatic Correspondence Which Preceded the European War in 1914* (London, 1914).

5. Salomon may be referring to Albert Einstein, whom she met at some point.

6. Martin Luther (1483–1546); Paul Gerhardt (1607–1676).

7. During the First World War, disputes over the cost and the availability of bread became increasingly contentious in Berlin. See Belinda J. Davis, *Home Fires Burning: Food, Politics, and Everyday Life in World War I Berlin* (Chapel Hill: University of North Carolina Press, 2000).

8. The Women's International League for Peace and Freedom originated in April 1915 at the Women's Peace Congress in the Hague, where an International Committee of Women for Permanent Peace was founded. The delegates resolved to come together for a second Congress, which was scheduled to occur in Zurich during the peace conference that took place in Paris after the First World War. The WILPF proper was founded at this meeting, in May 1919. Jane Addams served for many years as its president.

9. Theobald von Bethmann Hollweg (1856–1921) served as imperial chancellor between 1909 and 1917. The German high command, which was seeking to annex vast territories to the German Empire, forced him to give up his office because of his relatively moderate positions.

CHAPTER 11

1. Largely because of disagreements within the Social Democratic Party about the war effort, in 1917 a minority formed the Independent Social Democratic Party.

2. The program was actually known as the Hindenburg Program, after Paul von Hindenburg, who served, in effect, as the supreme commander of the German armed forces during the second half of the war, although quartermaster general Erich Ludendorff was the dominant force in the military establishment. The program, which the government began to implement in August 1916, focused on the need to increase weapons production.

3. On annexationist sentiment in Germany at the time, see the classic work by Fritz Fischer, *Germany's Aims in the First World* (New York: Norton, 1967).

CHAPTER 12

1. Following an October 3 German offer, an armistice was finally negotiated between November 8 and 11. The German delegation received peace terms at Ver-

sailles on May 7, 1919, and a peace treaty was signed on June 28. The blockade was then lifted.

2. Hjalmar Horace Greeley Schacht (1877–1970) was a prominent financier. He held official positions both during the years of the Weimar Republic and during the years of the Third Reich.

3. The interval was actually a little over two months (see chap. 12, n.1).

4. Friedrich Ebert (1871–1925) served as a member of the Reichstag beginning in 1912 and succeeded August Bebel as leader of the Social Democratic Party after Bebel's death in 1913. Ebert was elected president of the Weimar Republic (so named because its constitution had been hammered out in the city of Weimar) on February 2, 1919.

5. Otto Meissner (1880–1953), a civil servant, adhered to values that were basically antirepublican. Paul von Hindenburg (1847–1934), the supreme commander of German forces during the First World War, was elected president of the republic in 1925 and reelected in 1932. After appointing Hitler as Reich chancellor in 1933, Hindenburg died in the summer of 1934; the office of president was abolished, with Hitler absorbing its functions into his own office.

6. Walter Rathenau (1867–1922) was the head of one of Germany's leading electrical companies and the man in charge of efforts to coordinate industrial production during the First World War. He served as minister for reconstruction for half a year in 1921 and as foreign minister from February until June 1922, when he was assassinated by right-wing and anti-Semitic terrorists.

7. The German *Tariflöhne,* which Salomon would have had in mind, means "wages established through collective bargaining."

8. Ben B. Lindsey and Wainwright Evans, *The Companionate Marriage* (New York: Garden City Publishing, 1927). Lindsey, a Colorado Progressive, advocated birth control, woman suffrage, and "trial marriages."

9. The Munich "beer-hall putsch" attempt on November 9, 1923, for which Hitler received a light sentence under conditions that enabled him to write his autobiographical and propagandistic *Mein Kampf* (first published in 1925).

10. Gustav Stresemann (1878–1929) founded the conservative German People's Party in 1918. After serving briefly as chancellor, he served between 1923 and 1929 as Germany's foreign minister. He is remembered for having worked to promote better relations between Germany and other countries in the West.

11. Matthias Erzberger (1875–1921) was a Catholic politician whom nationalists despised, among other reasons, because of his having signed the Versailles Peace Treaty. Rosa Luxemburg (1871–1919), Karl Liebknecht (1871–1919), and Kurt Eisner (1867–1919) were all left-wing socialists (Luxemburg and Liebknecht helped found the German Communist Party) who lost their lives during the period of revolutionary turmoil that immediately followed the end of the First World War.

CHAPTER 13

1. Dorothy Buxton and Eglantine Jebb (1876–1928), both members of the Society of Friends (or Quakers), had founded a Save the Children Fund in England. Jebb drafted a "Children's Charter" that the League of Nations approved in 1924.

2. Before becoming president of the United States in 1929, Herbert Hoover (1874–1964) had become famous for his efforts between 1914 and 1923 as a governmental official to alleviate hunger in Europe.

3. Carolena Wood (1871–1936) was an American Quaker, a social worker, and a philanthropist.

4. Betsy Kjelsberg (1886–1950) served as president of the Norwegian Women's League between 1922 and 1938 and as vice president of the International Council of Women between 1926 and 1938.

5. Agnes von Zahn-Harnack (1884–1950) was a Berlin teacher and school administrator who served as president of the German Council of Women from 1931 until it was dissolved in 1933.

6. Julia Lathrop (1858–1932), a coworker for twenty years with Jane Addams at Hull House, served as the first head of the federal Children's Bureau from 1912 to 1921 and as president of the National Conference of Social Work in 1918–19. In 1925, she was named as an adviser to the Child Welfare Committee of the League of Nations.

7. Peter Kropotkin, *Mutual Aid: A Factor in Evolution* (New York: McClure, 1902). Parts of this work were first published (in English) in 1890. A refugee from czarist Russia, Kropotkin (1842–1921) made a great name for himself as an advocate of nonviolent anarchism, which was based on a belief in society as a naturally harmonious entity, before returning to Russia in 1917.

8. The story appears in Thomas Carlyle's widely read *Past and Present* (1843).

9. Junkers were members of aristocratic families who had large landed estates. Many held high positions in the Prussian army.

10. Mary Antin, *The Promised Land* (Boston and New York: Houghton Mifflin, 1912), a descriptive and celebratory work about the United States that focuses on the experiences of Jewish immigrants.

11. Alice Salomon, *Kultur im Werden: Amerikanische Reiseeindrücke* [Culture in Evolution: Travel Impressions of America] (Berlin: Ullstein,1924).

12. A forerunner of the United Nations, the League was established in 1919 at the urging of Woodrow Wilson in connection with the Peace of Paris.

13. The Soviet Union was admitted to the League in 1934. Litvinov headed the first Russian delegation. Having invaded Finland early in 1939, the Soviet Union was expelled from the League later that year.

14. Germany gained admission to the League in 1926 and left in 1933.

CHAPTER 14

1. Thirteen volumes were published between 1930 and 1933. The title of the series was "Forschungen über Bestand und Erschütterung der Familie in der Gegenwart." They focused on problems relating to homelessness and the plight of single and working mothers.

2. These men were thinkers who enjoyed high reputations in a variety of fields, including philosophy and theology as well as the natural sciences.

## CHAPTER 15

1. Theodor Wolff (1868–1943) was a founder of the German Democratic Party in 1918 and the chief editor of the *Berliner Tageblatt,* a liberal newspaper, between 1906 and 1933, when he emigrated to France.

2. Electoral support for the Nazis seems to have increased more rapidly—at least in Protestant areas—among women than among men between 1932 and 1933. In part owing also to the fact that female voters outnumbered male ones in the electorate as a whole, by July 1932 the Nazis were receiving more votes overall from women than from men, and by March 1933 they received a larger share of the female vote than of the male vote. The difference between levels of female and male support for National Socialism, however, was not large, and until 1933 the Nazis did not gain majority support among members of either sex except in a few strongholds. See Helen L. Boak, "'Our Last Hope': Women's Votes for Hitler—A Reappraisal," *German Studies Review* 12 (1989): 289–310; see also Julia Sneeringer, *Winning Women's Votes: Propaganda and Politics in Weimar Germany* (Chapel Hill: University of North Carolina Press, 2002).

3. There were only two Reichstag elections in 1932, but there were also two presidential elections, making a total of four elections at the national level.

4. Kurt von Schleicher (1882–1934) and Heinrich Brüning (1885–1970) served as chancellors shortly before Hitler came to power. Both opposed Hitler, but neither can be credited with having supported parliamentary democracy.

5. The Nazis had received 37.4 percent of the vote in July 1932 before falling to 33.1 percent in November. Their share of the vote rose to 43.9 percent in March 1933, their maximum share in a contested election.

6. Franz von Papen (1879–1969) held the chancellorship for six months in 1932 and later served as vice chancellor under Hitler.

7. Alfred Hugenberg (1865–1951) was a businessman and leader of the Conservative Nationalist Party. Junkers were members of aristocratic families who had large landed estates.

## CHAPTER 16

1. Moses Mendelssohn and Gotthold Ephraim Lessing lived in the eighteenth century; Felix Mendelssohn-Bartholdy in the first half of the nineteenth century. Robert (1857–1917) and Franz (1865–1935) von Mendelssohn worked as bankers in Berlin. They frequently entertained musicians, artists, and intellectuals.

2. Gerhart Hauptmann (1862–1946) was a dramatist, novelist, and poet. He occupied a leading position in German literature for many years.

3. Rudolf Serkin (1903–91) was a famous pianist and teacher. Having first performed in the United States in 1933, he settled there permanently in 1939.

4. Max Liebermann (1847–1935) was a leader of the Berlin Secession, whose members revolted against academic traditions in German art.

## CHAPTER 17

1. This event was not actually a pogrom but was a one-day national boycott, after which German Jews mistakenly hoped for a return to normal conditions. On the second event to which Salomon refers, see chap. 20, n. 5.
2. The best known of the early camps was established in Dachau, just outside Munich.
3. Often referred to as the Nuremberg Laws, these decrees deprived Jews of their rights as citizens and forbade intermarriage between Jews and non-Jews. These measures served as an early milepost on the route toward the Holocaust. In general, see Marion A. Kaplan, *Between Dignity and Despair: Jewish Life in Nazi Germany* (New York: Oxford University Press, 1998).
4. Between 450,000 and 600,000 "non-Aryan" Germans fled from the expanding territory of the Third Reich between 1933 and 1939. Decisions regarding whether to leave were usually reached only after much soul-searching. For more detail, see Kaplan, *Between Dignity and Despair*, 62–73. On the difficulties that many Jews experienced in trying to gain admittance to the United States, see David Wyman, *Paper Walls: America and the Refugee Crisis, 1938–1941* (Amherst: University of Massachusetts Press, 1968).

## CHAPTER 18

1. Several other members of the faculty also resigned, and at least two emigrated. Charlotte Dietrich, whom Salomon had chosen as her replacement in 1925, joined the Nazi Party in 1933 and remained director of the school until 1945.
2. Hilde Lion (1893–ca. 1960), a teacher of youth workers who had headed the academy since 1929. She soon emigrated to England.
3. On professionals' support for National Socialism, see Konrad H. Jarausch, *The Unfree Professions: German Lawyers, Teachers, and Engineers, 1900–1950* (New York: Oxford University Press, 1990).
4. Bronislaw Hubermann (1882–1947), a prominent violinist who emigrated in 1933, later founding the Israel Philharmonic Orchestra; Richard Strauss (1864–1949), a prominent composer and conductor, who served briefly under the Nazis as an official in charge of musical affairs; Bruno Walter (1876–1962), a prominent conductor who was forced by the Nazis to leave Germany.
5. A quite unflattering portrait of German professors and other intellectuals appears in Joachim C. Fest, *The Face of the Third Reich*, trans. Michael Bullock (New York: Pantheon, 1970), 249–62.

## CHAPTER 19

1. Thomas Mann (1875–1955), the greatest German novelist of the twentieth century, having been on vacation in Switzerland in early 1933, remained there after Hitler's accession to power. He frequently denounced the Nazi regime in speeches

and essays. In 1936, the regime withdrew his citizenship, and later that year the University of Bonn withdrew an honorary doctorate that it had awarded him in 1919. He moved to the United States in 1938, becoming an American citizen in 1944.

2. In 1934, Martin Niemöller (1892–1984), a submarine commander in the First World War, ignored Nazi orders to retire from his pastoral position and subsequently became a leader among Protestants who resisted Nazi efforts to "coordinate" the Christian churches (see chap. 22, n.1). Arrested in 1937, he was detained in concentration camps until 1945, reemerging during the postwar years as a prominent figure in church affairs.

## CHAPTER 20

1. Salomon is probably referring to Gertrud Scholz-Klink; for extensive discussion of Scholz-Klink's role in the Third Reich, see Claudia Koonz, *Mothers in the Fatherland: Women, the Family, and Nazi Politics* (New York: St. Martin's, 1987).

2. Alfred Rosenberg (1893–1946) was one of several men who ostensibly exercised overall control over cultural and ideological policy in Nazi Germany. He was best known for his *Der Mythus des 20. Jahrhunderts* (The Myth of the Twentieth Century; 1934), in which he expounded the principle of Germanic racial superiority. Maintaining this superiority entailed in his view not only strong anti-Semitism but also combating low birth rates among Germans.

3. Joseph Goebbels (1897–1945) was the minister of propaganda in Nazi Germany.

4. The "Röhm putsch," or "night of the long knives." Ernst Röhm (1887–1934), the commander of the paramilitary storm troopers (the SA), and several hundred others whom Hitler regarded as threats to his power were rounded up and shot.

5. The Reichskristallnacht (Night of Broken Glass), a night of widespread violence by Nazis against Jews and Jewish property, during which many Jews were killed, synagogues were destroyed, and store windows were smashed.

6. Alice Salomon, *Soziale Führer: Ihr Leben, ihre Lehren, ihre Werke* (Leipzig: Quelle & Meyer, 1932).

7. Alice Salomon, *Heroische Frauen: Lebensbilder sozialer Führerinnen* [Heroic Women: Portraits of Social Leaders] (Zürich: Verlag für Recht und Gesellschaft, 1936).

8. Salomon, *Education for Social Work* (see Introduction, note 9).

## CHAPTER 21

1. Adolf Hitler's autobiography, *Mein Kampf,* first published in 1925, enjoyed canonical status in the Nazi movement, and it was reprinted numerous times.

2. On social work during the Third Reich, see Hans-Uwe Otto and Heinz Sünker, eds., *Soziale Arbeit und Faschismus* (Frankfurt a.M.: Suhrkamp, 1989).

262  Notes to Pages 205–16

Many social workers played important parts in efforts to marginalize people who were considered threats to the health and well-being of society as a whole and did so in ways that complemented Nazi persecution of racial and ethnic minorities.

3. On the Strength through Joy program, which constituted a major effort both to increase workers' satisfaction with their lives and the Nazi regime and to increase economic productivity through a wide array of leisure-time activities, see Ronald Smelser, *Robert Ley: Hitler's Labour Front Leader* (Oxford: Berg, 1988).

4. Sterilization was part of a far-flung program of negative eugenics through which the Nazis sought to promote the "health" of the German people by preventing the birth of "misfits." The program contrasted sharply with earlier efforts by social workers, among others, to promote a positive eugenics that would entail improving the living conditions of mothers and their families. According to current estimates, about 250,000 people were sterilized in Nazi Germany. See Robert N. Proctor, *Racial Hygiene: Medicine under the Nazis* (Cambridge: Harvard University Press, 1988), 95–117; and Gisela Bock, "Sterilization and 'Medical' Massacres in National Socialist Germany: Ethics, Politics, and the Law," in *Medicine and Modernity: Public Health and Medical Care in Nineteenth- and Twentieth-Century Germany,* ed. Manfred Berg and Geoffrey Cocks (New York: Cambridge University Press, 1997), 149–72.

5. Americans began to experiment with sterilization of the "unfit" in the late nineteenth century, and by the end of the 1920s laws supporting it were on the books in twenty-four states. In the United States, the total number of sterilizations peaked in the 1930s. Its subsequent decline was traceable in part to the bad publicity that surrounded the Nazi program, but a few states still have sterilization laws on the books. About 60,000 individuals have been sterilized in this country. See Daniel J. Kevles, *In the Name of Eugenics: Genetics and the Uses of Human Heredity* (Berkeley and Los Angeles: University of California Press, 1985), 111–17.

CHAPTER 22

1. On the Confessing Church, see Victoria Barnett, *For the Soul of the People: Protestant Protest against Hitler* (New York: Oxford University Press, 1992). The church emerged in 1934 as a result of efforts by Martin Niemöller (see chap. 23) and other Protestant leaders to establish a basis for defending Protestantism against encroachments by theologians who were sympathetic to National Socialism. The Confessing Church did not, however, pose a challenge to the Nazi regime's political goals.

2. Hans Kerll (1887–1941).

CHAPTER 23

1. Hans Christian Asmussen (1898–1968).

CHAPTER 24

1. A public statement critical of the Nazi regime.

2. Fiorello La Guardia (1882–1947), mayor of New York City, 1933–45; George William Mundelein (1872–1939), archbishop of Chicago starting in 1915.

3. Max Warburg (1867–1947) was a highly regarded private banker. Like Salomon, he emigrated to the United States in the 1930s.

4. Henry George (1839–97) was an American economist who sought to base all taxation on unearned increases in the value of land. He received strong support from voters in an unsuccessful effort to become mayor of New York City in 1886.


APPENDIX A


Delivered as a lecture at a convention of German women's groups in Berlin in 1912 under the title "Die Bedeutung der Frauenbewegung für das soziale Leben." Published in Salomon, *Was wir uns und anderen schuldig sind,* 127–34. Translated by Andrew Lees.

1. Benjamin Disraeli, *Sybil; or, the Two Nations* (1845; London: Oxford University Press, 1926), 67.

2. Oda Olberg was a prominent turn-of-the-century theorist in German socialist women's groups.

3. On the International Council of Women, which was founded in the late nineteenth century, see Rupp, *Worlds,* 15–21.


APPENDIX B

This essay was written in English sometime during the early part of the Second World War. A note on the original typescript (which, like the document on which this volume is based, resides in the Leo Baeck Archive in New York City) refers to the year 1942. The statements annotated in notes 1 and 3 suggest that Salomon wrote the essay somewhat earlier. In any case, however, it was almost certainly one of the last things she wrote. It remained unpublished during her lifetime.

1. The three dictators were presumably Adolf Hitler, Benito Mussolini, and Joseph Stalin. The fact that Salomon seems to be referring to Stalin suggests that she wrote the essay before the attack by Germany on the Soviet Union that took place in June 1941.

2. Edith Cavell, born in 1865, was executed in 1915, having pled guilty to a charge of harboring and aiding escaped prisoners.

3. After their failure to be seated with men on the main floor at the World Antislavery Convention in London in 1840 (they were told that they would have to sit in the balcony and that they could not speak), Lucretia Mott and Elizabeth

Cady Stanton took the lead in organizing a Women's Rights Convention that met in Seneca Falls in upstate New York in 1848.

4. The International Council of Women, in which Salomon played a leading role, was established in 1888.


APPENDIX C

This document does not appear in the version of Salomon's autobiography that resides in the Leo Baeck Institute. It comes from a slightly earlier version held in Berlin by the archive of the German Central Institute for Social Questions. It was brought to my attention by Joachim Wieler, who argued persuasively that even though Salomon eventually omitted this material, as did Rolf Landwehr and Rüdeger Baron from their German version of Salomon's autobiography, it deserves publication here. Whether one wishes to accept Salomon's view of "the minds of the Germans," it is important to understand how she situated herself late in life in relation to dominant trends in the country in which she grew up and spent most of her adult life.